Structural Transformation as Development

Anis Chowdhury · Zulfan Tadjoeddin ·
Yogi Vidyattama

Structural Transformation as Development

Path Dependence and Geopolitics

palgrave
macmillan

Anis Chowdhury
School of Business
Western Sydney University
Sydney, NSW, Australia

Zulfan Tadjoeddin
School of Social Sciences
Western Sydney University
Sydney, NSW, Australia

Yogi Vidyattama
School of Politics, Economics
and Society
University of Canberra
Canberra, ACT, Australia

ISBN 978-981-97-9091-3 ISBN 978-981-97-9092-0 (eBook)
https://doi.org/10.1007/978-981-97-9092-0

This Palgrave Macmillan imprint is published by the registered company Springer Nature Singapore Pte Ltd.
The registered company address is: 152 Beach Road, #21-01/04 Gateway East, Singapore 189721, Singapore

If disposing of this product, please recycle the paper.

Preface

While no single factor can explain the state of underdevelopment, we believe in the path dependence of development determined by initial conditions. In almost all of the countries included in this book, the initial conditions were the result of their long colonial experiences. The curse of initial conditions and path dependence persists due to neo-colonial arrangements between former colonies and colonial powers as well as global economic governance architecture designed by Western powers. Nobel Laureate Simon Kuznets' observation, in his 1971 Nobel Lecture, resonates: "obstacles to … transformation were, and still are being, imposed on the less developed regions by the policies of the developed countries".

We believe that continued underdevelopment and exploitation are against the United Nations Declaration on the Right to Development. The Declaration affirms "an inalienable human right and that equality of opportunity for development is a prerogative both of nations and of individuals who make up nations". It calls for all States to "co-operate with each other in ensuring development and eliminating obstacles to development".

We believe that solidarity among developing countries, often collectively referred to as the "Global South" or "Third World", is crucial for structurally underdeveloped countries to break away from path dependence. Without solidarity, it will be impossible to reform the global economic governance architecture that continues to disadvantage them.

This became so clear during the COVID-19 pandemic crisis, when poor countries were denied access to vaccines, drugs, testing and other treatments using the Trade Related Intellectual Property Rights (TRIPS) of the World Trade Organisation (WTO).

We also believe that in accordance with the UN Declaration on the Right to Development, countries need to have solidarity among their citizens. Democratic and accountable governments have to respond to citizens' development aspirations and hence have an urgency to demand reform of the neo-colonial arrangements that disadvantage them. Solidarity among the countries of the Global South resists attempts by Northern powers to divide and rule.

We reject extreme deterministic views that attribute structural underdevelopment to culture or geography. Instead, we believe in the role of agency of citizens and States in determining their destiny. We, therefore, deplore policy conditionality that ties aid to the donor community's preferred policies and projects and thereby limits the policy space of developing countries.

We also reject a "one-size-fits-all" policy approach. The UN Declaration on the Right to Development affirms States' right and duty to formulate appropriate national development policies. A rigid "one-size-fits-all" approach can be extremely harmful, particularly for transition economies. There is no blueprint for structural transformation and systemic transition. Learning by doing is key when "crossing the river by feeling the stones".

It is false to believe that citizens' agency can be expressed only through unfettered markets. Therefore, we argue for the guiding role of the State that responds to citizens' development aspirations in structural transformation. This is especially the case because structural transformation is now much more challenging as countries have to be mindful of equity and environmental sustainability. Countries cannot simply follow the pattern or path traversed by already-developed countries.

Similarly, it is false to believe that the expression of citizens' agency implies the superiority of individual property rights to communal ownership. Citizens' agency implies that they can choose from a variety of arrangements or social compacts to achieve their development aspirations.

We reject the appeal for authoritarianism for a developmental State, which implies a false dichotomy between democracy and development. Authoritarian developmental States are rare; unable to handle crises and hence likely to collapse; inept for innovation and hence likely to stagnate.

Therefore, we argue for an inclusive or participatory developmental State where citizens interact with the State without fear and prejudice; and where the State empowers citizens and widens citizens' choices. In other words, democratic consolidation and building of State capabilities should be organically linked.

We conceptualised this book during our consultancy work for the United Nations Economic and Social Commission for Asia and the Pacific (UN-ESCAP, Bangkok) and the United Nations Office of the High Representative for the Least Developed Countries, Landlocked Developing Countries and Small Island Developing States (UN-OHRLLS, New York). Our understanding of the wider issues of development, systemic transition, democratisation and the State's role deepened during our work at the United Nations Support Facility for Indonesian Recovery (UNSFIR, Jakarta). The familiarity with structural transformation issues of the countries analysed in this book was gained during Anis Chowdhury's tenure as Director of the Macroeconomic Policy and Development Division at the UN-ESCAP and a Senior Official at the United Nations Department of Economic and Social Affairs (UN-DESA). Our profound thanks to these United Nations entities without implicating any for the views expressed in this book.

Finally, we thank our publisher, Palgrave Macmillan, first for accepting our book proposal, and then for bearing with our repeated requests for an extension of the deadline to submit the manuscript.

We dedicate this book to the Global South solidarity movement and development aspirations of the Third World's toiling masses.

Sydney and Canberra, Australia
May 2024

Anis Chowdhury
Zulfan Tadjoeddin
Yogi Vidyattama

Contents

Abbreviations

AFC	Asian Financial Crisis
ASEAN	Association of Southeast Asian Nations
BRI	Belt and Road Initiative
DAC	Development Assistance Committee
ECI	Economic Complexity Index
ECOSOC	The United Nations Economic and Social Commission
EEU	Eurasian Economic Union
EU	European Union
GFC	Global Financial Crisis
IMF	International Monetary Fund
ITO	International Trade Organisation
LDCs	Least Developed Countries
LLDCs	Landlocked Developing Countries
ODA	Official Development Assistance
OECD	Organisation for Economic Cooperation and Development
SAARC	South Asian Association for Regional Cooperation
SAP	Structural Adjustment Programmes
SCO	Shanghai Cooperation Organisation
SIDS	Small Island Developing States
TNCs	Transnational Corporations
UNCTAD	United Nations Conference on Trade and Development
UN-DESA	United Nations Department of Economic and Social Affairs
UNDP	United Nations Development Programmes
UN-ESCAP	United Nations Economic and Social Commission for Asia and the Pacific

UN-OHRLLS	United Nations Office of the High Representative for the Least Developed Countries, Landlocked Developing Countries and Small Island Developing States
USSR	Union of Soviet Socialist Republics
WEF	World Economic Forum
WTO	World Trade Organisation

List of Figures

List of Tables

CHAPTER 1

Introduction: Context and Overview

"…the spread of modern economic growth, despite its worldwide partial effects, is limited in that the economic performance in countries accounting for three-quarters of world population still falls far short of the minimum levels feasible with the potential of modern technology" (Simon Kuznets, 1971 Nobel Lecture, republished in 1973)

Ever since the United Nations defined development as, "growth *plus* change (italics in the original); change, in turn is social and cultural, as well as economic and qualitative as well as quantitative" (UN, 1962, pp. 2–3) in 1961 at the start of the United Nations First Decade of Development and categorised 24 mostly decolonised poor countries as "least developed" in 1971 at the beginning of the United Nations Second Decade of Development, structural change remained elusive in these countries. The 1971 list of least developed countries (LDCs) included 17 African newly independent countries—Benin, Botswana, Burkina Faso, Burundi, Chad, Ethiopia, Guinea, Lesotho, Malawi, Maldives, Mali, Niger, Rwanda, Somalia, Sudan, Uganda, United Republic of Tanzania; 4 landlocked Asia countries—Afghanistan, Bhutan, Lao People's Democratic Republic (Lao, PDR), Nepal; 2 Asia–Pacific Small Island Developing States (SIDS)—Maldives, Samoa; one Arab country—Yemen and

A. Chowdhury et al., *Structural Transformations as Developing Africa, Asia, and the Pacific*, https://doi.org/10.1007/978-981-97-9092-0_1

one Latin American country—Haiti. New countries were included in the list since 1971, and disappointingly the number stood at 44 in 2024.[1]

These LDCs were identified for special support measures by the donor and international community. These include favourable market access to industrial country markets, concessional development finance in addition to grants and agreed aid target, technical and capacity building supports. The LDCs together with their development partners identified priority areas and adopted 10-year action programmes at the initiative of the United Nations in order to accelerate their transformation. The first such action programme, known as Substantial New Programme of Action, was adopted at the first United Nations Conference on the LDCs in Paris in 1981. Since then, four-decade-long action programmes have been adopted focusing on different priority areas with a view to achieving agreed development targets.[2]

Despite such heightened attention, only 7 countries—Botswana (1994), Cabo Verde (2007), Maldives (2011), Samoa (2014), Equatorial Guinea (2017), Vanuatu (2020), Bhutan (2023)—could qualify to graduate out of the LDC category.[3] São Tomé and Príncipe are scheduled to graduate in 2024; Bangladesh, Lao PDR and Nepal in 2026 and Solomon Islands in 2027. Among them only 4 succeeded during the most recently concluded Istanbul Programme of Action (2011–2020) which had an ambitious target of halving the number of LDCs by 2020.

Being landlocked and small island developing states (SIDS), many of the LDCs are also supported by complementary 10-year programmes of action for these categories of countries.[4] Yet, the majority of the LDCs failed to structurally transform their economies. Even those LDCs which graduated out of the LDC category remain highly vulnerable and face uncertain development prospects with high poverty and rising inequality.

[1] Visit the website of the United Nations Department of Economic and Social Affairs (UN-DESA), https://www.un.org/development/desa/dpad/least-developed-country-category/creation-of-the-ldc-category-and-timeline-of-changes-to-ldc-membership-and-criteria.html for the list of LDCs.

[2] For comprehensive programmes of action for LDCs, visit https://www.un.org/ldcportal/content/comprehensive-programmes-action-ldcs.

[3] The graduated year is in the parenthesis.

[4] Visit the website of the United Nations Office of the High Representative for the Least Developed Countries, Landlocked Developing Countries and Small Island Developing States (OHRLLS), https://www.un.org/ohrlls/.

How can one explain such a dismal failure or "stubborn" structural underdevelopment? What are the barriers to their structural transformation or development? How can they overcome these barriers? What role should citizens and States play in structural transformation.

In this book, we seek to answer these and related questions for African and Asian LDCs (Chapters 4 & 5, respectively) and remote Pacific SIDS (Chapter 7). We begin with discussing conceptual issues in Chapter 2, followed by a discussion on the stylised facts and some key features of structurally underdeveloped countries in Chapter 3.

We also analyse five Central Asian countries and Azerbaijan (Chapter 6). These former Soviet republics offer interesting insights into structural transformation. They are landlocked countries; but became "landlinked", being part of a larger economic and political union—Union of Soviet Socialist Republics (USSR). Seventy years of Soviet central planning integrated these economies not only among themselves, but also with the rest of the former Soviet republics. "An intensive interregional exchange of goods among the former Soviet republics, and so interrepublican trade had become a major factor in their interdependence", as Ünal Çeviköz (1994, p. 45) observed.

The strong emphasis on industrialisation during the Soviet era also transformed their primary resource-dependent economies, with a great degree of product specialisation. On average about 20% of their gross material product (the measure of GDP used during the Soviet era) came from industry. This integration and interdependence were ruptured with the collapse of the Soviet Union in 1991 and the emergence of former Soviet republics as independent States. Not only these Central Asian former Soviet republics suddenly transformed from landlinked to landlocked, but also all of them, except Uzbekistan, suffered severe economic collapse and deindustrialised during their transition to a market-oriented economy. They now face the disadvantages of landlockedness and uncertainty of commodity price fluctuations.

Thus, our questions with regard to these Central Asian transition economies are: what can they do to overcome the disadvantages of landlockedness; how can they re-industrialise and diversify their economies away from primary resource dependence and what can the Central Asian transition economies and the African and Asian LDCs learn from each other's experiences?

Structural Underdevelopment—The Debate

Pioneering development economists, such as Ragnar Nurkse, Walt Rostow, Albert Hirschman, Gunnar Myrdal, attributed underdevelopment primarily to the lack of capital, resulting in a low level of productivity leading to low income and low savings and thus a "vicious circle" or "circular causation" of "low-level equilibrium trap". For them, the solution was straightforward—a "big push" of investment with external help, primarily aid and foreign direct investment—to break the trap. The argument in favour of aid and external capital was formalised in the so-called two-gap models, pioneered by Hollis Chenery and his associates (Michael Bruno; Alan Strout).

This saw newly decolonised poor countries vigorously demanding assured transfer of external funds from rich countries during the 1960s at different United Nations fora. The World Council of Churches suggested a target of 1% of rich countries' Gross National Income (GNI) to be transferred to poor countries as official aid and private capital to which all rich countries—the members of the OECD's Development Assistance Committee (DAC)—subscribed. The target was later fine-tuned to 0.7% as official aid and 0.3% as private capital, totalling the agreed target, of 1% of GNI.[5] Alas, only 6 countries have ever met the target, and the OECD average has never exceeded 0.4%.[6]

Despite the failure to meet the agreed official development aid (ODA) target, the donor community shifted the focus of discussion to aid effectiveness. The donor community largely blames the lack of

[5] In 1969, the Pearson Commission—in its report *Partners in Development*—proposed a target of 0.7% of donor GNP to be reached "by 1975 and in no case later than 1980". This suggestion was taken up in a UN resolution on 24 October 1970. DAC members generally accepted the 0.7% target for official development assistance (ODA), at least as a long-term objective, with some notable exceptions: Switzerland—not a member of the United Nations until 2002—did not adopt the target, and the US stated that it did not subscribe to specific targets or timetables, although it supported the more general aims of the Resolution. A target of ODA of 0.75% of Gross National Product (GNP) was proposed to be reached by 1972, based on work by Nobel-Prize winning Jan Tinbergen, who estimated the inflows required for developing economies to achieve desirable growth rates.

[6] Sweden was the first country to meet the target in 1974, joined by the Netherlands in 1975. Norway and Denmark reached it in 1976 and 1978, respectively, and Luxembourg reached it in 2000—they have consistently met the target since, while Finland achieved it once, in 1991. In fact, Sweden, Norway, Luxembourg, Denmark and the Netherlands have all reached or exceeded the 0.7% target.

good governance and absorptive capacity of poor recipient countries for aid ineffectiveness, thus absolving themselves for their failure to meet commitments. Rich countries' disregard of their aid commitments not only results in large shortfalls of development finance, but also causes uncertainty or unpredictability of aid. Both adversely impact planning and implementation of development projects, and thus contribute to poor absorption or utilisation of aid.

Some leading development economists attribute the causes of development failure to poor countries' difficult culture or ethnicity, unfortunate geography and weak institutions. For example, it is argued that ethnic similarities can encourage positive enterprise development, while conflict due to ethnic differences is a bane to development. Thus, William Easterly and Ross Levine (1997) claimed that a significant cause of Sub-Saharan Africa's "growth tragedy" is ethnic fragmentation. Ingeniously, they related everything under the sky that may possibly impair growth, such as low schooling, underdeveloped financial systems, insufficient infrastructure, distorted foreign exchange markets, to high ethnic diversity!

Cultural or sociological explanation for development has a long history, pioneered by early twentieth-century German sociologist, Max Weber, who advanced the idea that some socio-religious-cultural traits or ethics, such as Protestantism are more conducive to capitalist development than Catholicism. Such deterministic explanation re-emerged and came to prominence in the 1980s attempting to explain the spectacular transformation of East Asia. It is claimed that so-called "Asian values", rooted in Confucianism, encourage frugality (hence high savings), respect for authority (hence discipline), harmony (hence social-political stability) and hard work (hence high labour productivity) (see, for example, Wang, Smyth and Tan, 2000; Berger and Hsiao, 1988). The founder Prime Minister of Singapore, Lee Kuan Yew, held the view that these are essential ingredients of East Asia's economic growth success (see Barr, 2000 for a review of the debate). However, the 1997–98 Asian crisis, largely attributed to crony capitalism, has discredited the Asian values thesis.

The fact that nearly all countries in the tropics are underdeveloped while countries located in temperate zones all show a relatively high level of economic development led to the so-called geography hypothesis that countries in tropical regions grow more slowly than countries in temperate environments. For example, David Bloom and Jeffrey Sachs

(1998) attributed Africa's lacklustre growth performance to its unfortunate geography, pointing that a sizeable proportion of the African population is in tropical climates, infested with parasitic diseases such as malaria, which according to John Gallup and Jeffrey Sachs (2001, p. 85) "a large impact on the economy, such as foreign investment and economic networks within the country".

It is also argued that the climatic conditions in the tropics exert a negative effect on the productivity of agriculture due to, for example, the absence of frost periods allowing faster growth of bacteria which mineralise soil organic matter and hence lower soil quality. The high temperatures in the tropics also reduce the photosynthetic potential of plants and lead to higher plant respiration, which can cause a loss of agricultural productivity. Thus, John Gallup (1998) finds that tropical agriculture suffers a productivity decrement of 30–50% after controlling for factor inputs.

For resource-rich structurally underdeveloped African countries, it is often claimed that their natural resources are in fact a "curse"—manifested in several ways. For example, one major stumbling block to industrialisation or a dynamic manufacturing sector is the appreciation of exchange rates with the inflow of foreign currencies, particularly during the commodity price booms—the phenomenon often referred to as "Dutch disease" (Ianchovichina and Onder, 2017).

Natural resources often provide a fertile ground for corruption and reduce the levels of rule of law and quality of institutions (Norman, 2009; Collier and Gunning, 1999). Thus, the natural resource curse can also occur through poorer governance and corruption as in the case of Nigeria (Amin, 2009), a country ranked 154th least corrupt out of 180 countries in 2021 by Transparency International.

Another channel for a resource curse is violent conflict as claimed in research at the World Bank (Bannon and Collier, 2013) that the countries most likely to be blighted by conflict are those whose economies depend heavily on natural resources. It is claimed that greed and grievances related to natural resources, especially in an ethnically diverse society, are the root causes of violent conflict and civil war (Stewart, 2002).

Among other geographical factors identified as impediments to growth are landlockedness and remoteness which raise trade costs. Adam Smith, as early as 1776 in his *The Wealth of Nations*, postulated the influence of geographical location on economic growth. By raising transport costs, both landlockedness and remoteness from global centres of commerce limit the scope for international trade, which is critical for enlarging the market in order to reap the benefits of scale and specialisation as well as the transfer of technology and foreign direct investment.

Thus, geography, especially the smallness and remoteness, seems a curse for the Pacific Small Island Developing States (PSIDS) as highlighted in Chapter 7. They "are fragmented and 'sea-locked' with limited access to world markets, suffer from the challenges of smallness and geographic isolation" (World Bank, 2009, p. 3). Their income levels are influenced by their extreme isolation, and limited scope to tap economies of scale due to small populations and little arable land (Becker, 2012). They are also disproportionately vulnerable to climate change-related extreme weather conditions. Thus, geography is often regarded as their destiny.

The role of institutions has become one of the most popular research areas in development economics since the 1990s, popularised by Douglas North's 1993 Nobel Prize for his work on institutions. The International Monetary Fund (IMF)'s *World Economic Outlook* (April 2023) focused on growth and institutions, indicating "a resurgence of interest in this subject, including research into the sources of institutional differences across countries, the channels through which institutions may affect economic performance, and the quantitative importance of these links" (IMF, 2023, p. 95).

Jeffery Sachs (2003, p. 38) expressed concerns about "the vague concept of institution", and cautioned that "the debate over the role of institutions in economic development has become dangerously simplified". However, the adherents of the institutional school (e.g., Dani Rodrik, Arvind Subramanian, and Francesco Trebbi, 2004) claim that institutional quality "trumps" geography as an explanation of growth. William Easterly is also critical about the "geography matter" school and supports the institutionalists claiming, "destructive governments rather than destructive geography explain the poverty of nations" (Easterly, 2009).

However, despite the general acknowledgement that "institutions matter" for development, the nature of the relationship is still debated and contested (see Shirley, 2009). Moreover, interesting questions remain unresolved, for example,

- what specific set of institutions are optimal or desirable for economic growth, or which institutions must function effectively if countries are to develop;
- do countries need to build strong institutions first and growth will follow, or do they evolve together;
- why have so few countries been able to create and sustain the rules and norms that foster growth and social progress;
- how can poorer countries attain well-functioning institutions?

One of the main problems with the institutional explanation of underdevelopment is its predominance of market and private property rights or preference of individualism over collectivism. By default, it regards local practices and traditions, such as communal ownership or collectivist systems, as inferior or unconducive for development.

The United Nations Conference on Trade and Development (UNCTAD) attempted to simplify the barriers of structural transformation as a lack of "productive capacity", comprised of "productive resources, entrepreneurial capabilities and production linkages that together determine a country's ability to produce goods and services that will help it grow and develop".[7] Components of productive capacity include human capital, natural capital, energy, transport, information & communication technology, institutions, private sector and structural change. UNCTAD reports a high positive correlation between productive capacity index and per capita GDP, and a negative correlation between productive capacity and lack of merchandise exports diversification (i.e., high concentration in a few products). Thus, it concludes that the low productive capacity of LDCs is the main barrier to their structural transformation.

UNCTAD's emphasis on productive capacity is motivated by the pioneering development economists who emphasised the lack of financial, physical and human capital as mentioned earlier, and the criteria used by the United Nations for the LDC classification—(i) income, (ii) human assets and (iii) economic and environmental vulnerability. Each of the three criteria is measured by using key indicators which reflect long-term structural handicaps. If a country falls under threshold levels of these

[7] See UNCTAD, https://unctad.org/topic/least-developed-countries/productive-capacities-index.

three, it is eligible to be classified as an LDC. The graduation thresholds are set higher than the thresholds for inclusion to ensure that graduation is sustainable.[8]

However, the main problem with the UNCTAD's productive capacity explanation is that it is tautological—poor countries by definition have low productive capacity. Thus, the argument is circular—poor productive capacity constraints countries' income growth, and low-income constraints their ability to expand productive capacity; the result is a "low-level equilibrium trap", a terminology coined by Richard Nelson (1956). UNCTAD's solutions for breaking the trap are not dissimilar to the ones suggested by pioneering development economists as mentioned earlier. Among them, foreign aid, technical assistance and favourable market access to development countries play a critical role.

Our Take

While cultural, geographical and institutional factors may play a role, we reject determinism, for example, a country is doomed if it does not share Confucius or Protestant ethics. We also reject the extreme or dogmatic view that high ethnic diversity is the root cause of all the ills. Similarly, we reject the century-old derogatory geographic view of Charles-Louis Montesquieu (1689–1755) that the warm and humid climate of the South brings out only the worst in every person (Montesquieu, 1989, p. 231). We reject an equally dubious argument of Ellsworth Huntington who, in 1915, wrote, "The climate of many countries seems to be one of the great reasons why idleness, dishonesty, immorality, stupidity, and weakness of will prevail" (Huntington, 1915, p. 411).

We believe that no single factor can explain structural underdevelopment; thus, searching for a universal answer—or "one-size-fits-all"—explanation is futile. Nonetheless, we believe that some common threads bind them. Furthermore, we believe in "path dependence" of development and structural change. That is, initial conditions matter. Almost for all of them, except a few—e.g., Ethiopia, Afghanistan and Nepal—the initial conditions were determined by their colonial experiences.

Even these countries, which were not formally colonised, could not remain outside colonial influences; being landlocked, they either had to

[8] See UN-DESA, https://www.un.org/development/desa/dpad/least-developed-country-category/ldc-criteria.html.

sign compromising treaties with colonial powers occupying the neighbouring countries or faced constant threats of war and disruptions. For example, in 1896, a decade after the European powers began "scramble for Africa" and the border of Eritrea was drawn for Italy, it attacked Ethiopia. Beaten back by a well-armed Ethiopian force, Italy invaded Ethiopia again in 1936; declared it part of its colonial empire and conquered it during the Second World War (WW II). Super-power rivalry continued and a Soviet Union-backed coup in 1974 established Ethiopia as a Marxist–Leninist state under a military junta. Various opposition groups drawn from a specific ethnic background began armed resistance against the Soviet-backed Ethiopian junta army which was already fighting the Eritrean separatists, whose identity was defined by Italy's colonial rule (1882–1941). The civil war contributed to one of the world's worst famines during 1983–1985, affecting 7.75 million people (out of Ethiopia's 38–40 million) with approximately 300,000 to 1.2 million dead; 2.5 million internally displaced and 400,000 refugees leaving Ethiopia. Almost 200,000 children were orphaned (Glorgis, 1989).

Afghanistan shares a similar history. Between 1839 and 1842, British imperial forces fought a bitter war in Afghanistan, the campaign ending with Britain withdrawing from the country having suffered one of the worst military disasters of the nineteenth century. However, the Great Game between the Western powers and Russia involving Afghanistan continued ravaging the country and turning it into one of the world's poorest countries which was once thriving along the ancient silk road, with great cities like Kabul, Balkh, Bamiyan, Herat, Kandahar, Ghazni and Badakhshan.

The Treaty of Sagauli (1816) ended the Anglo-Nepalese War (1814–1816), known as the Gorkha War, fought between the Gorkhali army of the Kingdom of Nepal and the British forces of the East India Company (EIC). The Sugauli Treaty ceded some of the Nepalese-controlled territory to the EIC and rendered moot the degree of independence of Nepal. Although the 1923 Treaty helped Nepal to stay as an independent sovereign state in the immediate aftermath of India's independence in 1947, senior Indian politicians like Vallabhbhai Patel were reported to have wished to annex Nepal within India. However, India's influence over Nepal looms large.

The institutionalists admit that countries inherited poor institutions from their colonial masters. Countries that had valuable resources, people that could be enslaved or land suitable for plantation agriculture, enticed colonisers to design institutions to exploit these endowments (Shirley, 2009). The exceptions were the cases of settler colonisation of countries with a sparse population, where colonisers could ethnically cleanse the indigenous population to make their stay "safe". As observed by Daron Acemoglu, Simon Johnson and James Robinson (2001, 2002), only in such cases, Europeans settle in larger numbers bringing with them beneficial institutions. This observation finds support in Benjamin Mackenzie-Grieve (2024) in his Harvard University Master's thesis.

Beyond these few exception cases, the colonial powers created exploitative institutional arrangements which lacked accountability. Their success depended on the creation or patronisation of a compliant local elite class, which replaced colonial exploiters after decolonisation, thus has a vested interest in the continuation of unaccountable institutions. It is like a virus, transmitted from the colonial regime to the post-independence rulers as Tom Burgis (2015) observed. After reporting for nine years for the *Financial Times* on Africa, Burgis exposed how the extractive industries, owned by some of the world's biggest companies—among them blue-chip TNCs—turned into a hideous looting machine. He also exposed the West and former colonial powers' guilt of complicity in the raping of a continent and showed how even the World Bank is linked to this looting, by propping up awful regimes.

Indeed, military rulers in Africa were eulogised by Western civil-military relations experts as "modernising soldiers" (Adekanye, 1978). Getachew Fentahun (2023, p. 11) demonstrates that despite Western countries' professed use of aid for democratisation, "donors not only support but also align with authoritarians who reject liberal values". Thandika Mkandawire (2010, p. 1150) stated that "even if they swear by democracy, part of the aid establishment is still preoccupied with funding means and ways to insulate aid from encumbrance of democratic politics in democratic countries by creating what have been aptly termed authoritarian enclave". This suggests that aid is not a matter of democracy but a matter of donors' vested interest.

Throughout this book, we have highlighted the democratic deficit in the structurally underdeveloped Africa, South and Southeast Asia, Central Asia and the Pacific SIDS. In large part, this, too, is due to continued neo-colonialism. We mentioned earlier how the economic and political union with the former USSR and its sudden break-up determined the economies of Central Asian landlocked countries' initial conditions. Although these newly independent countries established formal democracies with regular elections, they remain largely autocratic, a legacy of the Soviet centralised one-party system. Jos Boonstra (2012) noted that Central Asian regimes have developed most of the institutions of a democracy; but they lack democratic practice, and democracy is seen by the leaders of Central Asia as a direct threat to their existence—a fear born out of the collapse of the USSR itself in trying to democratise and reform (Pomfret, 2021). Jonathan Eales (2021) analysed the rising tide of authoritarianism in Central Asia. The fear was reinforced by the deep economic collapse that the Central Asian countries witnessed in the first decade of their systemic transition.

We can also relate ethnic conflicts as well as border and resource disputes to the way the colonisers carved up continents, especially Africa, in their scramble for resources of the countries that are now structurally underdeveloped. As Robert Blanton, David Mason and Brian Athow noted (2001, p. 473), “European colonialism had profound, lasting, and wide-ranging effects on the development of contemporary African states. One of the most profound legacies of the colonial period has been ethnic conflict. When the European powers imposed formal territorial boundaries throughout the continent in 1885, seeds for ethnic conflict in post-colonial Africa were sown. Those boundaries were drawn with little or no consideration to the actual distribution of indigenous ethno-cultural groups. With the demise of colonial rule, the former colonies, with their colonial borders essentially intact, were transformed into some of the more ethnically fragmented states”. According to Tasew Gashaw (2017), “Improper border design and the partitioning of ethnic groups have contributed to underdevelopment, and instability in African states”.

One of the manifestations of neo-colonialism is geopolitical competitions of global and regional powers to draw poor countries to their spheres of influence. This fractures solidarity among the countries of the “Global South” or “Third World” and prevents effective regional cooperation among them for mutual benefits. For example, meaningful regional cooperation could not emerge in the African continent as the Pan-Africanist leaders were toppled by former colonial power conspired coup d’état that led to oppressive dictatorial regimes (discussed in more details in Chapter 4). As elaborated in Chapter 5, in the case of South Asia, the conflict between India and Pakistan, mainly linked to the Kashmir issue, and India’s hegemonic attitudes towards smaller neighbours rendered the South Asian Association for Regional Cooperation (SAARC) ineffective.

India's rivalry with China also adversely impacted landlocked Nepal's and Bhutan's development prospects.

Following the implosion of the USSR, the Central Asian transition countries immediately confronted the problem of settling their new (formerly internal) state borders, artificially drawn during the Soviet era with little consideration paid to ethnic or geographical features of the area (International Crisis Group, 2002). The process of demarcation of the ill-defined borders within the region, predominantly in the Fergana Valley, remains incomplete. Thousands of kilometres of borders still in dispute serve as a stumbling block for intra-regional cooperation and feed into tensions arising from time to time.

As discussed in Chapter 6, this has also created a fertile ground for geopolitical rivalries, especially when the region is strategically located, bordering China, Russia and Iran which are seen by the US as a new "axis of evil" (Taylor, 2024). Following its retreat from Afghanistan, and the Russia-Ukraine war, the US wants to deepen connections with Central Asian countries for its so-called "counter-terrorism" activities, and combating Russia's sanctions evasion. The region's vast energy resources also make it attractive to European nations. Meanwhile, China has deepened its presence in Central Asia with its Belt and Road Initiative (BRI).

The colonial legacies continue to disadvantage, especially the Sub-Saharan African States through neo-colonial arrangements, such as *CFA frank*, which forces the resource-rich, but poor former African colonies of France to use currency issued by France and deposit their foreign currency reserves with the French Treasury as a condition for France granting them independence. As elaborated in Chapter 4, such stringent control creates economic dependencies because it allows France to dictate the economic direction of its former colonies (Taylor, 2019; Yansane, 1978). James Wilson (2021) in his Ph.D. dissertation at the Oxford University has shown how this neo-colonial currency and reserve arrangement not only deprives them of the benefits derived from their natural resources, but also constrains their macroeconomic policy space. Luigi Di Maio, Italy's former deputy prime minister and minister of foreign affairs, observed in 2019: "France is one of those countries that by printing money for 14 African states prevents their economic development and contributes to the fact that the refugees leave and then die in the sea or arrive on our coasts".[9]

Condescending donor-recipient relations that tie aid to conditions and the post-WW II global economic governance architecture, such as the World Bank and the International Monetary Fund (IMF), also favour rich countries as the major share-holders of these institutions (Helleiner, 2002). While Chapter 7 narrates the damaging impact of condescending aid relations and highlights the limits of the neo-liberal policies in the Pacific SIDS, Chapter 4 sheds light on how, encouraged by the World Bank's "Berg Report", liberalisation and privatisation policy conditionality of IMF-World Bank structural programmes (SAP) during the 1980s and the 1990s caused great damage to Sub-Saharan Africa, often referred to as "lost decades of development" (Easterly, 2001). The IMF-World Bank aid conditionality and policy advices on industrialisation, trade, taxation and development finance are largely responsible for developing countries never-ending external debt distress (Chowdhury & Jomo, 2023).

In the absence of a blueprint for transition, a rapid change imposed by donors and the IMF/World Bank increased the risks and instabilities, thus greatly harmed Central Asian transition economies as highlighted in Chapter 6. According to Patrick Hamm, Lawrence King and David Stuckler (2012), mass privatisation programmes created a massive fiscal shock for post-communist governments, thereby undermining the development of private-sector governance institutions and severely exacerbating the transformational recession. Not only there was an unprecedented economic collapse, but also adult mortality increased and life expectancy dropped in most of these former Soviet republics during their transition (Brainerd, 2021). Michael Hudson (2021) described the phenomena as "Central Asia's neoliberal tragedy".

The Organisation for Economic Cooperation and Development (OECD), a rich country club, sets rules for international taxation, that favour rich countries. Using loopholes in these rules the transnational corporations (TNCs)[10] siphon off more money from poor countries than

[9] "African migration: Is the CFA franc forcing people to leave?", BBC News, 25 January, 2019, https://www.bbc.com/news/world-africa-46960532 (accessed 27/10/2023).

[10] Throughout this book, we shall refer to business organisations with operations in more than one country, as transnational corporations (TNCs), instead of commonly used

these countries receive as foreign aid (GFI, 2015). For example, in 2012, developing countries received a total of US$1.3 trillion, including all aid, investment, and income from abroad; but some US$3.3 trillion flowed out of them—US$2 trillion net outflow from the Global South to the Global North. Since 1980, these net outflows add up to US$16.3 trillion, roughly the GDP of the US! The bulk of this resource drain happened through illicit fund transfers by TNCs (US$13.4 trillion), facilitated by the World Trade Organisation (WTO)'s rule that requires custom officers to accept TNCs' trade invoices at face value except in very suspicious circumstances. The rest was due to interest payments.

In an attempt to maintain unfair trade, developed countries, in particular the US, scuttled the establishment of the International Trade Organisation (ITO), envisioned in the 1948 Havana Charter (Chowdhury & Jomo, 2018). Nearly half a century of efforts led to the creation of WTO in 1995 with a pledge to deliver pro-development international trade. However, developing countries have been completely sidelined in the WTO by the global powers (Walker, 2011). For example, Western countries used its trade-related intellectual property rights (TRIPS) to prevent developing countries' access to COVID-19 drugs, vaccines, tests and equipment, causing millions to die (Chowdhury & Jomo, 2021). The WTO is now permanently in a limbo, and its death is inevitable due to the US actions (Bloomberg, 2024; Johnson, 2019).

Lessons of History

Stylised facts and key features, reviewed in Chapter 3, reveal key lessons of history. Among them is the critical role of the State and policy space in determining a country's destiny. As highlighted by UNCTAD (2016, p. 1), "Market forces left alone cannot always drive the process of structural transformation and sustain economic growth; rather, they risk favouring specialization in low-productivity and low-value-added

term, multinational corporations (MNCs)—both generally headquartered in the Global North. MNCs predominantly produce for local or national markets, whereas TNCs distribute their production across countries and sell beyond any national or local market. Since the mid-1960s, TNCs have increasingly displaced MNCs, giving rise to growing global value chains across nations. Thus, TNCs are one of the principal drivers of globalisation and the most important beneficiaries of the liberalisation of investment and trade regimes, with rising influence on the development of the world economy and its constituent parts (UNCTAD, 1999).

economic activities, thus calling for government intervention". Like-wise, the World Bank's Growth Commission (2008, p. 5) noted, "Just because governments are sometimes clumsy and sometimes errant, does not mean they should be written out of the script. On the contrary, as the economy grows and develops, active, pragmatic governments have crucial roles to play".

A key second lesson is that countries cannot follow the historical pattern of structural transformation that now developed countries have traversed. This is especially the case for remote small island developing states. They have to find niche areas to develop which again needs the State's active role and ability to pursue independent policies. South-South cooperation and inclusive participatory policy making can play a critical role in this regard.

Finally, today's structurally underdeveloped countries confront much more challenging circumstances than what the mature economies had faced in their early stage of development. Now structurally underdeveloped countries face much more daunting task of maintaining environmental sustainability, especially in the face of climate change threats. They also have to be much more aware of social tensions that accompany growth and structural change. That is, they do not have the option of either "grow first and clean up later" or "grow first and distribute later" strategies.

Way Forward

We believe that solidarity—among and within the countries—is key to overcoming the challenge of initial conditions and path dependence created by colonial legacies and neo-colonial arrangements, including unfair global economic governance architecture. The Afro-Asia Conference in Bandung (Indonesia) gave hope to the newly decolonised countries; they united to:

- create the non-aligned movement (NAM) desiring to remain neutral in the damaging geopolitical rivalry between the two super-powers—the US and the USSR;
- organise United Nations Conference on Trade and Development (UNCTAD) and
- demand a new international economic order (NIEO)

in order to overcome unfavourable trade and financial relations with the rich world and end exploitative operations of transnational corporations (TNCs), especially in their natural resource sector.

The final communiqué of the Bandung Conference expressed, "general desire for economic co-operation among the participating countries on the basis of mutual interest and respect for national sovereignty"; "agreed to provide technical assistance to one another"; "recognized the vital need for stabilizing commodity trade"; recommended that: "Asian-African countries should diversify their export trade by processing their raw material, wherever economically feasible, before export"; promote "intra-regional trade" and provide "facilities for transit trade of landlocked countries".

The United Nations General Assembly resolution adopted in May 1974 to establish a New International Economic Order (NIEO) "based on equity, sovereign equality, interdependence, common interest and cooperation among all States, irrespective of their economic and social systems". The NIEO was hoped to "correct inequalities and redress existing injustices, make it possible to eliminate the widening gap between the developed and the developing countries and ensure steadily accelerating economic and social development and peace and justice for present and future generations". It also reaffirmed the target of 1% of the GNP of developed countries to be devoted to official assistance to the developing countries, and called for the accumulation of buffer stocks of commodities in order to offset market fluctuations, combat inflationary tendencies and ensure grain and food security.

As can be seen, the Bandung declaration and NIEO were about the desire of newly decolonised countries to structurally transform them and how that desire could be fulfilled. Unfortunately, they have been betrayed. What emerged instead was TNC-led super globalisation, supported by the donor community, including the IMF-World Bank. While the target aid promise remained unfulfilled, aid conditionality forced structurally underdeveloped countries to comply with TNCs' interests. The result has been continued centre-periphery relationships that ensured transfer of resources from poor to rich countries, and hence a widening gap between the developed and developing worlds.

Such betrayal was possible due to rich countries' time-tested "divide and rule" strategy that saw G7 expand to G20 to co-opt leading developing countries. Ironically, China, India and Indonesia, which played a leading role in creating the Bandung spirit and the Third World solidarity, are now in G20 to endorse the G7 agenda, for example, entrusting OECD to address TNCs' tax avoidance which disproportionately harms low-income countries (OECD, 2014). The result has been OECD's so-called "Inclusive Framework"—a deceptive term—and a "bad deal" for developing countries (McCarthy, 2022). *The* Economist (2015, 2022) called the deal "New rules, same old paradigm". The deal could have been better (Chowdhury & Jomo, 2019) and top economists condemned the IMF's arm-twisting of developing countries to adopt harmful OECD tax deal (Tax Justice Network, 2023).

The United Nations Economic and Social Commission (ECOSOC), which was designed to serve as the central forum for discussing international economic and social issues, and formulating policy recommendations addressed to member states and the United Nations System, has been marginalised by rich and powerful countries in favour of the IMF and the World Bank where they have share-holding power. Global economic and social agenda are now set at the World Economic Forum (WEF) set up by TNC leaders.

The G20 suffers from legitimacy deficits under international law as its institutional structure fails to respect the principle of a democratic and equitable international order as set forth in various United Nations instruments (Alexander, Lorez, Zobl and Thürer, 2014). This will not be resolved by co-opting the African Union (AU) and calling it G21. The WEF's organisational status is ambiguous, and it lacks accountability even to its own members, casting doubt on the legitimacy of such an influential organisation (McNeil, 2023). Neither the Bretton Woods Institutions (IMF-World Bank) nor the OECD is as inclusive as the United Nations or ECOSOC.

Structurally underdeveloped countries are unlikely to get fair treatment in these fora which lack legitimacy or inclusivity. Therefore, their solidarity is critical for them to be heard, and their interests protected. Solidarity among the structurally underdeveloped countries is needed to prevent "beggar thy neighbour" competition among themselves, which eventually harms everyone. They may also be drawn into dangerous geopolitical rivalry among regional and global powers in the absence of solidarity among themselves. On the other hand, by remaining neutral and united in the spirit of Bandung, they can leverage their collective bargaining power to benefit from the regional and global geopolitical games.

While no amount of domestic institutional reforms, for example, to improve governance or revenue collections, can outweigh the systemic disadvantages of global economic governance architecture and neocolonial arrangements, the countries still have to strive for efficiency, accountability and shared progress. As shown in Chapter 3, most of the structurally underdeveloped countries are ranked low in terms of liberal democracy. Therefore, domestically, the most damaging for structurally underdeveloped countries is their democratic deficits, even though many of these countries have some form of electoral democracy.

It is often argued that poor countries are not fit for liberal democracy; they need more discipline than democracy, according to the founding Prime Minister of Singapore Lee Kuan Yew. Undemocratic regimes may produce high growth for a while as a regime legitimising tool; but cannot satisfactorily mediate between "winners" and "losers" or respond to other forms of social changes and consequences that result from structural changes (see for example, Girling, 1988; Chowdhury and Islam, 1993 for discussion in the context of East and Southeast Asia). This requires a distributive fiscal system (i.e., taxes and subsidies/transfers/social security) that is socially and politically acceptable and at the same time financially sustainable or responsible. Failure to achieve that often leads to violent conflicts and socio-political instabilities that adversely impact growth. Authoritarian regimes also cannot create dynamism or sustain growth as they stifle free thinking and experimentation without fear, which is vital for innovation and entrepreneurship.

Democratisation is needed for within-country solidarity. Democracy, the rule of law and respect for human rights are hallmarks of resilient, inclusive and peaceful societies. By making the governments accountable, and allowing participatory policymaking, democracy ensures shared progress. More critically, in ethnically and regionally diverse societies, democracy allows for resolving social and regional discontents without violence. As the UN Secretary-General, António Guterres noted, "Strong democratic societies are places that are capable of self-correction—and self-improvement. They can enable change—even radical change—without bloodshed and violence. And crucially, they are centres for broad-based cooperation, rooted in the principles of equality, participation and solidarity".[11]

[11] UN press release, SG/SM/21752, 29 March, 2023, https://press.un.org/en/2023/sgsm21752.doc.htm (accessed 6/05/2024).

A united country is in a better position to withstand external pressure, be it from the donor community through aid conditionality or from global/regional powers through various concessions that can comprise economic and political sovereignty. Democratic accountability also extends to how countries interact with one another, and thus, ensures solidarity among countries and neutrality in the geopolitical rivalry. It is much harder to convince people in a democracy that war is necessary against another democratic country. Thus, the more open and accountable governments are to their fellow citizens, the less likely they are to use force against other States whose systems are similarly open.

Therefore, it is important to dispel the argument that a country at a lower level of development or income is not fit for democracy. Nobel Laureate Amartya Sen (1999, p. 4) reminded "A country does not have to be deemed fit for democracy; rather, it has to become fit through democracy". In other words, it is wrong to ask whether a country is fit for democracy. The development potential of democracy can be relevant for "countries with their varying histories and cultures and disparate levels of affluence" (Sen, 1999, p. 4). We have elaborated democracy's instrumental value in fostering structural transformation and sustainable development in Chapter 5 on South and Southeast Asia.

Summing Up

While various factors—culture, geography and institutions—mentioned in the literature—can cause structural underdevelopment creating a vicious circle of low-productive capacity-low-income, we reject extreme or deterministic views of different schools of thought. We also believe that geography and institutions offer a better explanation of structural underdevelopment than culture or particular values.

We emphasise initial conditions shaped by colonial past and continued path dependence due to neo-colonial arrangements between former colonial powers and their former colonies as well as lop-sided global economic governance architecture that favours rich countries. Poor or weak institutions as well as ethnic conflicts found in many structurally underdeveloped countries are also legacies of their colonial past. Of all the institutional weaknesses, the worst is their democratic deficits, making them more prone to both internal and external conflicts.

Time has come for the rising Global South to collectively work for the unfinished business of an NIEO that today has to take a more integrated and universal approach for people, planet and prosperity for sustainable and inclusive development. However, the developing South must lead by putting its own house in order and improving democratic governance to ensure wider freedom of its own citizens to re-establish legitimacy and trust through a new social contract that responds to the needs and hopes of all citizens; not just in form, but in substance.

The United Nations Declaration on Right to Development[12] provides all the instruments for achieving structural transformation for shared prosperity. It affirms citizens' rights to participation in making policies that affect their lives and livelihoods, highlights State's responsibility for "appropriate national development policies" and calls for states to cooperate for "ensuring development and eliminating obstacles to development". It also asks for States "to promote a new international economic order based on sovereign equality, interdependence, mutual interest".

In the spirit of Bandung, they have to work together for the prosperity of their people and to protect humanity's common good, especially our planet. They should recall the Bandung message, "All of us … are united by more important things than those which superficially divide us. … And we are united by a common determination to preserve and stabilize peace in the world....".[13]

References

Acemoglu, D., Johnson, S., & Robinson, J. (2001). The colonial origins of comparative development: An empirical investigation. *American Economic Review, 91*(5), 1369–1401.

Acemoglu, D., Johnson, S., & Robinson, J. (2002). Reversal of fortune: Geography and institutions in the making of the modern world income distribution. *Quarterly Journal of Economics, 117*(4), 1231–1294.

Adekanye, J. B. (1978). On the theory of the modernising soldier. *Current Review on Peace and Violence, 8*(1), 29–40.

Alexander, K., Karin, L., Martin, Z., & Daniel, T. (2014). *The legitimacy of the G20 - A critique under international law.* available at: http://ssrn.com/abstract=2431164.

12 General Assembly resolution 41/128, available at https://www.ohchr.org/Documents/Issues/Development/RTD_booklet_en.pdf (20/05/2024).

13 Open address of President Sukarno at the Bandung Conference of Non-Aligned States, April 18 1955, https://international.ucla.edu/institute/article/18432 (6/05/2024).

Amin, M. (2009). "Dutch disease vs. Nigerian disease." *World Bank Private Sector Development Blog*, 28 April, https://blogs.worldbank.org/psd/dutch-disease-vs-nigerian-disease (accessed 03/01/2021).

Bannon, I., & Paul, C. (2013). *Natural resources and violent conflict options and actions*. World Bank.

Barr, M. (2000). Lee Kuan Yew and the 'Asian Values' debate. *Asian Studies Review, 24*(3), 309–334.

Becker, C. (2012). *Small island States in the Pacific: The tyranny of distance?* IMF Working Paper WP/12/223 (September).

Berger, P., & Hsin-huang, M. H. (Eds.). (1988). *In search of an east Asian development model*. Transaction Books.

Blanton, R., David, M., & Brian, A. (2001). Colonial style and post-colonial ethnic conflict in Africa. *Journal of Peace Research, 38*(4), 473–491.

Bloom, D., & Sachs, J. (1998). Geography, demography, and economic growth in Africa. *Brookings Papers on Economic Activity, 2*, 207–295.

Bloomberg. (2024). The death of the WTO now looks inevitable. *Bloomberg Editorial Board*, 9 March, https://www.bloomberg.com/opinion/articles/2024-03-08/world-trade-organization-s-death-is-a-momentous-error?embedded-checkout=true (accessed 6/05/204).

Boonstra, J. (2012). Democracy in Central Asia: Sowing in unfertile fields? *EUCAM Policy Brief* No. 23 (May), https://www.files.ethz.ch/isn/143354/PB_EUCAM_23.pdf (accessed 2/05/2024).

Brainerd, E. (2021). Mortality in Russia since the fall of the Soviet Union. *Comparative Economic Studies, 63*(4), 557–576.

Burgis, T. (2015). *The looting machine: Warlords, oligarchs, corporations, smugglers, and the theft of Africa's wealth*. Harper Colins.

Çeviköz, Ü. (1994). A brief account of the economic situation in the former soviet republics of central Asia. *Central Asian Survey, 13*(1), 45–50.

Chowdhury, A., & Jomo K. S. (2018). Havana charter's progressive trade vision subverted. *Inter Press Service (IPS) Opinion Column*, 4 December, http://www.ipsnews.net/2018/12/havana-charters-progressive-trade-vision-subverted/ (6/05/2024).

Chowdhury, A., & Jomo K. S. (2019). OECD tax reform proposal could be better. *Inter Press Service (IPS) Opinion Column*, 15 October, http://www.ipsnews.net/2019/10/oecd-tax-reform-proposal-better/ (6/05/2024).

Chowdhury, A., & Jomo K. S. (2021). End vaccine apartheid before millions more die. *Inter Press Service (IPS) Opinion Column*, 23 March, https://www.ipsnews.net/2021/03/end-vaccine-apartheid-millions-die/ (6/05/2024).

Chowdhury, A., & Iyanatul, I. (1993). *The newly industrialising economies of East Asia*. Routledge.

Chowdhury, A., & Jomo, K. S. (2023). Chronicles of debt crises foretold. *Development and Change, 54*(5), 994–1030.

Collier, P., & Jan, G. (1999). Why has Africa grown so slowly. *Journal of Economics Perspectives, 13*(3), 324–376.

Eales, J. (2021). The rising tide of authoritarianism in Central Asia. *Australian Institute of International Affairs*, 6 May, https://www.internationalaffairs.org.au/australianoutlook/the-rising-tide-of-authoritarianism-in-central-asia/ (2/05/2024).

Easterly, W. (2009). Lost in the tropics: Sachs' misguided African geography. *VoxEU/CEPR Columns*, 1 June, https://cepr.org/voxeu/columns/lost-tropics-sachs-misguided-african-geography (1/05/2024).

Easterly, W. (2001). The lost decades: Developing countries' stagnation in spite of policy reform 1980–1998. *Journal of Economic Growth, 6*(2), 135–157.

Easterly, W., & Ross, L. (1997). Africa's growth tragedy: Policies and ethnic divisions. *Quarterly Journal of Economics, 112*(4), 1203–1250.

Economist. (2015). New rules, same old paradigm. *The Economist*, 10 October.

Economist. (2022). "Developing countries take tax talks to the UN", *The Economist*, 1 December

Fentahun, G. (2023). Foreign aid in the post-colonial Africa: Means for building democracy or ensuring Western domination? *Cogent Social Sciences*. https://doi.org/10.1080/23311886.2023.2241257

Gallup, J., & Jeffrey, S. (2001). The economic burden of malaria. *American Journal of Tropical Medicine and Hygiene, 64*(1–2 Suppl), 85–96.

Gallup, J. (1998). *Agricultural productivity and geography*. Harvard Institute for International Development.

Gashaw, T (2017). Colonial borders in Africa: Improper design and its impact on African borderland communities. *Wilson Center Blog*, 17 November.https://www.wilsoncenter.org/blog-post/colonial-borders-in-africa-improper-design-and-its-impact-on-african-borderland-communities (2/05/2024).

Giorgis, D. W. (1989). *Red Tears: War, famine, and revolution in Ethiopia*. Red Sea Press.

Girling, J. (1988). Development and democracy in Southeast Asia. *The Pacific Review, 1*(4), 332–340.

Global Financial Integrity (GFI). (2015). *Financial Flows and Tax Havens Combining to Limit the Lives of Billions of People*. Centre for Applied Research (Norwegian School of Economics), Global Financial Integrity, Jawaharlal Nehru University, Instituto de Estudos Socioeconômicos, Nigerian Institute of Social and Economic Research.

Hamm, P., Lawrence, K., & David, S. (2012). Mass privatization, State capacity, and economic growth in post-communist countries. *American Sociological Review, 77*(2), 295–324.

Helleiner, G. (2002). Developing countries in global economic governance and negotiation processes. In D. Nayyar (Ed.), *Governing globalization: Issues and institutions* (pp. 308–333). Oxford University Press.

Hudson, M. (2021). Central Asia's neoliberal tragedy. *Monthly Review online*, https://mronline.org/2021/10/18/central-asias-neoliberal-tragedy/ (accessed 2/05/2024).

Huntington, E. (1915). *Civilization and Climate*. Hamden.

Ianchovichina, E., & Harun, O. (2017). Dutch disease: An economic illness easy to catch, difficult to cure. *Brookings Future Development Blog*, 31 October, https://www.brookings.edu/blog/future-development/2017/10/31/dutch-disease-an-economic-illness-easy-to-catch-difficult-to-cure/ (accessed 03/01/2021)

International Crisis Group. (2002). Central Asia: Border disputes and conflict potential. *Asia Report* No.33, https://www.crisisgroup.org/europe-central-asia/central-asia/tajikistan/central-asia-border-disputes-and-conflict-potential (10/05/2024).

International Monetary Fund (IMF). (2023). *World Economic Outlook, April 2003: Growth and Institutions*. The International Monetary Fund.

Johnson, K. (2019). How Trump may finally kill the WTO. *Foreign Policy*, 9 December, https://foreignpolicy.com/2019/12/09/trump-may-kill-wto-finally-appellate-body-world-trade-organization/ (accessed 6/05/2024).

Kuznets, S. (1973). Modern economic growth: Findings and reflections. *American Economic Review, 63*(3), 247–258.

Mackenzie-Grieve, B. (2024). *The British Effect: Is colonial legacy a contributing factor to post-colonial democratization?* Master's thesis, Harvard University Division of Continuing Education.

McCarthy, J. (2022). A bad deal for development: Assessing the impacts of the new inclusive framework tax deal on low- and middle-income countries. *Brookings Global Working Pape*r #174 (May).

McNeill, D. (2023). The World Economic Forum: An unaccountable force in global health governance? *Global Policy, 14*(5), 982–789.

Mkandawire, T. (2010). Aid, accountability, and democracy in Africa. *Social Research, 77*(4), 1149–1182.

Montesquieu, C.-L. (1989). *The spirit of the laws*. Cambridge University Press.

Nelson, R. (1956). A theory of the low-level equilibrium trap in underdeveloped economies. *American Economic Review, 46*(5), 894–908.

Norman, C. (2009). Rule of law and the resource curse: Abundance versus intensity. *Environmental and Resource Economics, 43*(2), 183–207.

OECD. (2014). *Two-Part Report to G20 Developing Working Group on the Impact of BEPS in Low Income Countries*. https://www.oecd.org/tax/tax-global/report-to-g20-dwg-on-the-impact-of-beps-in-low-income-countries.pdf (accessed 6/05/2024).

Pomfret, R. (2021). Central Asian Economies: Thirty years after dissolution of the Soviet Union. *Comparative Economic Studies, 63*, 537–556.

Rodrik, D., Arvind, S., & Francesco, T. (2004). Institutions rule: The primacy of institutions over geography and integration in economic development. *Journal of Economic Growth, 9*(2), 131–165.

Sachs, J. (2003). Institutions matter, but not for everything. *Finance & Development* pp. 38–41.

Sen, A. (1999). Democracy as a universal value. *Journal of Democracy, 10*(3), 3–17.

Shirley, M. (2009). Institution and development. In M. Claude & S. Mary (Eds.), *Handbook of new institutional economics* (pp. 611–638). Heidelberg: Springer-Verlag Berlin.

Stewart, F. (2002). Root causes of violent conflict in developing countries. *British Medical Journal, 324*, 342–345.

Tax Justice Network. (2023). *Top economists condemn IMF arm-twisting countries to adopt harmful OECD tax deal.* 11 July, https://taxjustice.net/press/top-economists-condemn-imf-arm-twisting-countries-to-adopt-harmful-oecd-tax-deal (accessed 6/05/2024).

Taylor, A. (2024). "The desperate alignment of Russia, China, Iran and North Korea." *The Washington Post*, 17 April.

Taylor, I. (2019). France à fric: The CFA zone in Africa and neocolonialism. *Third Word Quarterly, 40*(6), 1064–1088.

UNCTAD (1999). *The social responsibility of transnational corporations.* https://unctad.org/system/files/official-document/poiteiitm21_en.pdf (accessed 10/05/2024).

UNCTAD. (2016). *Structural Transformation and Industrial Policy*, Virtual Institute Teaching Material, New York & Geneva: United Nations.

United Nations (UN). (1962). *The United Nations Development Decade: Proposals for Action.* The United Nations.

Walker, A. (2011). The WTO has failed developing nations. *The Guardian*, 15 November.

Wang, J., Russell, S., & Tan, D. H. (2000). The role of Confucian values in East Asian development: Before and after the financial crisis. *Journal of International and Area Studies, 7*(1), 115–135.

Wilson, J. (2021). *A Franc Appraisal: The Political Economy of Macroeconomic Policy in the CFA Zones.* Thesis submitted in partial fulfilment of the requirements for the Degree of Doctor of Philosophy Department of International Development, University of Oxford, Kellogg College.

World Bank. (2009). *Pacific Islands—Development in 3D.* World Bank.

World Bank Growth Commission. (2008). *The Growth Report: Strategies for Sustained Growth and Inclusive Development*. World Bank.

Yansane, A. (1978). Some problems of monetary dependency in French-speaking West African States. *Journal of African Studies, 5*(4), 444–470.

CHAPTER 2

Concepts and Issues

> "Structural transformation has different dimensions, especially changes in the composition of output, employment, exports and aggregate demand" (UNCTAD, 2014, p. 60).

For more than six decades since the United Nations (UN) broadened the definition of development as "growth *plus* change" in the proposals for actions during the First United Nations Decade of Development (1961–1970), the focus of policymakers as well as development economists shifted from narrow economic growth to "structural change", also referred to as "structural transformation". Thus, structural transformation and diversification are often seen as synonymous with development in its broader sense.

Yet the majority of the countries remain structurally underdeveloped. As recognised in the Istanbul Programme of Action for least developed countries (LDCs) (para 18, p. 9), "in many least developed countries structural transformation was very limited, and their vulnerability to external shocks has not been reduced".[1] Similarly, there has been very limited structural transformation in most landlocked developing countries (LLDCs), especially in Africa, as highlighted during the High-level

[1] https://undocs.org/en/A/CONF.219/7 (accessed 20/09/2023).

A. Chowdhury et al., *Structural Transformations as Developing Africa, Asia, and the Pacific*, https://doi.org/10.1007/978-981-97-9092-0_2

Africa regional review meeting of the Vienna Programme of Action for LLDCs.[2] The Pacific small island developing states (SIDS) also face various challenges concerning their structural transformation (Tateno & Bolesta, 2019).

On the other hand, landlocked Central Asian transition economies, except Uzbekistan, deindustrialised. As the United Nations Office of the High Representative for the Least Developed Countries, Landlocked Developing Countries and Small Island Developing States (UNOHRLLS, 2019) noted, the declines in the GDP shares of agriculture have not been followed by an expansion of more modern, productive and dynamic manufacturing sector. Instead, there has been premature deindustrialisation and "re-primarisation" with the natural resources sector becoming dominant. That is, the Central Asian transition economies have witnessed a regression or reversal of their Soviet era structural transformation.

Structural transformation is critical for "overcoming the curse of destiny" (Monga & Lin, 2019). Structural transformation is not only a source of higher productivity growth and rising per capita income, but also a mechanism that helps to achieve greater diversity of the economic structure, which creates a country's resilience to vulnerability to poverty and external shocks. Nobel Laureate Simon Kuznets noted half a century ago, "[I]t is impossible to attain high rates of growth of per capita or per worker product without commensurate substantial shifts in the shares of various sectors" (Kuznets, 1979, p. 130). As UNCTAD (2016, pp. 4–5) highlights, "Structural transformation can be particularly beneficial for developing countries because their structural heterogeneity—that is, the combination of significant inter-sectoral productivity gaps in which high-productivity activities are few and isolated from the rest of the economy—slows down their development".

However, structural transformation is not without challenges and undesirable consequences. For example, rapid growth that should come with structural transformation is often fossil fuel-based energy-intensive and hence can be contributing to greenhouse gas emissions (Kibria, Akhundjanov & Oladi, 2019). There can also be other consequences such as environmental pollutions or degradation and biodiversity losses. Rapid growth and structural transformation can cause massive internal dislocations leading to large-scale migration from rural to urban areas resulting

[2] https://www.uneca.org/stories/call-for-accelerated-action-to-support-structural-transformation-of-landlocked-developing (accessed 20/09/2023).

in unsustainable urbanisation as well as shifts in the relative position of different groups or classes of people resulting in rising inequality. Failure to manage these challenges can lead to social and political instability which can styme growth and hinder desired structural transformation.

Therefore, structural transformation requires careful management and guidance by the State. However, there are considerable debates regarding the nature of the role of the State. In this chapter, we discuss the concept of structural transformation and related issues including the challenges involved in structural transformation. This chapter also reflects on the debate concerning the role of the State in light of the historical experiences highlighted in Chapter 3.

What Is Structural Transformation

UN-OHRLLS defines structural transformation as "a process that involves the reallocation of economic activity from low value-added and low productivity activities and sectors to those of higher value added and high productivity".[3] Once ignited and sustained, this process can generate both static and dynamic economic gains. Static gains are usually defined as the rise in economy-wide labour productivity, as workers are increasingly employed in more productive sectors. Dynamic gains, which follow over time, accrue from skill upgrading and the positive externalities resulting from workers having access to better technologies and accumulating capabilities (McMillan & Rodrik 2011).

A joint report by United Nations Economic and Social Commission for Asia and the Pacific (ESCAP, 2016)[4] notes that the concept of structural transformation "is sometimes restricted to the reallocation of economic activity across the broad sectors of agriculture, manufacturing and services", whereas it is "multidimensional, including a reallocation of resources across products within sectors and across geographical areas as well as changes in the technology of production and social changes" (p. 58). This large-scale resource transfer from the least productive economic activities to more productive ones is driven by two dynamics:

[3] http://unohrlls.org/custom-content/uploads/2016/04/Ms.-Hertova-Structural-Economic-Transformation.pdf.

[4] Produced jointly with United Nations Environmental Programme (UNEP), United Nations University (UNU) and the Institute for Global Environmental Strategies (IGES).

(i) the rise of new activities (diversification) and (ii) the movement of resources from traditional activities to newer ones.

Structural transformation or structural change is a distinctive feature of sustained economic growth, resulting in rising living standards and declines in poverty. Central to the notion of structural transformation is compositional shifts in employment and output towards higher productivity sectors of the economy, sometimes referred to as "leading sectors" characterised by economies of scale, positive spillovers (or externalities) and higher backward-forward linkages.

Structural transformation or the re-orientation of a country's economic activities has traditionally been defined as movements of productive resources *between* sectors—from predominantly primary sectors, such as agriculture and simple resource extractions activities, to more complex tasks, such as manufacturing or value addition to resources. However, structural transformation can also occur *within* sectors, such as from small-holders peasant farming to large-scale commercial and mechanised agriculture, or from simple assembling to more sophisticated skill- and technology-intensive manufacturing. In simple terms, structural transformation means higher value addition activities and hence higher productivity.

In the case of less developed or developing countries, it is the "between" sectors structural transformation that is usually emphasised. This is the kind of structural transformation that historically happened in present-day developed countries and the newly industrialised countries of Asia. In these countries, the structural transformation had been "growth-enhancing" because labour has transferred from low to higher productivity sectors.

When growth dividend is shared and used to expand citizens' entitlements then growth-enhancing structural change becomes developmental—"growth *plus* change". This was precisely what happened in the East Asian "miracle" economies of Taiwan and South Korea during their fast growth phase. Their experience was regarded as miracle not just because of their spectacular growth, but also because the growth was widely shared and inequality remained stable, defying the historical pattern, known as Kuznets' (1955) "inverted-U" hypothesis—that is, inequality initially rises with growth before declining (Chowdhury & Islam, 1993, World Bank, 1993). As a result, there were widespread improvements in social indicators, such as life expectancy and literacy. Such shared growth also created an expanding middle class that provided the impetus for their successful democratisation (Chowdhury & Islam, 1993).

However, structural transformation may also occur in reverse directions—from higher productivity sectors to lower productivity activities as in the case of Sub-Saharan Africa (McMillan & Rodrik, 2011). "Reversed" structural transformation may also involve movement from complex manufacturing to extractive resources dependence as in some former Asian Soviet Socialist Republics, for example, Azerbaijan. Thus, in both Sub-Saharan Africa and former Asian Soviet Republics structural transformation is "regressive", lacking dynamism and increasing vulnerability of growth.

These countries experienced "premature deindustrialisation", meaning the declines in the share of manufacturing, in particular in GDP, before reaching the peaks seen in advanced countries during their early phase of industrialisation. For example, the peak of manufacturing sector's contributions to GDP—achieved in the 1960s—was around 36 per cent in Japan, 32 per cent in European Union and 30 per cent in industrial countries, before declining (Rowthorn & Ramaswamy, 1999), whereas in Sub-Saharan countries and some former Asian Soviet Republics, the manufacturing's GDP shares began declining after reaching around 20 per cent or even less.

Such premature deindustrialisation has also been described as "re-primarisation" or a return to extractive activities, a dominant feature of the colonial era, in the case of Latin American countries. In many cases, this happened due to policy advice—commonly referred to as "Washington Consensus"—from the World Bank and the International Monetary Fund (IMF), that discouraged active industry policy or State interventions and encouraged market-oriented policies. Critics of industry policy or State interventions often argued that governments cannot pick winners; hence countries should adhere to their comparative advantage in primary products. It has been justified as a first stage of the development process to accumulate the resources required for a productive, non-extractive economy.

Such arguments are described as "Commodities Consensus", a derivative of the so-called "Washington Consensus" (Svampa, 2012). However, in the words of Fernando Coronil (1997, p. 7), "Paradoxically, in pursuit of their comparative advantage, these nature-exporting nations are frequently recast in their old colonial role as sources of primary products, a role now rewritten in terms of the neoliberal rationality of globalizing capitalism. For them, neocolonialism follows postcolonialism".

Economies experiencing premature deindustrialisation or re-primarisation have lost internal dynamism, and growth has been more volatile and unsustainable due to commodity price fluctuations. These countries have become more vulnerable to external shocks, especially economic conditions in the developed world (Cooney, 2021). The instability of export earnings has been a particularly difficult problem, requiring periodic macroeconomic adjustments to adverse external developments when international reserves or the availability of foreign financing were inadequate. With a persistent balance of payments problems and mounting international debt obligations in many low-income countries, uncertain export prospects continue to pose difficult problems.

Countries may also find their growth-enhancing structural transformation stunted before fully transforming them into high-income developed countries. These countries are often said to be in a "middle-income trap", a term coined by Indermit Gill and Homi Kharas (2007). Most Latin American countries and some Asian countries, e.g., Malaysia, seem to be experiencing stunted structural transformation and are in a middle-income trap. Jesus Felipe (2012) identified that in 2010, 35 out of the 52 middle-income countries were in the middle-income trap—30 in the lower middle-income trap and 5 in the upper middle-income trap; 8 out of the remaining 17 middle-income countries were not in the trap in 2010, but were at the risk of falling into the trap.

Developmental Structural Transformation

Movements "in what direction" and "between what" are critical for structural transformation of developing countries to be growth-enhancing to cause their per capita income to converge with that of advanced high-income countries. More than half a century ago, Nobel Laureate Arthur Lewis (1954, 1955) developed a two-sector model to answer these questions.[5] For him the driver of economic development was a movement of labour—the factor of production abundant in developing countries—from the "traditional" or "non-capitalist" sector, featured by

[5] Lewis' model provided the basis for generations of economists, practitioners and policymakers concerned with economic development, thus earned him the Nobel Prize in Economics in 1979.

low productivity, low wage and widespread "disguised" unemployment to the "modern" or "capitalist" sector, characterised by higher productivity and higher wages. Lewis did not intend traditional to be synonymous with agriculture nor modern to be synonymous with manufacturing although for simplicity this is often how the model has been used (Sumner 2017).

Others—for example, Bruce Johnston and John Mellor (1961), Dale Jorgenson (1961) and Gustav Ranis and John Fei (1961)—also developed two-sector models with a "backward" agricultural sector and a modern industrial or capital-intensive one. In such models, income growth arises from exogenous technological change and population growth, which induce endogenous capital accumulation in the non-agricultural sector, all of which spur income growth and a steady outflow of labour from agriculture.

The basic conclusion of two-sector models is carried to multi-sectoral growth models. That is, starting from an initial condition of a workforce concentrated in relatively low-productivity agriculture, farm productivity growth drives labour and investible capital to higher productivity uses in the non-farm sector. Such a process fuels farmers' demand for non-farm products as farm productivity and income rise. This drives down relative food prices, thereby stimulating capital accumulation and broader economic growth that increasingly concentrates employment and output in the non-agricultural, modern sector.

None of these models, however, answered the important question: why the same factor of production would have different productivity in different sectors? Instead, they took it as a given aspect of the reality. Historically, the use of machines indeed began with the manufacturing sector, creating a big difference in labour productivity between this sector and the traditional agricultural sector.

One may ask why the historical reality of the eighteenth century would apply to the contemporary developing countries. We believe that it should not be the case, especially for SIDS or sparsely populated resource-rich LLDCs, such as Mongolia. These countries may be able to bypass the historical structural transformation pattern and specialise in niche activities, as did Switzerland in the past or Singapore, Hong Kong and Taiwan in recent decades. Such possibilities have become increasingly feasible with the advancement in technology, especially in the area of information and communications (ICT).

Dudley Seers (1963), another pioneer of development economics, identified a number of features for growth-enhancing and developmental structural transformation. Acquiring these features should structurally transform a developing country into a developed one. These features can be classified by:

- factors of production (e.g., a literate and mobile labour force who are mostly in employment; substantial quantities of skilled labours);
- sectors of the economy (e.g., manufacturing diversified and much larger than either agriculture or mining);
- public finance (e.g., reliance on direct taxes; outlays on social security);
- foreign trade (e.g., exports that have a large internal market and are sold to many countries with high price and income elasticities);
- household consumption (e.g., very few people below subsistence level and a moderately equal distribution of income post-tax);
- savings and investment (e.g., well-developed financial intermediaries; high investment) and
- "dynamic influences" (e.g., no chronic tendency to deficits; slow population growth and high urbanisation).

Simon Kuznets (1973) in his 1971 Nobel Prize ceremony lecture listed six inter-related characteristics of modern economic growth based on conventional measures of national product and its components, population, labour force and the like. They are:

- high rates of growth of per capita GDP;
- high rates of productivity (i.e., of output per unit of all inputs) growth
- high rates of structural transformation—shift away from agriculture to non-agricultural pursuits; from industry to services; a change in the scale of productive units, and a related shift from personal enterprise to impersonal organisation of economic firms, with a corresponding change in the occupational status of labour;
- rapid urbanisation and modernisation;
- rapid technological progress, especially in transportation and communication and
- lack of convergence between developed and developing worlds leaving "three-quarters of world population" falling "far short of the minimum levels feasible with the potential of modern technology".

Kuznets emphasised the role of science and technology in accelerating productivity growth and hence continued high growth of GDP per capita. He also emphasised rapid changes in production structure given the differential impact of technological innovations on production sectors, the differing income elasticity of domestic demand, and the changing comparative advantage in foreign trade.

What is sobering in Kuznets' observations is the lack of desirable progress in the developing world. He lamented that "obstacles to ... transformation were, and still are being, imposed on the less developed regions by the policies of the developed countries" (Kuznets, 1973, p. 250). Kuznets observations resonate with the critics of France's neo-colonial currency and reserve arrangements with its former colonies in Africa and neo-liberal orthodoxy promoted through the so-called Washington Consensus favouring a market-oriented approach over State interventions as highlighted in Chapters 1 and 4. The devasted impacts of neo-liberal Washington Consensus policies are also elaborated in Chapters 6 and 7 in the context of Central Asian transition LLDCs and Pacific SIDS, respectively.

Challenging Consequences

Structural transformation also carries some challenging or undesirable consequences. As highlighted by Kuznets, effective participation of the labour force in the modern economic system necessitates rapid changes in its location and structure, in the relations among occupational status groups, and even in the relations between labour force and total population. In the process, structural changes create "winners" and "losers" as elaborated in Chapter 2. Rapid growth and structural transformation also bring about "rapid changes in other aspects of society—in family formation, in urbanisation" (Kuznets, 1973).

Most challenging is unsustainable urbanisation and rising inequality—both horizontal (e.g., regional, rural–urban) and vertical (interpersonal)—in income and wealth. Large cities may become both centres of poverty and social collapse. There will be a tremendous burden on these cities for providing housing, sanitation, transportation and other basic amenities. Countries will face the dilemma of resource allocation between rural and urban sectors. There will be increased pressure to spend more on the provision of urban amenities at the expense of rural development. This will likely to increase both the push and pull factors leading to unsustainable rural–urban migration. Besides demographic pressure on amenities and environmental consequences—for example, pollutions and hazardous wastes—rapid urbanisation is also associated with rising expectations, what Kuznets (1973) termed as "man's views on his role and the measure of his achievement in society".

In general, structural change has a far-reaching impact on inequality as workers move from low-productivity activities to high-productivity activities, and people migrate from rural to urban areas. Technological progress has often been a structural driver of inequality as skilled workers are better able to adopt and thereby increasing the skill premium and widening the wage gap between skilled and unskilled workers. Broader structural change, such as demographic transition, can also impinge upon inequality. In the absence of well-functioning pension systems, demographic change worsens inequality.

Foreign trade can exacerbate inequality by rewarding industries and firms which are able to compete in the global marketplace while punishing those which cannot. Foreign direct investment (FDI) or the operations of transnational corporations (TNCs) can also worsen inequality as they tend to pay higher wages than the local enterprises (Cox, 1976). Where MNCs operate in special economic zones (SEZs), labour oppression is common as union activities are often either prohibited or restricted.

Armida Alisjahbana, Kunal Sen, Andy Sumner and Arief Yusuf (2022) termed growing inequality associated with rapid growth and structural transformation "the developer's dilemma" that most countries face. Growing inequality and rising expectations are often an explosive mix leading to increased violent social conflict and political instability. Such developments can derail development progress.

Both urbanisation and industrialisation also demand an increasing amount of energy. It has been long recognised that economic growth affects climate change, air and water pollution, land conversion and biodiversity loss, at least during the initial phase of growth and structural transformation when countries rely on older technologies and cannot afford mitigation measures. Manufacturing is still today the main engine for economic growth due to its large economic multiplier and technological opportunities (UNIDO, 2016, 2018). However, manufacturing is directly and indirectly responsible for a large share of overall environmental pressures, raising concerns for the environmental sustainability of manufacturing-based development.

A country's economy is based on its stock of "easy to use" natural resources, during its initial phase of economic expansion. Constant exploitation of natural resources causes damage to the environment. At the same time, because of high costs countries cannot easily switch to alternative renewable energy sources. As a result, fossil fuel remains the main source of energy for industrialisation. Thus, developing countries face another dilemma between pursuing industrialisation and environmental sustainability as well as climate change mitigation. A study of industrialisation's influence on the environment quality for 20 low-income countries in Sub-Saharan Africa during 1980–2018 found that structural transformation is associated with considerable damage to the environment quality (Awad, 2021).

Challenges of Developmental Structural Transformation

Today's LDCs, LLDCs and SIDS face a much more daunting task of structural transformations than the developed countries at their early phase of transformation. As emphasised by Kunal Sen (2019), a large majority of present-day developing countries may not be able to follow the historical trajectory that developed countries followed.

This is for several reasons. For example, while Pacific SIDS are in the class of their own confronting the challenge of remoteness and smallness, almost all SIDS are extremely vulnerable to climate change and degradation of ocean. For them, it seems that geography is their destiny. Although we reject extreme "geographical determinism", Pacific SIDS' structural transformation and development prospects are influenced by their peculiar geography—remoteness, smallness and being islands disproportionately impacted by climate change. That is, their policy choices have to be cognisant of their peculiar geography and extreme climate change vulnerability (more on this later in Chapter 7).

Second, structural transformation in present-day developing countries cannot ignore commensurate agricultural and rural development, and concentrate on industrial diversification only. Although the GDP and employment shares of agriculture have declined in almost all developing countries, agriculture is still the largest employer, and poverty is concentrated in mainly rural areas. Therefore, the neglect of agriculture and rural development will lead to out migration, and hence increase pressure on unsustainable urbanisation, youth unemployment and informalisation. A lagging agriculture sector can hamper industrialisation as it can create shortages of food (wage goods) as well as raw materials for agro-based industries. Large low-productivity agricultural and informal sectors also constrain the ability to enhance tax revenues for structural transformation. All of these will seriously impair poverty reduction.

Third, today's SIDS, LDCs and LLDCs also face a much more adverse external environment. In addition to problems such as commodity price volatility in the international markets and declining terms of trade of primary and standardised manufactured products, the emergence of global value chain (GVC) poses new kinds of challenges and opportunities for the structurally underdeveloped countries. The fact that production is increasingly taking place within global production networks and consequently is fragmented across countries, rather than occurring in a single country or a single firm as was previously the case, means that countries have to develop niche areas to be able to face increased competition from other low-cost production location, and to avoid damaging "no-win" competition among themselves by racing to the bottom.[6]

On the other hand, the pandemic and rapid technological revolution have also revealed limitations of the GVC-dependent structural transformation pathway. The pandemic has seriously disrupted the global supply chains, forcing many countries consider to rebuild their local domestic production facilities. Moreover, as capital becomes cheaper and more productive than labour, the fourth industrial revolution could lead to significant "reshoring" of global manufacturing to advanced economies as they substitute labour for capital (Fish & Spillane, 2020; McLaughlin & Peterson, 2023; Raza et al., 2021; Vinoski, 2024).

Fourth, these countries are further challenged by the fact that they have to be conscious of planetary boundaries and hence their structural transformation has to be environmentally sustainable. Shared prosperity has to be also an integral part of the transformation process. That is, the present-day structurally underdeveloped countries simply cannot follow the old path of "grow first, distribute and clean up later". Their path must significantly deviate from "business as usual" and uphold environmental and labour standards in order to achieve Agenda 2030 for

[6] UNCTAD (2016) highlights the implications of GVCs for five impact areas relevant for developing countries: (a) local value capture; (b) upgrading and building long-term productive capabilities; (c) technology dissemination and skill-building; (d) social and environmental impact and (e) job creation, income generation and quality of employment.

Sustainable Development Goals (SDGs). Therefore, Nazrul Islam and Kenneth Iversen (2018) argue that structural change has to be "transformative" that provides greater space for inclusion and interaction of all three dimensions of sustainable development—economic, social and environmental.

However, according to Hausmann and Rodrik (2007), Hausmann and Klinger (2007), Hidalgo and Hausmann (2009), diversification is a path-dependent process. What product mix a country will produce in the future is determined by not only its initial conditions in terms of capabilities, such as availability of trained manpower or quality of institutions, but also products it produces today, largely due to "learning by doing effects".

Hausmann and Rodrik (2006, p. 21) argue that such dependence on pre-existing capabilities means that "purely market-based structural transformations will be too slow as it will involve jumps that are fewer in number and shorter in distance than would be socially optimal". There may not be enough incentives to accumulate the required capabilities for new activities because of coordination failures.

The structurally underdeveloped countries need a "big push" towards cleaner and resource-efficient technologies, as well as radical measures to make the process pro-poor and inclusive. In other words, integrated development strategies are needed for an inclusive and sustainable structural transformation. Furthermore, as Richard Nelson (1956, p. 894) showed in his "low-level equilibrium trap" model, "even if production techniques are not improved and even in the absence of a crash investment program, the trip may still be escaped in the socio-political environment is favorable". Nelson also noted, "historically, escape has been achieved through the simultaneous use of several means" (p. 903).

Therefore, State has to play an active role in not only create an enabling regulatory and institutional environment for the private sector, but also design integrated development strategies for investments in social and natural capital, infrastructure choices, employment opportunities, human capital formation and technological changes to achieve sustainable consumption and production patterns in line with the SDGs. The very adoption of internationally agreed Programmes of Action is a recognition of the critical role that States have to play in structural change in structurally underdeveloped countries—LDCs, LLDCs and SIDS.

The Role of the State[7]

Historically the State played a central role either indirectly as a provider of public goods, such as an enabling policy and regulatory environment, or directly as an entrepreneur producing goods and services and innovating new ways. The State also provided a vision for change, and remains a significant user of goods and services. In the recent past, the State has been more visible, especially in the rapid transformation of Northeast and Southeast Asian newly industrialised economies, thus being referred to as "Developmental State". However, questions have been raised about the ability of other structurally underdeveloped countries, especially those in Africa and SIDS to emulate developmental States of East Asia.

Views about States' appropriate role also vary as with historical experiences—past and recent. Since the 1980s, the role of States has been diluted with the ascendance of neo-liberalism at the back of debt crises and economic stagnation, often seen as being contributed by States' suppression of markets and direct participation in the economy. Yet, the States' role remained critical, pursuing liberalisation policy reforms. This section provides a brief overview of the evolving role of the State.

Theoretical Perspectives on States' Role

Gunnar Myrdal (1957) observed that modern and integrated nation-states learnt how to oppose the blind operation of forces that cause low-level equilibrium traps and undermine development. They also endowed themselves with a set of countervailing measures to neutralise the undesired effects of cumulative causation and prevent the rise of inequality. For Myrdal, the emergence of a new role for the State has been the result of a long historical process, which has transformed the old "Oppressor State" into a "Welfare State". During this process, there has been continuous interaction among economic growth, increased democracy, social and political reforms, State intervention, improved social and economic conditions and so on.

[7] Following Rueschemeyer and Evans (1985, 46), the State will be seen as a "set of organizations invested with the authority to make binding decisions for people and organizations juridically located in a particular territory and to implement these decisions using, if necessary, force".

Two different theoretical perspectives provided the logic for States' direct role in the economy—both at the micro and macro levels—during the post-World War II (WW II) period (Chang & Rowthorn, 1995):

1. Welfare economics
2. Keynesian macroeconomics

However, at the heart of both perspectives was market failures. Analytically, at the microeconomic level, market failures are the results of externalities causing deviations between private costs (benefits) and social costs (benefits). These deviations can lead to under-(over-) investment in socially desirable (undesirable) sectors. Arthur Pigou's analytical work in the 1930s showed that such market failures can be resolved by intervention instruments, e.g., taxes and subsidies. These are the subject matters of modern welfare economics.

At the macro level, market failures occur due to coordination failures and asymmetric information causing "effective" demand to deviate from aggregate demand needed to maintain full employment. Government's fiscal and monetary policies are justified to influence effective demand in order to maintain full employment and smoothen business cycles. Keynesian macroeconomics also has a welfare economics aspect since well-designed progressive taxes and transfers (e.g., social security payments) being part of its act as automatic stabilisers (European Parliament, 2010).

Both perspectives came under attack from the monetarist-new classical paradigm which viewed taxes and subsidies as distortionary and disincentives for work and investment (Toye, 2018). Fiscal deficits and public debts are believed to "crowd out" private investment as both public and private sectors compete for investable funds. Additionally, expansionary fiscal and monetary policies are blamed for inflation and balance of payments problems without any long-term impact on employment and output as "rational" economic agents respond to neutralise policy measures to stabilise the economy.

Development Economics and Neo-classical Counter Revolution

For the early development economists of the 1950s and 1960s, sustained growth was a complex process of economic, social and political transformation. The pioneers of development economics, such as

Paul Rosenstein-Rodan (1943, 1961), Ragnar Nurkse (1953), Albert Hirschman (1958), Gunnar Myrdal (1957) and others believed that industrialisation was a necessary condition for long-term growth in the developing countries. They argued that a "big-push" State intervention was indispensable to break a "low-level equilibrium trap" or "vicious circle" of low income-low savings and low investment. State intervention was also argued to address pervasive market failures (such as growing economic disparity and exclusion) and the constraints due to outright absence of markets.

When the Keynesian statist position came under attack from the monetarist-new classical school, the ascending neo-liberal school used neo-classical political economy to argue that "government failures" were much more important than the market failures that had justified state intervention in the first place (see for example, Bhagwati, 1982; Krueger, 1990; Srinivasan, 1988). Ahluwalia and Little (1998) is an excellent collection of articles on this issue in the context of India. The neo-classical political economists, such as Ronald Findlay and John Wilson (1984), see the State as a "leviathan", especially in the context of developing countries, and an agent serving the private interests of various powerful interest groups from inside and outside of the state apparatus. Hence, state interventions do not lead to the achievement of a common good but to the proliferation of self-interested bureaucrats, non-market rents and "directly unproductive rent-seeking" activities which are harmful to growth.

Neo-classical counter revolution in development economics was complete by the 1980s with a simpler view that growth is a matter of "getting policies right"—be it for a landlocked country, such as Uganda, or unstable country such as Afghanistan, or transitioning economy, such as Azerbaijan. The right policies meant lower fiscal deficits; lower import tariffs; fewer restrictions on international trade and capital flows and a greater role for markets in allocating resources, regardless of history, political economy or local institutions.

The new dominant paradigm of stabilisation, liberalisation, privatisation and deregulation was embodied in the structural adjustment programmes (SAP) of the International Monetary Fund (IMF), supported by the World Bank. While under the new dominant paradigm—which came to be known as "Washington Consensus"[8]—the

[8] John Williamson first coined the term, "Washington Consensus" in 1989. See Williamson (2008) for a short history of the Washington Consensus.

state's sphere has been reduced as much as possible, there arose a new agenda of "good governance".

Ironically, the good governance agenda as a prerequisite for development was found to be too onerous for the States which were reduced to the bare-bone with SAP conditionality on their ability to spend and raise revenues. While spending is seen as harmful to macroeconomic stability, taxing is a disincentive for investment. The World Bank's Doing Business Report, thus, encouraged competitive tax cuts, but at the same time advocated reforms which needed revenues.

Lessons of SAP and World Bank's Re-inventing States' Role

The two decades (1980s & 1990s) of SAP were described as "lost decades" for development which saw deindustrialisation and at the same time declines in investment in agriculture (Easterly, 2001). Stabilisation, privatisation and liberalisation reforms failed to ignite promised sustained growth spurt as cuts in public investment were not matched by increased private investment as was assumed. Reviewing the lessons, the World Bank (2005) concluded, "slow growth and multiple crises were symptoms of deficiencies in the design and execution of the ... reform strategies that were adopted in the 1990s with macroeconomic stability as their centrepiece" (p. 93).

Thus, the World Bank Growth Commission (2008, p. 5) observed that advice to "stabilise, privatise and liberalise" defined the role of government too narrowly. Nonetheless, the Bank's Growth Commission favoured a pro-market stance; yet it argued for "active, pragmatic governments" in unlocking barriers to sustained growth and structural transformation.

By "active and pragmatic" governments, the Growth Commission means "effective" government, following Arthur Lewis (1955, p. 376), "[G]overnments may fail either because they do too little, or because they do too much". This still favours a minimalist position of the State, responsible only for providing basic public goods, including enabling regulatory frameworks, for markets as "natural" institutions capable of producing long-term structural transformation. The Growth Commission did not tell when governments' actions could be "too little" or "too much". It suggested a trial-and-error approach *a la* Deng Xiaoping's dictum, "cross the river by feeling for the stones", and state interventions when transaction costs—such as, as the cost of defining and enforcing property rights—are too high. The World Bank has emphasised institutional building (including the increase in state capacities) as one of the basic elements of a development policy.

Obviously, the State or Government cannot do everything. As Dani Rodrik (2004, p. 28) asserts, the State has to foster "strategic cooperation between the private and public sectors which, on the one hand, serves to elicit information on business opportunities and constraints and, on the other hand, generates policy initiatives in response".

Structuralist/Institutionalist School

Out of the disappointing experiences of the SAP's minimalist role of the State emerged the structuralist/institutionalist school. Justin Lin (2012) floated the concept of new structuralist model which does not significantly depart from mainstream thoughts. It retains the neo-classical vision of rational individuals as the centre of economic analysis and views institutions as optimal responses to the need for vital information for individual action. As with the World Bank, it keeps free markets as the ideal benchmark and presumes that when transaction costs are not too high markets are the most efficient way of resource allocation.

An alternative institutionalist analysis of state intervention has emerged following the work of Max Weber, Karl Polanyi and Alexander Gerschenkron and more contemporary authors such as Alice Amsden, Robert Wade, Pranab Bardhan, Fernando Cardoso, Enzo Faletto, Peter Evans, Ha-Joon Chang, Robert Rowthorn and Dani Rodrik. They argue that:

1. there is no reason to believe in the "institutional primacy of the market" or to take free markets as the ideal point of reference;
2. economic success or failure depends on a range of socially specific institutions and not just on the efficiency of the market;
3. case studies offer important insights into the theory of state intervention and
4. neo-classical assumption that less intervention is always better is not sustainable; the relevant factor is what states do and how they do it.

Ha-Joon Chang and Robert Rowthorn (1995, p. 34) believe that the theory of State should take into account the role of the state as "designer, defender, and reformer of many formal and informal institutions" and should incorporate three basic elements:

1. the study of politics;
2. the role of the state as creator and manipulator (both in a positive and negative sense) of institutions and
3. the role of the state as entrepreneur.

State's Role in Developmental Structural Transformation

Both historical and contemporary experiences suggest seven different, but inter-related, roles of the state in the process of structural transformation: the State as creator of institutions, the State as policy reformer, the State as guardian of macroeconomic stability, the State as guardian of environmental sustainability, the state as guardian of social stability and manager of conflicts, the state as entrepreneur and the state as productive factor enhancer.[9]

The State as Creator of Institutions

One of the essential functions of the State is to build various formal and informal institutions as emphasised by Douglas North—the 1993 Nobel Prize winner. North (1991, p. 97) argued, "Institutions provide the incentive structure of an economy; as that structure evolves, it shapes the direction of economic change towards growth, stagnation, or decline". He further reasoned that rational and wealth-maximising individuals lack complete information and have difficulties monitoring and enforcing agreements. Institutions can provide information and reduce transaction costs, thus encouraging economic activity.

[9] UN-CTAD (2016) elaborated four roles of the State in the context of industrial policy for structural transformation. They are: regulator and enabler; financier; producer and consumer and innovator. The six role identified here subsumes them. For example, the regulator and enabler role is covered in the State's roles as creator of institutions, policy reformers and guardian of macroeconomic stability.

This implies that the appropriate role of the State is, on the one hand, designing or strengthening those political institutions that assure better communication between the State and society,[10] and on the other, the establishment of new coordination principles and rules in the economy. The process of structural transformation is characterised by radical changes in the pattern of interdependence between various social actors (workers, capitalists from different sectors, etc.) and the State is the only institution that has the ability to legalise the new property rights and relations of power (Chang & Rowthorn, 1995). When doing so, the State does not only react to market outcomes but also tries to influence the direction of the structural changes. This happens, e.g., when it introduces regulations into the labour market or restricts the mobility of financial assets (Chang, 1993).[11]

The State as Policy Reformer

The State has the fundamental responsibility to design development strategies. As mentioned earlier, during the heydays of neo-liberalism or so-called Washington Consensus, governments were advised to pursue market-friendly strategies that depend on the international division of labour dictated by countries' resource endowments. Such strategies were misleadingly interpreted as "minimize tariffs, maximize privatization, maximize liberalization of finance, with the assumption that the more of these changes the better, at all times and in all places" (World Bank, 2005, p. 11). This was not found very encouraging for structural transformation in many low-income countries as well as resource-rich transition economies.

[10] Such as strengthening the judicial and legislative institutions, enforcing rules that consolidate an effective structure of political parties, creating informal channels of communication with relevant social groups, etc.

[11] The Scandinavian States, for example, forced the modernisation of firms in low-wage sectors through the institutionalisation of a solidaristic wage scheme in the labour market (Chang, 1994b). Singapore, too followed a similar model of compulsory contributions to the Central Provident Fund and Skill Development Funds to force industrial restructuring towards skill-intensive, higher value-added activities. Several East Asian countries used the state-controlled financial sector to channel credits to desired activities. The recognition of the state as a builder of institutions rejects the idea that markets are natural institutions that develop spontaneously. Markets are, in fact, political institutions (Chang, 1994a) and are shaped by premeditated actions of different actors, such as the state, labour unions and large corporations.

As the World Bank's, 2005 study noted, reforms of the 1990s focused on the efficient use of resources as the predominant source of growth. The pro-market reforms were aimed at enabling better use of existing capacity, thereby establishing the basis for sustained long-run growth. However, such reforms did not provide sufficient incentives for expanding productive capacity or to drive structural transformation as the dominant source of growth. Thus, whereas market-friendly reforms can help achieve efficiency gains, they may not put an economy on a sustained growth path unless they also enhance production incentives, accelerate physical and human capital accumulation and boost productivity.

However, there is no one-size-fits-all policy reform guidebook. A reforming government needs to recognise country-specific characteristics and identify the binding constraints to growth. It needs to adopt strategies for creating competitive advantage through integrated policies for agriculture, manufacturing, trade, finance, human resources, technology, etc., which are crucial for accelerated and successful structural transformation.

Although the State has the sole responsibility to initiate and implement policy reforms, it must not act alone. Policy reforms will have maximum political feasibility if they are nationally owned. For this, policy reforms should be genuinely participatory involving various stakeholders in social dialogues. This function becomes more relevant in the State's role as a conflict manager.

The State as Guardian of Macroeconomic Stability

The fact that the State has the sole authority on fiscal and monetary matters, it must ensure macroeconomic and financial sector stability. Macroeconomic volatility and unpredictability damage private-sector investment, and hence, growth and structural transformation. For example, very high inflation is clearly damaging to investment and growth. Bringing inflation down is also very costly in terms of lost output and employment. But how high is very high? Some countries, for example, Republic of Korea, Indonesia and China, have grown for long periods with persistent inflation of 15–20 per cent. Many also ran budget deficits for extended periods; some nursed high ratios of debt-to-GDP. But this public debt did not get out of hand, not least because the economy grew faster than the stock of public liabilities.

Therefore, as the World Bank (2005) acknowledged based on the lessons learned from the 1990s, macroeconomic stability should not be always interpreted narrowly as very low inflation or "zero" fiscal deficits for all countries. There are many ways to achieve macroeconomic stability other than restrictive fiscal and monetary policies. Income policy and social dialogues to prevent wage-price spirals could be part of policy tools for macroeconomic stability.

The State also has to consistently pursue counter-cyclical policies to prevent adverse impacts of short-term fluctuations in economic activities. Progressive redistributive fiscal policy and monetary policy that supports financial inclusion go a long way in the State's role in managing conflicting claims of different actors, especially labour and capital.

The State as Guardian of Environmental Sustainability

Simon Kuznets (1973) warned in his 1971 Nobel Lecture, economic growth can have many negative consequences, such as rapid unsustainable urbanisation and deterioration of the environment, including fast depletion of natural resources and biodiversity. Ronald Coase who was awarded the 1991 Nobel Prize in economics, challenged the idea that the only way to address the negative consequences of economic activities was through government intervention. Coase (1960) argued that pre-empting negative consequences with regulations can be more costly and distorting than the market solutions. He emphasised that the appropriate role of the State is to properly define and enforce property rights for optimal market-based solutions.

This line of argument was carried forward by George Stigler—the 1982 Nobel Prize winner. He argued that regulators can be captured by vested interest (Stigler & Friedland, 1962; Stigler, 1971). Much earlier than both Coase and Stigler, Arthur Pigou (1932) argued in favour of State's fiscal role (taxing and subsidising) to address negative consequences of economic activities. A related concept in this regard is the existence of a so-called Kuznets' "inverted-U" environmental curve as a natural consequence of economic growth process until countries are rich enough to deal with it. That is, in the early stages of economic growth, environmental quality declines; but the trend reverses after some level of per capita income.

However, continued and alarming deteriorations of the environment affecting biodiversity and rising greenhouse gas emissions impacting climate change has led to a paradigm shift in the old development model—"grow first, clean up later". The fact that all States have committed to the United Nations Agenda 2030 for Sustainable Development Goals (SDGs), is a recognition of the reality that market-based solutions are not optimal and there is a need for a more direct or regulatory role of the State. For example, in the case of greenhouse gas emissions, carbon taxes or carbon trading schemes need to be supplemented by carbon emissions caps if emissions must fall by 45% below 2010 levels by 2030 in order to limit global warming to 1.5 °C—the goal set by the Paris Agreement.

The State as Guardian of Social Stability and Manager of Conflicts

Structural transformation of the patterns of production and employment usually creates dislocations of resources. Neo-classical economists, thus, favour flexible markets, especially of labour, on the assumption of perfect or quasi-perfect factor mobility. But in practice, many factors are either immobile (physical capital) or have many problems adjusting to the new situation (workers). If the adjustment process is slow (which is likely to happen), affected agents will use non-market actions, such as strikes or bribery, to redress the situation. This may lead to conflicts in the economy (Chang, 1994b) and may put the whole process of change on hold.

Structural transformation also creates "winners" and "losers". As Simon Kuznets cautioned in his 1971 Nobel Lecture, "The continuous disturbance of pre-existing relative position of the several economic groups is pregnant with conflict" (Kuznets, 1973, p. 252). Generally, winners are dispersed and disorganised while losers are often concentrated in particular sectors or industries; losers are also organised as they see the change as an existential threat. The losers, therefore, will try to block structural transformation at any cost. Therefore, some mechanisms have to be in place to compensate the losers.

There are also other types of conflicts, e.g., between resource-rich and resource-poor regions of a country (see for example, Murshed & Tadjoeddin, 2009; Tadjoeddin, 2012). While nation building and balanced development require the transfer of resources from the rich areas to the poor areas, the resource-rich regions may aspire otherwise and may see such transfer as exploitative (Murshed, Tadjoeddin & Chowdhury, 2009). Creating a vision for an inclusive society and national solidarity is a crucial political task. Failure to achieve this may end up in social and political unrest, and even damaging armed conflict, leading to a failed State.

The two central economic conflicts over income distribution that need to be specifically addressed are the conflict between capital and labour (the Marxian conflict) and the conflict between industry and finance (the Keynesian conflict) (Banuri & Amadeo, 1991). Ha-Joon Chang (1994b) distinguishes four different ways in which the State can intervene:

1. accept the market solution;
2. challenge market outcomes and give protection to specific groups in society;
3. reset the public agenda and change the number of problems that are considered political and
4. use general policies (e.g., monetary policy or fiscal policy) that seem neutral but in fact favour certain groups in society, or compensate losers without specifying their identity

Accepting the market outcome is only possible when there is a strong State capable of protecting property rights by whatever mechanisms are required. For example, in the early phase of East Asian developmental States, attenuation of labour rights and repression of wage were common features. However, repression may not be sustainable in the longer run as it worsens inequality and increases political instability (Banuri & Amadeo, 1991). Challenging market outcomes and giving protection to specific groups in society includes such measures as subsidising large corporations in trouble to avoid major job losses and to make possible it's gradual restructuring, but can be too onerous for the State and tends to discriminate in favour of powerful groups in society. Many of the neo-liberal policy recommendations associated with liberalisation try to manage conflict using the third mechanism. The deregulation of the labour market and the deliberate effort to reduce the power of trade unions, for example, can be easily understood as attempts to influence the outcome of the labour/capital conflict and assure downward wage flexibility (Banuri & Amadeo, 1991). The fourth approach includes many of the policies that are part of the welfare state, particularly unemployment benefits and income support schemes. These instruments have been critical to reduce social conflict and increase the legitimacy of the capitalist system.

In order to be successful as conflict manager, the state should create "the institutions and arrangements in which various social groups can cooperate with each other in the economic life of the country" (Banuri & Amadeo, 1991, p. 30). Within this perspective, promoting a strong trade union movement and a solid structure of political parties may be very positive for the economy (Rodrik, 1999).

All these institutions and arrangements, however, may not be very effective if social divisions are too intense and inequality is too high. Public policies that contribute to its reduction and assure a fair level of income for all will be a crucial instrument in the management of conflict. They should be promoted by the state not just for reasons of social justice but also as a way to provide insurance to the members of society and encourage industrial investment and technological innovation (Chang, 1994b).

The State as Entrepreneur

One of the most fruitful insights of the pioneers of development economists was the idea that underdevelopment is caused by massive coordination failures, inhibiting complementary investments (Ray, 1998). Thus, Rosenstein-Rodan proposed "big push", Hirschman suggested the strategy of "unbalanced growth" and Nurkse favoured balanced growth in both industrial and agricultural sectors. To a large extent, their ideas are consistent with the findings of some modern formal models that the existence of pecuniary externalities, generated by imperfect competition with large fixed costs, may lead to the multiplicity of long-run equilibria and poverty traps (Murphy, Shleifer, & Vishny, 1989). In those circumstances, "a (state) program that encourages industrialization in many sectors simultaneously can substantially boost income and welfare" (ibid, p. 1024).

Structural change "requires more than choosing from a pre-existing choice set. It requires formulating the choice set itself, namely, providing a vision for the future" (Chang, 1994b, p. 298). The potential productive structure of an economy is not pre-determined by comparative advantages derived from its current factor endowments. But, creating competitive advantages is a substantial component of the process of development (Evans, 1995) and implies a decision on what sectors are strategic for the economy. This election has to consider factors such as a sector's "backward" and "forward" linkages with other sectors (or its extent of sectoral interdependence), its potential for further technological innovations, its elasticity of demand in both domestic and international markets, etc., but also involves a certain level of speculation about the future.

Defining a vision for the future requires the gathering of information and obtaining a certain level of consensus among different agents in the economy. The State, due to its unique position in society, may be the only agent with the potential to carry out such an entrepreneurial mission. Governments have, indeed, performed this kind of entrepreneurial function during the process of development in all Western and late industrialising countries, such as Singapore, the Republic of Korea and even in Japan.

As the experience of Singapore demonstrates, the definition of a vision and the election of leading sectors are particularly important for small economies. Attempts to develop a large industrial sector composed of many different activities are likely to fail in small economies because the domestic market will not be able to generate enough demand. Moreover, they may also suffer from a critical capability shortage to engage in too many diverse activities. As a result, small economies are usually much more open to trade and depend on a few specific sectors for success in the global market.

The State may use different instruments to perform its role as entrepreneur. Peter Evans (1995) distinguishes four different types of state interventions used to promote new industrial capacity:

1. custodial interventions involving the creation and enforcement of rules and regulations;
2. direct involvement in productive activities, usually through the creation of public enterprises;
3. midwifery—to induce domestic entrepreneurs to make investments in target sectors using a variety of policies that reduce the risk and uncertainty of such investments and
4. husbandry—to support firms in strategic sectors and to assure their consolidation and technological growth.

While the first one directly follows from the State's role as institutions builder, the rest follow from its role as policy givers and are essential elements of industry policy. Although direct involvement in production through public enterprises has proven successful on different occasions, it is very risky and likely to lead to an inefficient over-extension of the public sector. On the other hand, the last two types of intervention, midwifery and husbandry, are usually more effective. Although signalling that a certain sector is important for the State is sometimes sufficient, subsidies, complemented by protection, have been the midwifery instrument most commonly used by late industrialising countries. Empirical analysis shows that, to be effective, these subsidies need to be subject to concrete performance standards in terms of output, exports or other relevant variables (Jomo, 2013). They also presuppose the existence of an active and developed capitalist class that is willing to follow the signals sent by the State. In countries where the entrepreneurial class is small or underdeveloped, this type of intervention may be less successful, and the State has to participate directly in production.

The State as Enhancer of the Productive Capacity

Improving the productive capacities of the economy is a necessary (but not sufficient) condition for the creation of new comparative advantages. This requires, in particular, an increase in public infrastructure and an assurance of the provision of quality education, particularly at the primary level.

The role of the State in this regard is very important and has been acknowledged by mainstream economists (see, for example, World Bank, 1997). Many empirical studies support the idea that public investment has a "crowding-in effect" and stimulates private capital via complementarities (Shapiro & Taylor, 1990). As noted earlier, the SAP during the 1980s and the 1990s and the excessive policy emphasis on the narrowly defined macroeconomic stability have led, however, to its dramatic reduction. Sustaining economic growth in the future will require higher public investment in infrastructures which could be financed in many countries by an increase in progressive direct taxation.

Increasing public spending on education is also very important for structural change. Improving the skills of workers may be required to avoid bottlenecks in the development of new sectors. However, the assumption that more highly skilled workers will be automatically used in an economy cannot be accepted (Taylor, 1996). Thus, the availability of educated and skilled workers is not a sufficient condition for long-term economic development. In the absence of adequate aggregate demand and economic activities, this may result in high educated unemployment and skill atrophy. Therefore, although the role of the State as economic capacity enhancer is very important, it is clearly insufficient if it is not accompanied by its other roles.

Thus, Margaret McMillan, Dani Rodrik and Claudia Sepúlveda (2016) identify two broad development challenges:

- The "structural transformation" challenge: How to ensure that resources flow rapidly to the modern economic activities that operate at higher levels of economic productivity.
- The "fundamentals" challenge: How to accumulate the skills and broad institutional capabilities needed to generate sustained productivity growth, not just in a few modern industrial sectors but also across the entire range of services and other non-tradable activities.

Finally, it should be noted that complexity of structural transformation suggests that the old dichotomy between the market versus the State is no longer valid. Both have to work together to evolve ecosystems that are geared towards the solution of practical problems to ensure growth-enhancing structural transformation. Duncan Green (2008) has gathered examples of how engaged citizens can offer effective solutions to practical problems.

References

Ahluwalia, I. J., & Little, I. M. D. (Eds.). (1998). *India's economic reforms and development: Essays for Manmohan Singh*. Oxford University Press.

Alisjahbana, A., Kunal, S., Andy, S., & Arief, Y. (Eds.). (2022). *The Developer's Dilemma: Structural transformation, inequality dynamics, and inclusive growth*. Oxford University Press (for the UNU-WIDER).

Awad, A. (2021). Structural transformation versus environmental quality: The experience of the low-income countries in Sub Saharan Africa. *International Journal of Energy Economics and Policy, 11*(6), 479–548.

Banuri, T., & Edward, A. (1991). Policy, governance, and the management of conflict. In T. Banuri (Ed.), *Economic liberalization: No Panacea. The Experience of Latin America and Asia*. Clarendon Press.

Bhagwati, J. (1982). Directly unproductive profit-seeking (DUP) activities. *Journal of Political Economy, 90*(5), 988–1002.
Chang, H.-J. (1993). The political economy of industrial policy in Korea. *Cambridge Journal of Economics, 17*(2), 131–157.
Chang, H.-J. (1994a). *The political economy of industrial policy*. McMillan Press.
Chang, H.-J. (1994b). Explaining 'flexible rigidities' in East Asia. In T. Killick (Ed.), *The flexible economy: Causes and consequences of the adaptability of national economies.* Routledge.
Chang, H.-J., & Robert, R. (1995). *The role of the state in economic change*. Clarendon Press.
Chowdhury, A., & Iyanatul, I. (1993). *The Newly Industrialising Economies of East Asia*. Routledge.
Coase, R. (1960). The problem of social cost. *Journal of Law and Economics, 3*(1), 1–44.
Cooney, P. (2021). *Paths of development in the Southern Cone*. Palgrave Macmillan.
Coronil, F. (1997). *The Magical State. Nature, money and modernity in Venezuela*. The University of Chicago Press.
Cox, R. (1976). Labor and the multinationals. *Foreign Affairs, 54*(2), 344–365.
Easterly, W. (2001). The lost decades: Developing countries' stagnation in spite of policy reform 1980–1998. *Journal of Economic Growth, 6*(2), 135–157.
ESCAP. (2016). *Transformations for sustainable development: Promoting environmental sustainability in Asia and the Pacific*. UNESCAP.
Evans, P. (1995). *Embedded autonomy: States and industrial transformation*. Princeton University Press.
Felipe, J. (2012). Tracking the middle-income trap: What is it, who is in it, and why? *ADB Economics Working Paper Series*, No. 306, March, https://www.adb.org/sites/default/files/publication/29804/economics-wp-306.pdf (accessed 24/08/2023).
Findlay, R., & John, W. (1984). *The political economy of leviathan*. Institute for International Economic Studies.
Fish, A., & Honora, S. (2020). *Reshoring advanced manufacturing supply chains to generate good jobs.* Brookings (Metropolitan Policy Program).
Gill, I., & Homi, K. (2007). *An East Asian renaissance: Ideas for economic growth*. World Bank.
Green, D. (2008). *From poverty to power: How active citizens and effective states can change the world* (2nd ed.). Oxfam.
Hausmann, R., & Dani, R. (2006). *Doomed to choose: Industrial policy as predicament*. Harvard University, September, https://drodrik.scholar.harvard.edu/publications/doomed-choose-industrial-policy-predicament (accessed 24/08/2023).

Hausmann, R., & Bailey, K. (2007). *The structure of the product space and the evolution of comparative advantage*. CDI Working Paper No.146, April. Harvard University, Center for International Development, https://www.hks.harvard.edu/centers/cid/publications/faculty-working-papers/structure-product-space-and-evolution-comparative-advantage (accessed 24/08/2023).

Hidalgo, C., & Ricardo, H. (2009). *The building blocks of economic complexity*. CID Working Paper No. 186. Harvard University, Center for International Development, https://www.hks.harvard.edu/centers/cid/publications/faculty-working-papers/building-blocks-economic-complexity (accessed 24/08/2023).

Hirschman, A. (1958). *The strategy of economic development*. Yale University Press.

Islam, N., & Kenneth, I. (2018). *From "Structural Change" to "Transformative Change": Rationale and Implications*. DESA Working Paper No. 155 , ST/ESA/2018/DWP/155, https://www.un.org/esa/desa/papers/2018/wp155_2018.pdf (27/05/2024)

Johnston, B., & John, M. (1961). The role of agriculture in economic development. *American Economic Review, 51*(4), 566–593.

Jomo, K. S. (2013). The best approach to economic development is pragmatism. In P. Dutkiewicz & R. Sakwa (Eds.), *22 Ideas to fix the world conversations with the World's Foremost Thinkers*. New York University Press.

Jorgenson, D. (1961). The development of a dual economy. *The Economic Journal, 71*(282), 309–334.

Kibria, A., Sherzod, A., & Reza, O. (2019). Fossil fuel share in the energy mix and economic growth. *International Review of Economics & Finance, 59*(C), 253–264.

Krueger, A. (1990). Government failures in development. *Journal of Economic Perspectives, 4*(3), 9–23.

Kuznets, S. (1973). Modern economic growth: Findings and reflections. *American Economic Review, 63*(3), 247–258.

Kuznets, S. (1979). Growth and structural shifts. In W. Galenson (Ed.), *Economic growth and structural change in Taiwan: The Postwar experience of the Republic of China*. Cornell University Press.

Kuznets, S. (1955). Economic growth and economic inequality. *American Economic Review, 45*, 1–28.

Lewis, A. (1954). Economic development with unlimited supplies of labour. *The Manchester School, 22*(2), 139–191.

Lewis, A. (1955). *Theory of economic growth*. Allen and Unwin.

Lin, J. Y. (2012). *New structural economics: A framework for rethinking development*. The World Bank.

McLaughlin, E., & Dana, P. (2023). A reshoring renaissance is underway. *MIT Sloan Management Review*, 2 Nov. https://sloanreview.mit.edu/article/a-reshoring-renaissance-is-underway/ (accessed 7/03/2024).

McMillan, M., & Dani, R. (2011). Globalization, structural change and productivity growth. *National Bureau of Economic Research (NBER) Working Papers* 17143.

McMillan, M., Dani, R., & Claudia, S. (Eds.). (2016). *Structural change, fundamentals, and growth: A framework and case studies*. International Food Policy Research Institute.

Monga, C., & Justin, Y. L. (2019). Introduction: Structural transformation—Overcoming the curse of destiny. In M. Célestin & Y. L. Justin (Eds.), *The Oxford handbook of structural transformation*. Oxford University Press.

Murphy, K., Andrei, S., & Robert, V. (1989). Industrialization and the big push. *Journal of Political Economy, 7*(5), 1003–1026.

Murshed, S. M., & Zulfan, T. M. (2009). Revisiting the greed and grievance explanations for violent internal conflict. *Journal of International Development, 21*(1), 87–111.

Murshed, S. M., Zulfan, T. M., & Anis, C. (2009). Is fiscal decentralization conflict abating? Routine violence and district level government in Java, Indonesia. *Oxford Development Studies, 37*(4), 397–421.

Myrdal, G. (1957). *Economic theory and under-developed regions*. Duckworth.

Nelson, R. (1956). A theory of the low-level equilibrium trap in underdeveloped economies. *American Economic Review, 46*(5), 894–908.

North, D. (1991). Institutions. *Journal of Economic Perspectives, 5*(1), 97–112.

Nurkse, R. (1953). *Problems of capital accumulation in underdeveloped countries*. Oxford University Press.

European Parliament. (2010). *The role of the social protection as economic stabiliser: Lessons*. https://ftp.iza.org/report_pdfs/iza_report_31.pdf (accessed 22/10/2023).

Pigou, A. (1932). *The economics of welfare* (4th ed.). Macmillan.

Ranis, G., & John, F. (1961). A theory of economic development. *American Economic Review, 51*(4), 533–565.

Ray, D. (1998). *Development economics*. Princeton University Press.

Raza, W., Jan, G., Hannes, G., Jürgen, E., & Nico, P. (2021). *Post Covid-19 value chains: Options for reshoring production back to Europe in a globalised economy*. European Union.

Rodrik, D. (2004). *Industrial policy for the twenty-first century*. Harvard University, September 2004. https://drodrik.scholar.harvard.edu/files/dani-rodrik/files/industrial-policy-twenty-first-century.pdf (accessed 24/08/2023).

Rodrik, D. (2007). Industrial development: Some stylized facts and policies. In *Industrial Development for the 21st Century: Sustainable Development Perspectives*. New York: United Nations.

Rodrik, D. (1999). *The new global economy and developing countries: Making openness work.* Overseas Development Council, distributed by Johns Hopkins University Press.

Rosenstein-Rodan, P. (1961). Notes on the theory of the 'big Push.' In H. S. Ellis & H. C. Wallich (Eds.), *Economic development for Latin America.* St. Martin's.

Rosenstein-Rodan, P. (1943). Problems of industrialisation of Eastern and South-Eastern Europe. *The Economic Journal, 53*(210/211), 202–211.

Rueschemeyer, D., & Peter, E. (1985). The State and economic transformation: Toward an analysis of the conditions underlying effective intervention. In P. Evans (Ed.), *Bringing the State Back In* (pp. 39–43). Cambridge University Press.

Seers, D. (1963). The limitations of the special case. *Bulletin of the Oxford Institute of Economics and Statistics, 25*(2), 77–98.

Sen, K. (2019). Structural transformation around the world: Patterns and drivers. *Asian Development Review, 36*(2), 1–31.

Shapiro, H., & Lance, T. (1990). The State and industrial strategy. *World Development, 18*(6), 861–878.

Srinivasan, T. N. (1988). *Food aid: A cause, or symptom of development failure or an instrument for success?* (p. 554). Yale University, Discussion Paper No.

Stigler, G. (1971). The theory of economic regulation. *Bell Journal of Economics and Management Science, 2*(1), 3–21.

Stigler, G., & Claire, F. (1962). What can regulators regulate: The case of electricity. *Journal of Law and Economics, 5*(1), 1–16.

Svampa, M. (2012). Resource extractivism and alternatives: Latin American perspectives on development. *Journal für Entwicklungspolitik, XXVIII*(3-2012 S), 43–73.

Tadjoeddin, M. Z. (2012). Conflict, natural resources and development. In G. Brown & A. Langer (Eds.), *The Elgar Companion to Civil War and Fragile States* (pp. 110–124). Edward Elgar.

Tateno, Y., & Andrzej, B. (2019). *Structural transformation in Asia-Pacific small island developing States. MPDD Policy Briefs* PB100, UN-ESCAP. https://www.unescap.org/resources/mpfd-policy-brief-no-100-structural-transformation-asia-pacific-small-island-developing (accessed 20/09/2023).

Taylor, L. (1996). *Growth and Development Theories* (mimeo).

Toye, J. (2018). The counterrevolution in development economics. *History of Political Economy, 50*(S1), 269–285.

UNCTAD. (2014). *The Least Developed Countries Report 2014: Growth with structural transformation: A post-2015 development agenda.* UNCTAD.

UNCTAD. (2016). *Structural Transformation and Industrial Policy*, Geneva: UNCTAD Virtual Institute Teaching Material University, Center for International Development https://unctad.org/system/files/official-document/gds2016d1_en.pdf (accessed 24/08/2023).

UNIDO. (2016). *Industrial Development Report 2016*. United Nations Industrial Development Organization.

UNIDO. (2018). *Industrial Development Report 2018*. United Nations Industrial Development Organization.

UNOHRLLS. (2019). *Review of Progress made in structural economic transformation in Euro-Asian landlocked developing countries (LLDCs)*. April, https://www.un.org/ohrlls/sites/www.un.org.ohrlls/files/review-of-progress-made-in-structural-economic-transformation-final-24-oct.pdf (9/05/2024).

Vinoski, J. (2024). *Covid is fading, but reshoring isn't*. Forbes, 25 January, https://www.forbes.com/sites/jimvinoski/2024/01/25/covid-is-fading-but-reshoring-isnt/?sh=10ab9a68f536 (accessed 7/03/2024).

Williamson, J. (2008). A short history of the Washington Consensus. In N. Serra & J. Stiglitz (Eds.), *The Washington consensus reconsidered* (pp. 14–30). Oxford University Press.

World Bank. (1993). *The East Asian Miracle: Economic growth and public policy*. Oxford University Press.

World Bank. (1997). *World Development Report, 1997: The State in a Changing World*. Oxford University Press.

World Bank. (2005). *Economic Growth in the 1990s: Learning from a decade of reform*. World Bank.

World Bank Growth Commission. (2008). *The Growth Report: Strategies for sustained growth and inclusive development*. World Bank.

CHAPTER 3

Stylised Facts and Key Features

"The movement of workers from agriculture to manufacturing to services has been the path of structural transformation in all economies that comprise the high-income... This path of structural transformation has received a great deal of attention among economists and underpins most of the theoretical understanding of structural transformation" (Kunal Sen, 2019, p. 2)

This chapter reviews the pattern of structural transform observed in both old and newly industrialised countries as captured in the above quote. One enduring question is whether the present day structurally underdeveloped countries, especially remote small island developing states (SIDS) and landlocked developing countries (LLDCs) with sparse populations, can emulate the historical path.

One key stylised fact, often ignored, is the role of the State. Thus, this chapter highlights the State's role in structurally developed industrialised countries of the North—the UK, US, Germany and France, and in East Asia and Northeast Asia—Japan, South Korea, Taiwan and Singapore.

This chapter also presents some key features of structurally underdeveloped countries. By definition, structurally underdeveloped countries have inadequate financial, physical and human capital; they suffer from low productive capacity. These countries are also found to suffer from democratic deficits. As alluded in Chapter 1, there is considerable debate

A. Chowdhury et al., *Structural Transformations as Developing Africa, Asia, and the Pacific*, https://doi.org/10.1007/978-981-97-9092-0_3

regarding whether countries can simultaneously address their underdevelopment and democratic deficits.

Historical Stylised Patterns

Historically successful structural transformation has been a distinctive feature of economic growth resulting in a sustained period of rising income and living standards coinciding with changes in the distribution of economic activity across three broad sectors of an economy—agriculture, industry, and services—as documented by Simon Kuznets (1955, 1966), Hollis Chenery and Moshe Syrquin (1975). The development or transformation trajectory of advanced or developed economies is characterised by a decline in the relative share of the primary sector in the gross domestic product (GDP) and a rise in the share of industry (manufacturing, mining and quarrying, construction and utilities). It is also found that after a certain level of per capita income, the GDP share of industry plateaus or even falls while that of services rises (see Fig. 3.1). Such historical trajectory is also characterised by: (i) all economies exhibit declining employment in agriculture, (ii) all economies exhibit a hump-shaped share of employment in industry and (iii) all economies exhibit an increasing share of employment in services (Sen, 2019).

By classifying economies as either structurally developed, structurally developing or structurally underdeveloped, Kunal Sen (2019) claims that such historical or stylised path of structural transformation may no longer be the route to economic development in low-income economies. He documented a different path of structural transformation in structurally underdeveloped economies where agriculture is still the largest sector in terms of the share of employment. In these structurally underdeveloped economies, workers move directly from agriculture to non-business services, which as a sector does not have the same productivity gains as manufacturing. A large part of the activity in the non-business service sector is in the informal sector, including self-employed or household enterprises in trade, hotels and restaurants and personal services (e.g., fruit and vegetable street vendors).

Furthermore, for structurally underdeveloped economies, the low productivity of the manufacturing sector provides a more challenging setting for both economic growth and structural transformation. Thus, he calls for rethinking the theoretical premises behind much of the conventional or historical approach to structural transformation and

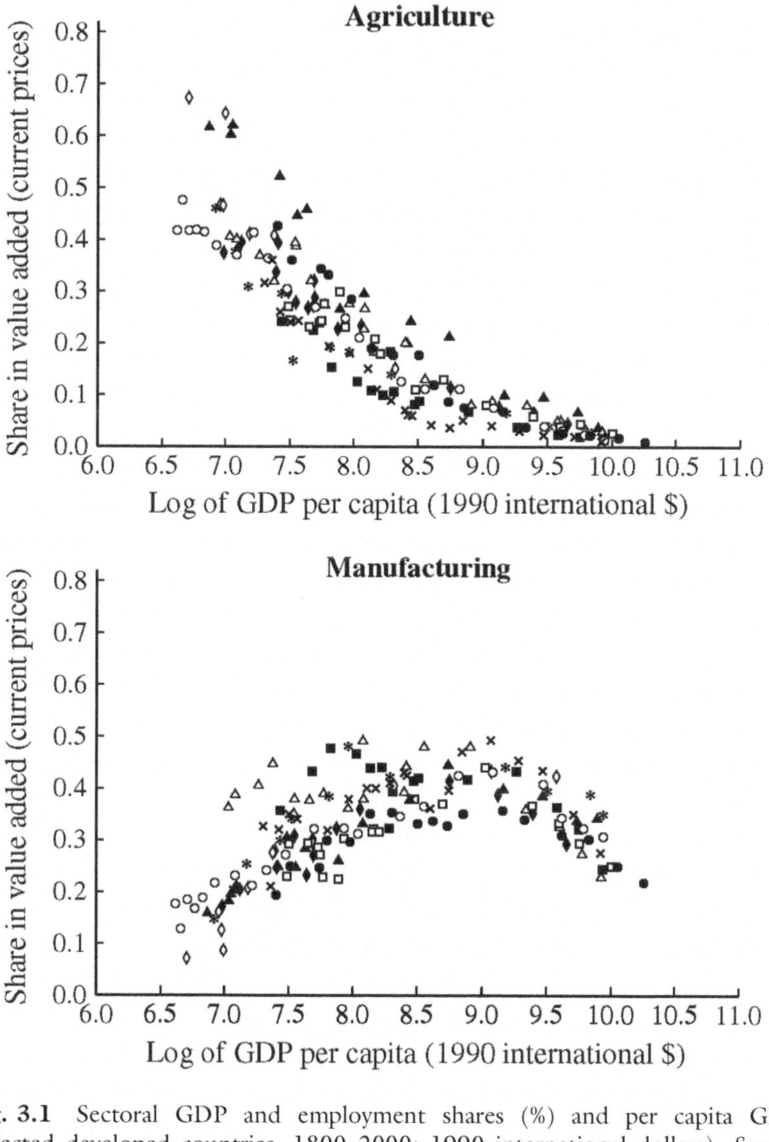

Fig. 3.1 Sectoral GDP and employment shares (%) and per capita GDP (selected developed countries, 1800–2000; 1990 international dollars). *Source*: Herrendorf, Rogerson and Valentinyi (2013, Fig. 1)

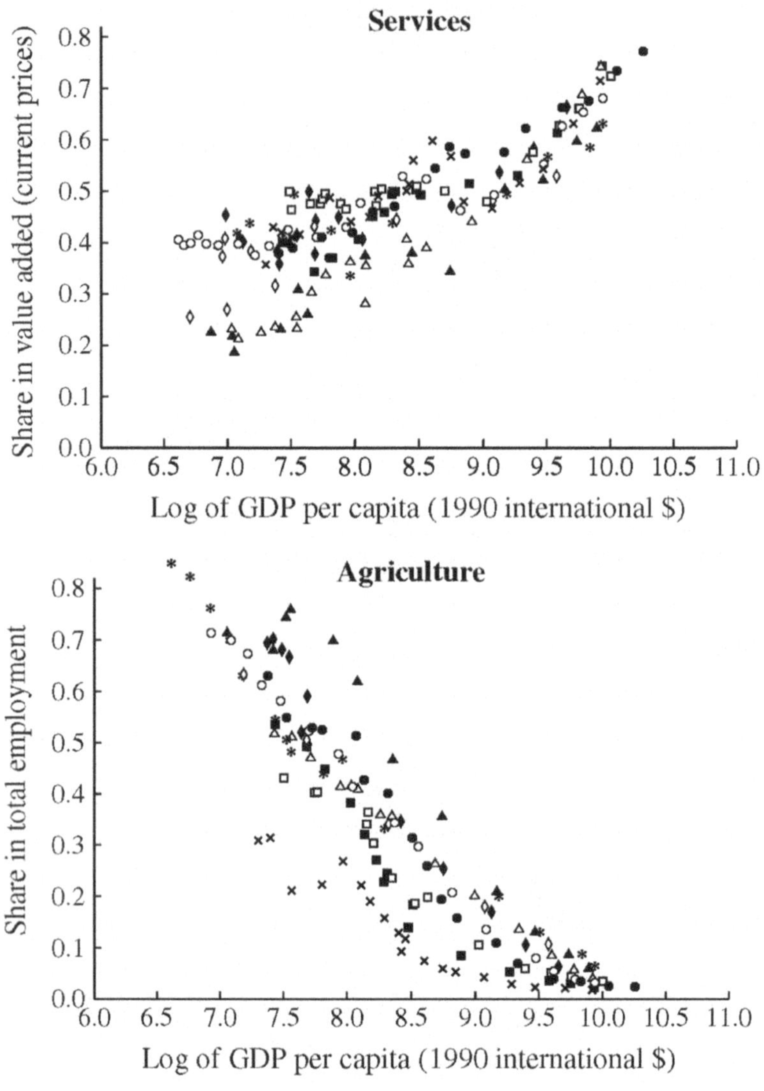

Fig. 3.1 (continued)

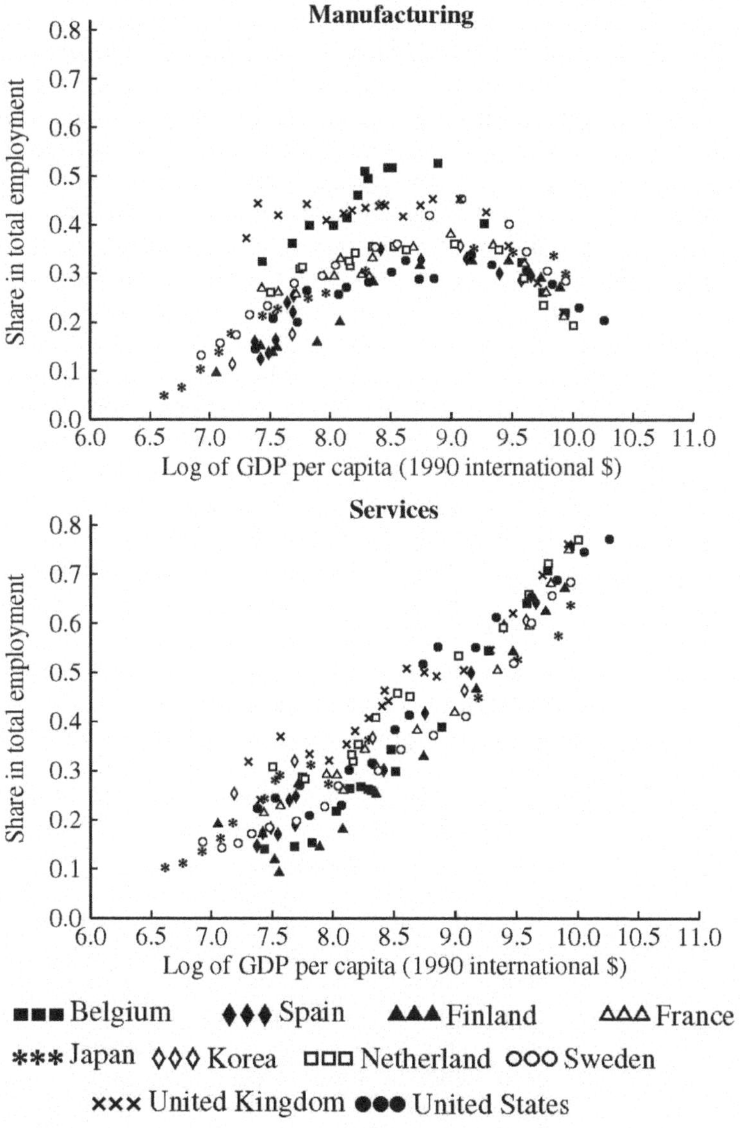

Fig. 3.1 (continued)

argues for the identification of alternate causal mechanisms to explain the different types of structural transformation observed in the developing world. According to Kunal Sen, for structurally underdeveloped low-income economies, whatever limited possibilities they may have for manufacturing-driven structural transformation must be focused on policies that can increase the manufacturing sector's productivity, and on exploring options for growth that are based on the non-business service sector, which remains the major sector of employment outside agriculture.

As highlighted in Chapter 2, structural transformation can generate both static and dynamic gains. The static gain is the rise in economy-wide labour productivity as workers are employed in more productive sectors. Dynamic gains, which occur over time, result from skill upgrading and positive externalities due to workers having access to better technologies and accumulating capabilities. A successful structural transformation process simultaneously generates productivity growth within sectors and shifts labour from lower to higher-productivity sectors, thereby creating more, better-remunerated, more formal and higher productivity jobs to reduce poverty and inequality. However, the link between structural transformation and reductions in poverty and inequality is neither a straightforward nor a foregone conclusion.

Structural Transformation, Poverty Reduction and Inequality

The uncertainty about the poverty reduction impacts of structural transformation is due to at least two reasons. First, the causality between structural transformation and growth can run from both directions. That is, while structural transformation can lead to growth acceleration, structural changes also result from the growth process itself. As levels of income rise, the demand for agricultural products relatively declines because of their low-income elasticity of demand; but demand for manufacturing goods increases until after reaching a reasonably high level of income because of their higher income elasticity of demand. Second, industrialisation has been generally found to generate highly unequal income and wealth distribution effects in the short run (Kuznets, 1955), and it is well-known that the rise in inequality dents the impact of growth on poverty reduction.

Thus, as can be seen from Fig. 3.2, there is no obvious association between GDP shares of manufacturing and poverty rates across middle- and low-income countries nor is there any clear correlation with inequality. However, when the GDP shares of manufacturing exceed 20 per cent, a positive correlation seems to appear with the Gini coefficient, implying that structural transformation may exacerbate inequality.

The experience of successful North and Southeast Asian countries shows that growth can cause rapid declines in poverty if inequality can be kept at a low level during the structural transformation process. With land reforms both the Republic of Korea and Taiwan Province of China began their high growth phase since the mid-1960s with a very low level of inequality (Gini of around 0.30). This saw rapid declines in poverty until about mid-1980s. Indonesia had a similar experience of poverty reduction, as it too had low inequality in the early 1970s when its growth took-off. The phenomenon of "shared growth" and rapid poverty reduction lasted until about the late 1980s when the pace of liberalisation reforms accelerated, marking a phase of growing inequality that reduced the growth elasticity of poverty reduction (Islam & Chowdhury, 2001).

Two corollaries follow from the above observations on the link between structural transformation and poverty reduction. First is the sectoral productivity differences. Since earnings are influenced by productivity, this differential has implications for cross-sector earnings, and hence inequality. Indeed, average wages tend to be higher (lower) in sectors with higher (lower) productivity. Second is the variation of employment shares across sectors. The implication is that the differential performance of sectors should have implications for the extent of new employment opportunities generated, earnings, inequality and thus poverty. Therefore, growth will have a larger impact on poverty when it is driven by sectors that employ a large proportion of an economy's rank and file workers (such as agriculture). However, growth can also be driven by structural transformation involving a reallocation of workers from low productivity (and low earnings) sectors to higher productivity (higher earnings) sectors. Structural transformation and growth that are driven by such a reallocation should also be poverty reducing (see McMillan & Rodrik, 2011; Aggarwal & Kumar 2012).

This shows that structural transformation for poverty reduction is not without challenges. "Structural change in sectoral shares may not always produce desired sectoral structure of employment. A structural change in the sectoral share may actually be associated with a rise in poverty unless it is matched by a desired structural change in employment" (Aggarwal & Kumar, 2012, p. 12). Therefore, careful policy formulation

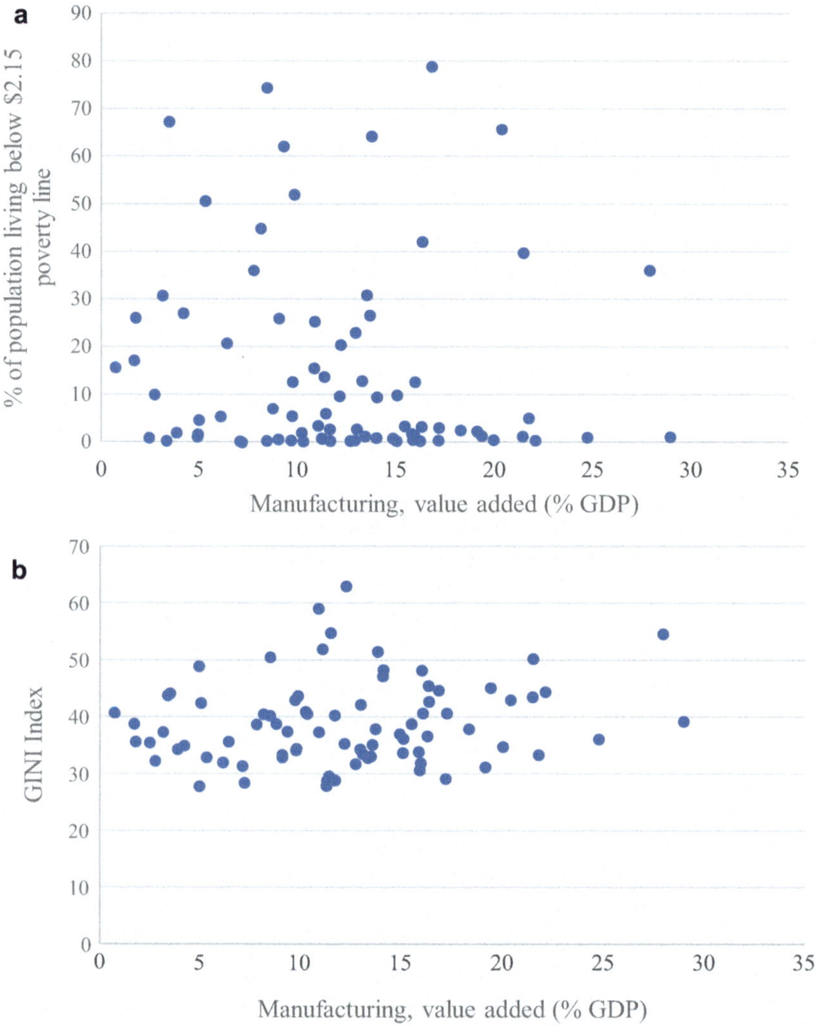

Fig. 3.2 **a** Manufacturing shares and poverty, $2.15 a day (2017 PPP) (% of population) (2022). *Source*: World Bank online database. **b** Manufacturing shares and inequality (Gini index) (2022). *Source*: World Bank online database

is critically important to ensure the expansion of productive and decent jobs, to enhance the productivity of rural and agricultural sectors where the majority of the poor work and live, and to prevent inequality from rising during the process of structural transformation.

The State's Historical Role

The State remains a key agent in structural transformation—either by direct interventions or by providing enabling environments and institutions. In the early stage of development, the State's role was predominantly direct interventions with tariffs, subsidies and public investments. At a later stage, the State's role varies from direct interventions to indirect enablers.

As documented by Douglas Dowd (1971), even in the case of England, traditionally described as a bastion of free market, State played a significant role, especially since late nineteenth century when other economies were catching up with, or had surpassed it. Britain was no longer the pre-imminent economic power by the close of the nineteenth century, and hence "wage earners, farmers, merchants and industrialists sought to protect themselves from the market through organisation and politics intended to supersede the free market, whose domestic and foreign pressures had become destructive" (Dowd, 1971, p. 5).

In France, Germany and the US, the State intervened to protect their new or "infant" industries from the competition of more mature British industries. Herbert Fisher (1896, p. 341) observed, "It is a commonplace of economic history that during the last thirty years a wave of protectionism has spread over Europe and America". Nikolaus Wolf (2018) reviewed the literature that discusses the role of protectionism in the political space of the continental Europe and the US where the political parties arguing for protections for their infant industries won elections. Asaf Zussman (2002) discussed the macroeconomic perspective of the rise of German protectionism in the 1870s.

As elaborated by Robert Wade (2014a, 2014b), Alexander Hamilton, the first Secretary of the US Treasury, in his eighty-plus page *Report on Manufacturers* pioneered the infant industry argument. Hamilton argued that new or "infant" industries in the US could not become competitive with others in the international market unless the government supported them with subsidies or allowances at least for some initial time period. Hamilton also suggested stamping out competition through import duties or, in an extreme case, the banning of competing imported products completely.

As documented by Simone Tagliapietra and Reinhilde Veugelers (2020), European States intervened increasingly in economies devastated by two World Wars. Until about the late 1950s, "The State played a major role in steering resources, not only under the dictatorships in Europe, but also in more traditionally liberal countries including France and Belgium" (Tagliapietra & Veugelers, 2020, p. 17). Christian Grabas and Alexander Nützenadel (2013) provided a brief history of industrial policies in Europe. They observed an interventionist industrial policy approach implemented in most European countries after 1945—prevailing persistently until the 1990s—fostered economic structural change.

The State also played a critical role in the newly industrialised countries of East Asia, including Japan, as documented in World Bank (1993), Chowdhury and Islam (1993) and Chang (2002). Therefore, building state capabilities is critically important. However, this should not be confused with the donor community's so-called "good governance" agenda as argued in Chapter 2. Besides lacking a clear definition, the good governance agenda is over-whelming for fiscally and human resource constrained structurally underdeveloped countries. While State capability building requires fiscal space, the good governance agenda ironically constrains it. Donor conditionality also constrains policy space by tying aid to donor favoured projects or policy reforms that may not be congruent with the development priorities of the recipient countries.

Key Features of Structurally Underdeveloped Countries

In this section, we highlight low productive capacity and democratic deficits as key economic and governance features of structurally underdeveloped countries. We also discuss their ramifications.

Low Productive Capacity

One key economic feature of structurally underdeveloped countries is their low productive capacity, which normally means lack of skilled labour force, capital and technology or physical infrastructure. United

Nations Conference on Trade and Development (UNCTAD) has developed productive capacity index (PCI) combining three dimensions—(a) productive resources, (b) entrepreneurial capabilities and (c) production linkages—that together determine a country's ability to produce goods and services" (UNCTAD, 2006). As can be seen from Fig. 3.3, almost all developed countries have high productive capacity, while it is low in most LDCs. Productive capacity of LLDCs and SIDs lies in the intermediate range.

There is a high positive correlation coefficient between PCI and GDP per capita (0.90), implying a circular causation between them. The low level of income constrains a country's ability to develop its productive capacity, even when it is well-endowed, for example with natural resources or working-age population. This, in turn, restricts a country's economic growth, resulting in low GDP per capita. Thus, there is a vicious circle: low income–low productive capacity–low income.

The circular causation can also run from low productivity to low income. For example, low productive capacity means low GDP per capita which in turn constraints a country's ability to develop its productive

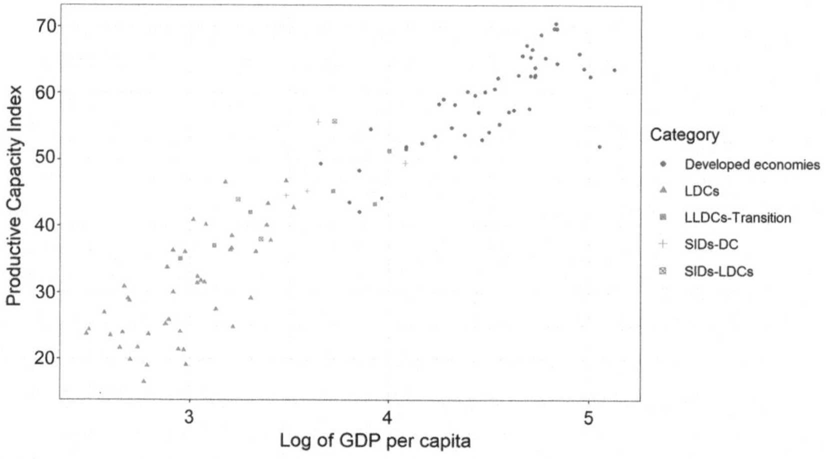

Fig. 3.3 Low productive capacity of structurally underdeveloped countries. *Source*: UNCTAD productive capacity database (https://unctad.org/topic/least-developed-countries/productive-capacities-index)

capacity, trapping it in a low-income, low productive capacity situation, which Richard Nelson (1956) called a "low-level equilibrium trap".

A similar picture is also present in the World Bank's Human Capital Index (HCI). The index measures the amount of human capital that a child born today can expect to attain by age 18, given the risks of poor health and poor education that prevail in the country where she lives. Poor countries' health and education systems are weak which can only generate low human capital which in turn constraints structural transformation and income growth.

Two interrelated key features of structurally weak or underdeveloped countries are low "economic complexity" and high concentration of merchandise (or, less diversified) exports. An inadequate or lack of productive capacity implies that countries are unable to engage in high skilled and technology-intensive activities; thus, their economic structure is less sophisticated or complex (Fig. 3.4), and their merchandise exports are concentrated in a few primary products (Fig. 3.5).

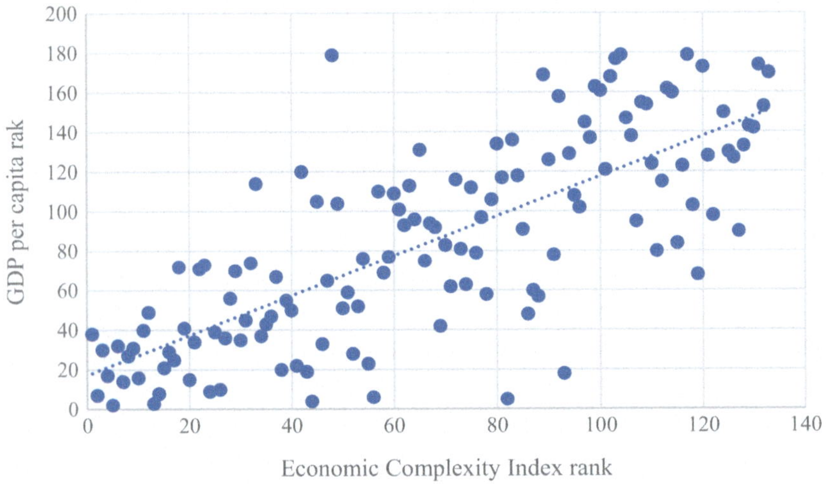

Fig. 3.4 Low-income levels of structurally underdeveloped countries with low economic complexity (2022). *Source*: ECI ranks, *Harvard Growth Lab* (https://atlas.cid.harvard.edu/rankings); Per capita GDP ranks, *worldometer* (https://www.worldometers.info/gdp/gdp-per-capita/)

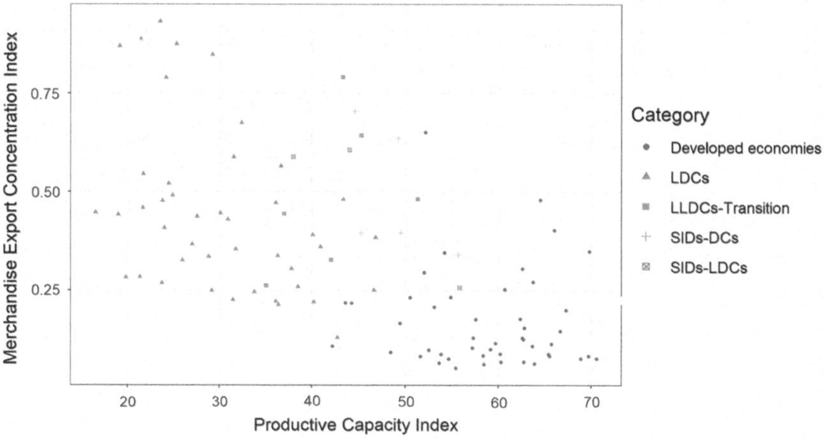

Fig. 3.5 Merchandise export concentration of structurally underdeveloped countries with low productive capacity. *Source*: UNCTAD productive capacity database (https://unctad.org/topic/least-developed-countries/productive-capacities-index)

A country's productive capacity and economic complexity go hand in hand. Harvard Growth Lab (at Harvard Kennedy School) has constructed the Economic Complexity Index (ECI) for countries based on the diversity and complexity of their export basket in order to assess the state of a country's productive knowledge. ECI captures the diversity and sophistication of the productive capabilities embedded in the exports of each country. As highlighted earlier, there is a vicious circle between low productive capacity and low-income levels. High-income countries with high productive capacity are able to produce more complex and diverse products. Thus, there is a high positive correlation (0.76) between country rankings in terms of their ECI and per capita GDP (Fig. 3.4) and a high positive correlation (0.077) between income levels and the number of diverse products exported (Fig. 3.6).

Arnelyn Abdon, Marife Bacate, Jesus Felipe and Utsav Kumar (Abdon et al, 2010) find that the major exporters of more complex products are

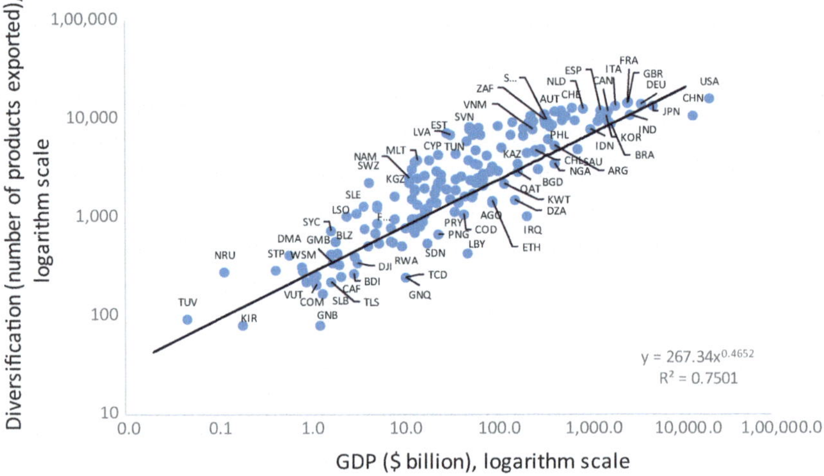

Fig. 3.6 Higher GDP associates with diversification (no. of products exported), 2019. *Source*: CONTRADE data

the high-income countries and the major exporters of less complex products are the low-income countries.[1] Also, export shares of the more (less) complex products increase (decrease) with income. Similarly, Clovis Freire (2012) shows that poorer countries' exports are limited to low complexity products, while a rich country exports products with a wide range of complexity, even though rich countries may produce low complexity products just as the poorer countries. In short, successful structural transformation results in a more diversified economy in present day developed countries.

Simon Kuznets (1973) noted in his Nobel Lecture, "A country's economic growth may be defined as a long-term rise in capacity to supply increasingly *diverse economic goods* to its population, this growing capacity based on *advancing technology* and the institutional and ideological adjustments that it demands" (emphasis added). As Justin Lin (2012, p. 3) pointed out, "all countries that remain poor have failed to achieve

[1] Abdon et al. (2010) find that: (1) the *most complex products* are in machinery, chemicals and metals, while the *least complex products* are raw materials and commodities, wood, textiles and agricultural products; (2) the *most complex economies* are Japan, Germany and Sweden, and the *least complex economies* are Cambodia, Papua New Guinea and Nigeria.

structural transformation, that is, they have been unable to diversify away from agriculture and the production of traditional goods into manufacturing and other modern activities". In fact, the less developed a country is, the lower is its structural transformation measured by relative sectoral GDP/employment shares. It is also found that countries' level of development correlates highly with the number of sophisticated/high value added products they produce and export, indicating the degree of its structural transformation (see Figs. 3.4 and 3.6).

Figure 3.6 shows that small island developing states (SIDS) of Tuvalu (TUV), Kiribati (KIR), Solomon Islands (SLB), Vanuatu (VUT) and Nauru (NRU) as well as Timor-Leste (TSL) in Asia and the Pacific, and Guinea-Bissau (GNB), Comoros (COM), Central African Republic (CAF) and Sao Tome Principe (STP) in Africa at the lowest end of GDP have the least number of export products. On the other end of the spectrum, advanced industrial countries such as the US, Great Britain (GBR), France (FRA), Italy (ITA), Canada (CAN) and Japan (JPN) have the largest number of export products. In a series of papers, Hidalgo et al. (2007), Hidalgo and Hausmann (2009) explained economic development as a process of learning how to produce (and export) more complex products.[2]

The LDCs form the largest set of structurally underdeveloped countries. Besides low levels of income and extreme environment as well as economic vulnerability, these countries have low human capital assets, meaning high under-5 (infant) and maternal mortality rates, malnutrition and low educational attainment. These factors feed into low productive capacity and create a vicious circle resulting in a low-level equilibrium trap. As can be seen from Fig. 3.7, African LDCs have generally lower human capital assets, and there is a wide variation among countries. Human assets of Chad, Central African Republic, Niger and Somalia and South Sudan are very low.

[2] Hausmann, Hwang and Rodrik (2007) suggested two simple empirical measures of *product* and *economic* complexity (or sophistication). First, the *complexity of a product*, represented by the income level associated with that product, is calculated as a weighted average of the income per capita of the countries that export the said product. The weight is the index of revealed comparative advantage. Second, *Economic (or country) complexity*, representing the productivity level associated with a country's export basket, is calculated as a weighted average (where the weight is the share of the product in the country's export basket) of the complexity of the products exported by the country.

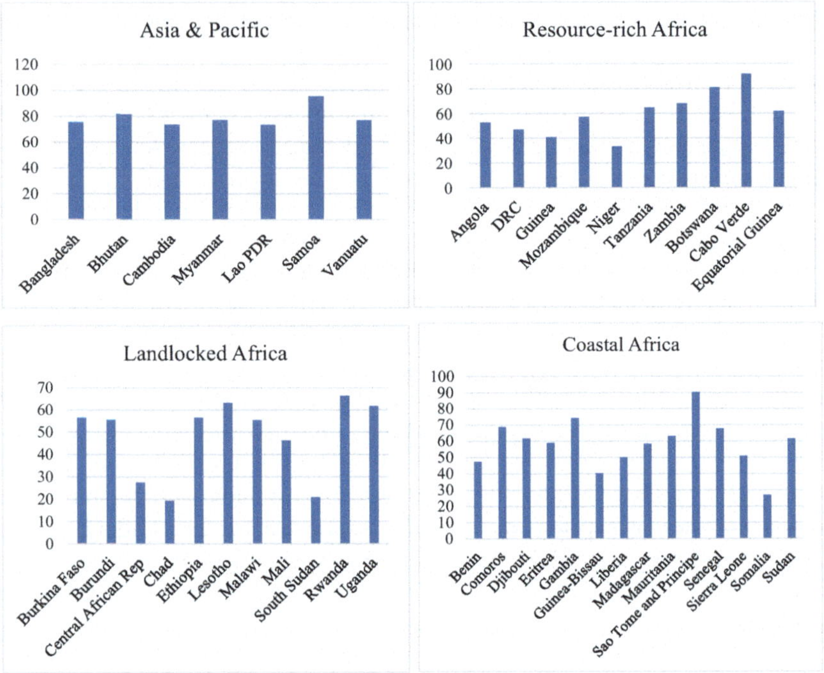

Fig. 3.7 Human capital index of LDCs (2021). *Source*: UN Department of Economic and Social Affairs, https://www.un.org/development/desa/dpad/least-developed-country-category/ldc-criteria.html

Botswana, Cabo Verde and Equatorial Guinea have graduated from the LDCs status. Both Botswana and Cabo Verde have higher human assets as they invested their resource income in the health and education sectors. Equatorial Guinea which graduated from the LDC status based on its high resource income but has low human capital. Nevertheless, the structural transformation of all three graduated countries remains weak and hence these countries are extremely vulnerable to shocks, especially from commodity price volatility.

Democratic Deficits

"Democratic deficit" is a term used to denote a situation where institutions and their decision-making procedures may suffer from a lack of citizen participation and accountability. We use the "Varieties of Democracy (V-Dem) Index" to assess democratic deficits. The V-Dem Index for liberal democracy is produced by V-Dem Institute at the University of Gothenburg by using a multidimensional and disaggregated dataset that reflects the complexity of the concept of democracy as a system of rule that goes beyond the simple presence of elections. It distinguishes between five high-level principles of democracy: electoral, liberal, participatory, deliberative and egalitarian and collects data to measure these principles. The V-Dem Institute then combines the "core" institutions of electoral democracy with the liberal dimension—constraints on the executive by the legislature and the judiciary, and the rule of law ensuring respect for civil liberties—to obtain the index (V-Dem Index) for liberal democracy in individual countries. The index varies from 0 (no democracy) to 1 (full democracy).

Figure 3.8 is a scatter plot of county ranks in terms of liberal democracy (V-Dem Index) and per capita income in the year 2022. As can be seen from Fig. 3.8, democratic deficits highly correlate with underdevelopment. This may give an impression that democratic deficits are almost a defining governance feature of most of the structurally underdeveloped countries, while stable and well-functioning democracy seems to be a luxury that only rich countries can afford—the so-called "Lee hypothesis".

However, a closer look at the data reveals exceptions; there is a good number of countries that are low on the per capital GDP rank but have reasonable liberal democratic rankings. For example, Malawi—a small landlocked African LDC—ranked 156th in terms of per capita GDP; but placed at 59 for its liberal democracy. Similarly, Vanuatu—a Pacific SIDS—has a low GDP per capita rank (138), while ranked 37 on liberal democracy index. These poor countries demonstrate that reasonable participatory liberal democratic governance can be achieved at low levels of income.

Figure 3.9 presents the 2023 V-Dem Index for the countries that we focus in this book. In Africa, Cabo Verde scores above 0.60, while three countries (São Tomé and Príncipe, The Gambia and Lesotho) score marginally higher than 0.50. Five African LDCs—Malawi, Senegal,

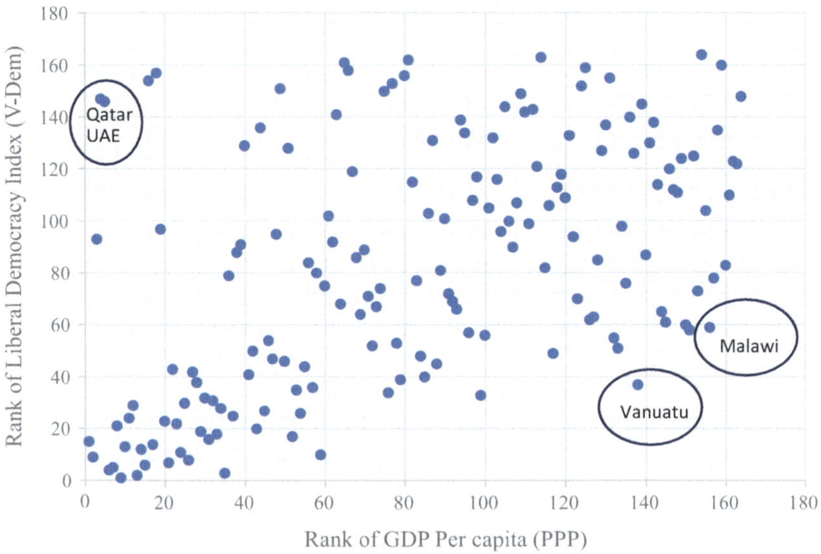

Fig. 3.8 Rank of Liberal Democracy Index (V-Dem) and Rank of GDP per capita (PPP) (2022). *Source*: World Bank data and Varieties of Democracy (V-Dem), https://www.v-dem.net/

Liberia, Zambia and Tanzania—also have reasonable rankings (above 0.4). In South Asia, Nepal shines with a score of 0.52, while Bhutan scores 0.44. Timor-Leste with a score of 0.51 stands out in Southeast Asia, while Vanuatu is a star performer in the Pacific. These countries confirm our earlier observation that liberal democracy does not have to be a "luxury" affordable only in high-income countries. Low-income LDCs can also afford reasonable liberal democratic institutions.

Evidence presented in Figs. 3.8 and 3.9 also reveals some disturbing facts. For example, Bangladesh which has recorded impressive economic growth since the early 2000s, scores very poorly on liberal democracy; and so is Cambodia. The same is true for middle-income countries of Central Asia—all six countries of our focus perform poorly. What is more alarming is that most of these countries have regressed or made a "u-turn" after some periods of democratisation, and some turned into electoral autocracy (or *de-facto* one-party rule).

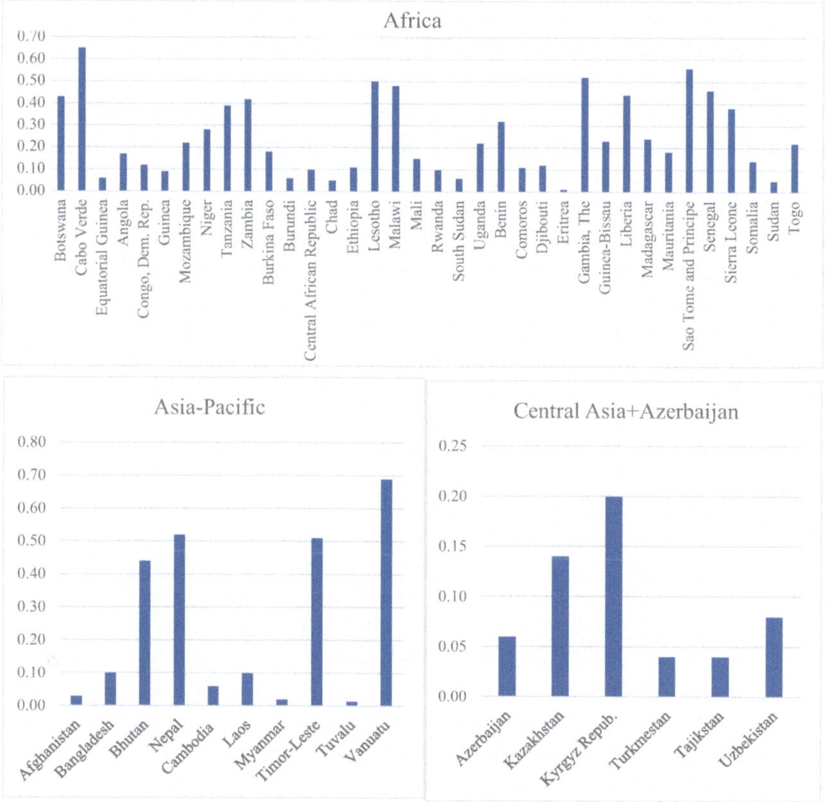

Fig. 3.9 Democratic deficits in structurally underdevelopment countries, Liberal Democracy Index (V-Dem) (2023). *Source*: Democracy Report 2024: Democracy Winning and Losing at the Ballot, V-Dem Institute, https://www.v-dem.net/documents/44/v-dem_dr2024_highres.pdf (10/05/2024). Note: A total of 164 countries are ranked from 1 to 164 from the highest score of Liberal Democracy Index and the highest value of GDP per capita to the lowest

The recent survey data (2021/2022) of Afrobarometer from 28 countries reveal that fewer than half (46%) of Africans say their country is a full democracy or a democracy with minor problems, and even fewer (38%) say they are satisfied with the way democracy works in their country. Both ratings have declined since 2014/2015—the perceived extent of democracy is down by 4 percentage, while satisfaction has dropped by

7 points. As noted by Afrobarometer CEO Joseph Asunka, "The supply side of democratic governance—the failure of governments to deliver—is the main challenge of Africa's democratic governance".[3]

In Chapter 1, we have attributed the lack of democratic governance to colonial legacies and continued neo-colonialism, especially in Africa. However, William Gumede (2017) argues that at the heart of the governance failures of many African independence and liberation movements turned governments was, and still is, their inability to effectively transform from resistance movements into effective democratic governing parties.

Central Asian countries, including Azerbaijan, still could not shred off their authoritarian Soviet-era legacy. They have not adequately developed the social institutions and laws required to allow democracy to fully flourish, and alarmingly, they are going backwards in many respects, reflecting a wider and very concerning global trend.

The authoritarian past and wider global trend can also explain the democratic deficits and slides in the Southeast Asian LDCs—Cambodia, Lao and Myanmar. Rounaq Jahan (2003) called Bangladesh's situation as "imperilled democracy", where, "Murder, intimidation, suppression, and harassment of political opponents worsened the atmosphere of vendetta and violence that has marked the country's politics in the past few decades". Ali Riaz (2022) observed Bangladesh's slide in autocracy as "the end of a democratic success story". The sharp democratic slide in Bangladesh is explicable, especially when its people have a long history of democratic struggle. It is a puzzle for a country born through a liberation war fought for people's democratic rights.

One burning question is: can Bangladesh and Cambodia sustain their recent decades' high growth when they are effectively becoming a one-party state? The regimes in both countries justify their authoritarian turn claiming its necessity for development. We are aware of the complex and varied relations between democracy and development. In fact, the relation between democracy and development is widely debated. We have reflected on this debate in Chapter 2 and elaborated democracy's instrumental value in producing stable growth and successful structural transformation in Chapter 5 in the context of South and Southeast Asian LDCs.

[3] https://www.afrobarometer.org/articles/democracy-in-crisis-africas-long-standing-democracies-under-pressure-afrobarometer-ceo-warns/ (23/05/2024).

References

Abdon, A., Marife, B., Jesus, F., & Utsav, K. (2010). Product complexity and economic development. *The Levy Economics Institute Working Paper* No. 616, https://papers.ssrn.com/sol3/papers.cfm?abstract_id=1677442 (accessed 24/08/2023).

Aggarwal, A., & Nagesh, K. (2012). Structural change, industrialization and poverty reduction: The case of India. In *South and South-West Asia Development Papers* 1206, ESCAP South and South-West Asia Office, https://www.unescap.org/sites/default/files/SSWA_Development_Paper_1206_Nov2012.pdf (accessed 24/08/2023).

Chang, H.-J. (2002). *Kicking away the ladder: Development strategy in historical perspective*. Anthem Press.

Chenery, H., & Moshe, S. (1975). *Patterns of development, 1950–70*. Oxford University Press.

Chowdhury, A., & Iyanatul, I. (1993). *The newly industrialising economies of East Asia*. Routledge.

Dowd, D. (1971). *The State, Power and the Industrial Revolution, 1750–1914*. The Union for Radical Political Economics.

Fisher, H. (1896). The protectionist reaction in France. *The Economic Journal, 6*(23), 341–355.

Freire, C. (2012). Building productive capacities: Challenges and opportunities for least developed countries. *UN-ESCAP MPDD Working Papers* WP/12/02. https://www.unescap.org/sites/default/files/wp-12-02_1.pdf (accessed 24/08/2023).

Grabas, C., & Alexander, N. (2013). Industrial policies in Europe in historical perspective. *WWW for Europe Working Paper* No. 15, https://www.econstor.eu/handle/10419/125670 (accessed 19/05/2024).

Gumede, W. (2017). The democracy deficit of Africa's liberation movements turned governments. *Politikon, 44*(1), 27–48.

Hausmann, R., Jason, H., & Dani, R. (2007). What you export matters. *Journal of Economic Growth, 12*(1), 1–25.

Herrendorf, B., Richrad, R., & Akos V. (2013). Growth and structural transformation. In *National Bureau of Economic Research Working Paper* No. 18996, April, https://www.nber.org/system/files/working_papers/w18996/w18996.pdf (accessed 24/08/203).

Hidalgo, C., & Ricardo, H. (2009). The building blocks of economic complexity. *CID Working Paper No. 186.*Harvard University, Center for International Development, https://www.hks.harvard.edu/centers/cid/publications/faculty-working-papers/building-blocks-economic-complexity (accessed 24/08/2023).

Hidalgo, C., Bailey, K., Barabási, A.-L., & Ricardo, H. (2007). The product space conditions the development of nations. *Science, 317*(5837), 482–487.

Islam, I., & Anis, C. (2001). *The political economy of East Asia: Post crisis debates*. Oxford University Press.

Jahan, R. (2003). Bangladesh in 2002: Imperilled democracy. *Asian Survey, 43*(1), 222–229.

Kuznets, S. (1973). Modern economic growth: Findings and reflections. *American Economic Review, 63*(3), 247–258.

Kuznets, S. (1955). Economic growth and income inequality. *American Economic Review, 45*(1), 1–28.

Kuznets, S. (1966). *Modern economic growth: Rate, structure and spread*. Yale University Press.

Lin, J. Y. (2012). *New structural economics: A framework for rethinking development*. The World Bank.

McMillan, M., & Dani R. (2011). Globalization, structural change and productivity growth. In *National Bureau of Economic Research (NBER) Working Papers* 17143.

Nelson, R. (1956). A theory of the low-level equilibrium trap in underdeveloped economies. *American Economic Review, 46*(5), 894–908.

Riaz, A. (2022). Bangladesh's quiet slide into autocracy: The end of a democratic success story. *Foreign Affairs*, 29 April.

Sen, K. (2019). Structural transformation around the world: Patterns and drivers. *Asian Development Review, 36*(2), 1–31.

Tagliapietra, S., & Reinhilde, V. (2020). *A Green Industrial Policy for Europe*. Brussels: Bruegel. https://www.jstor.org/stable/resrep28602.7 (accessed 19/05/2024).

UNCTAD. (2006).*The Least Developed Countries Report 2006: Developing Productive Capacities*. New York & Geneva: United Nations.

Wade, R. (2014a). *The developmental state: New perspectives. For meeting of JICA/IPD task force on industrial policy & transformation*. Jordan, June 5–6, https://policydialogue.org/files/events/robert_wade_paper.pdf (accessed 19/05/2024).

Wade, R. (2014b). The mystery of U.S. industrial policy: The developmental state in disguise. In J. M. Salazar-Xirinachs, & R. Kozul Wright (Eds.), *Transforming economies: Making industrial policies work for growth, jobs and development* (pp. 379–400). ILO-UNCTAD.

Wolf, N. (2018). Protectionism: Historical perspectives. *VoxEU/CEPR Blog*, 11 June, https://cepr.org/voxeu/blogs-and-reviews/protectionism-historical-perspectives (accessed 19/05/2024).

World Bank. (1993). *The East Asian miracle: Economic growth and public policy*. World Bank.

Zussman, A. (2002). *The rise of German protectionism in the 1870's:A macroeconomic perspective.* Stanford Institute for Economic Policy Research (Stanford University) Discussion Paper No. 01–19 (January), https://siepr.stanford.edu/publications/working-paper/rise-german-protectionism-1870s-macroeconomic-perspective (accessed 19/05/2024).

CHAPTER 4

Africa's LDCs: Victims of Colonialism and Neoliberalism

> "The true explanation for the slowness of industrial development in Africa lies in the policies of the colonial period. Practically all our natural resources, not to mention trade, shipping, banking, building, and so on, fell into, and have remained in, the hands of foreigners seeking to enrich alien investors, and to hold back local economic initiative." (Kwame Nkrumah, 1963, p. 24)

Walter Rodney in his 1972 book, *How Europe underdeveloped Africa*, detailed how Africa was deliberately exploited and underdeveloped by European colonial powers. One of his main arguments is that Africa developed Europe at the same rate that Europe underdeveloped Africa. As development is path-dependent, most African structurally underdeveloped countries' development trajectory is determined by their colonial past. Ironically, the former French colonies are still tied to France though neo-colonial currency arrangements and other colonial powers maintained their exploitative arrangements through elite control of the State, often resorting to coups to topple nationalist governments.

Tom Burgis in his 2015 book, *The Looting Machine*, exposes how Africa's natural resource deposits attract a global network of traders, bankers, corporate extractors and investors who combine with venal political cabals to loot the States' value. The looting has accelerated in recent decades as never before with the rising global demand for Africa's

A. Chowdhury et al., *Structural Transformations as Developing Africa, Asia, and the Pacific*, https://doi.org/10.1007/978-981-97-9092-0_4

resources. Thus, a handful of Africans are becoming rich, but the vast majority, like the continent as a whole, is being fleeced. The result is a catastrophic social disintegration and not just a continuation of Africa's past as a colonial victim.

Burgis (2015) notes that in 2010, fuel and mineral exports from Africa were worth US$333 billion, more than seven times the value of the aid that went to the continent. He further notes that for every Frenchwoman who dies in childbirth, 100 die in Niger alone, the former French colony whose uranium fuels France's nuclear reactors. In resource-rich African countries, a large chunk of government revenue comes from resource rents, thus the governments do not feel accountable to their people. In these rentier states, people are largely serfs. The resource curse is not merely some unfortunate economic phenomenon. What is happening in Africa is systematic looting.

In the context of the above, this chapter analyses the growth experiences of structurally underdeveloped African countries, including those that graduated from their LDC status and their structural transformation. It reveals that the majority of structurally underdeveloped African countries could not capitalise on the commodity price boom of the early years of the new millennium that lasted until about 2014, albeit interrupted by the global financial crisis (GFC) of 2008–2009. Their high growth did not accompany much structural transformation. Their economies remain less diversified with correspondingly little complexity and low productive capacities. As a result, they experienced "boom-bust" growth, being adversely affected by falling commodity prices since the GFC.

Africa's Boom-Bust Growth

Growth returned to Africa's highly diverse structurally underdeveloped countries at the dawn of the new millennium after two lost decades as the majority of them managed to grow at an average rate of around 5% during 2000–2010 (Table 4.1). However, as mentioned earlier, the continent's commodity price led growth spurt was not accompanied by the desired structural transformation.

The continent's progress was disrupted by the GFC. African LDCs' recovery from the GFC was much more subdued than that of Asian LDCs due to over-dependence on commodity exports. Many African LDCs were also hit by other shocks such as deadly Ebola epidemics and droughts as well as a surge in armed conflicts during 2011–2020. Countries that

Table 4.1 Average Annual Real GDP Growth Rates (%), 2000–2020

Country	*2000–05*	*2006–10*	*2011–15*	*2016–19*	*2020*
Graduated African LDCs					
Botswana	3.4	4.8	4.9	3.7	− 8.7
Cabo Verde	7.2	6.0	1.5	4.7	− 14.8
Equatorial Guinea	28.3	6.6	0.4	− 6.6	− 4.2
Resource-rich African LDCs					
Angola	8.3	8.5	4.5	− 1.4	− 5.6
Congo, Dem. Rep	2.1	5.6	7.8	4.1	1.7
Guinea	3.0	3.2	4.6	8.2	4.9
Mozambique	7.3	7.5	7.1	3.3	− 1.2
Niger	3.5	5.4	5.9	5.9	3.6
Tanzania	6.6	6.1	6.4	6.2	2.0
Zambia	5.8	8.7	5.2	3.3	− 2.8
Landlocked African LDCs					
Burkina Faso	5.6	5.5	5.4	6.2	1.9
Burundi	1.7	4.5	2.7	0.8	0.3
Central African Republic	1.2	4.9	− 4.5	4.0	0.9
Chad	14.2	4.9	4.9	− 0.9	− 1.6
Ethiopia	6.5	10.9	10.2	8.5	6.1
Lesotho	3.0	3.8	4.4	1.2	− 8.4
Malawi	2.1	7.4	4.1	3.5	0.8
Mali	5.9	4.6	3.6	5.2	− 1.2
Rwanda	8.2	8.3	7.3	7.0	− 3.4
South Sudan		5.3	− 9.0		
Uganda	6.1	8.1	5.4	5.3	3.0
Coastal African LDCs					
Benin	4.2	3.9	4.6	5.6	3.8
Comoros	3.7	2.9	3.0	3.3	− 0.2
Djibouti			7.4	7.0	1.2
Eritrea	1.7	− 0.7	8.7		
Gambia	3.3	4.3	0.5	4.8	0.6
Guinea-Bissau	2.4	3.4	3.3	5.1	− 2.4
Liberia	− 3.1	7.2	5.1	0.0	− 3.0
Madagascar	3.0	2.9	2.7	4.3	− 7.1
Mauritania	2.8	3.8	4.5	3.2	− 0.9
Sao Tome and Principe	5.0	5.9	4.5	3.3	3.0
Senegal	4.4	3.4	4.5	6.4	1.3
Sierra Leone	7.9	5.2	5.2	4.8	− 2.0
Somalia			11.4	6.5	2.5
Sudan	6.4	6.5	2.9	1.0	− 3.6
Togo	0.8	3.4	6.1	5.0	1.8

World Bank online data; Somalia, African Development Bank, *African Economic Outlook* (various issues) are members of a monetary union have limited policy space, especially in monetary and exchange rate policies to deal with shocks. Rising external debt also limited fiscal policy space for many. The COVID-19 pandemic has also taken its toll.

First Decade (2000–2010): Commodity Price Boom Busted by Global Financial Crisis

Of African LDCs, oil exporters (Angola, Chad, Equatorial Guinea and Sudan) and mineral producers (the Democratic Republic of the Congo—DRC, Guinea, Mali, Mauritania, Mozambique and Zambia) benefited most from the surge in demand for commodities, mainly from the emerging economies of China, India and Brazil. African LDCs also benefited most from the growth in foreign direct investment (FDI) to LDCs, which rose from $4.1 billion to $32.4 billion between 2001 and 2008. African LDCs accounted for almost half of that total (UNCTAD, 2010).

International trade had a decisive influence on the economic performance of structurally underdeveloped economies. While the value of export of merchandise from the LDCs grew five-fold from 2000 to 2008, the volume exported increased by only 97% (UNCTAD, 2011). This illustrates the strong effect of commodity prices on the export boom of LDCs during the 2000s. However, such a trend led to an increased dependence of LDC economies, particularly in Africa, on primary commodities (UNCTAD, 2017). This not only hindered their structural transformation but also increased their vulnerabilities (UNCTAD, 2014).

This became evident in the wake of the 2008–2009 GFC. The Asian LDCs fared better than African LDCs both during the crisis and afterwards. The economies of Asian LDCs slowed marginally to 5.1% in 2009 from 5.4% in 2008 and rebounded to around 6.3% growth in 2010. Asian LDCs' performed better for two main reasons: (i) the overall dynamism of developing economies in Asia—especially China and India, during the crisis and after—and (ii) their less dependence on primary commodities, or some industrialisation and structural transformation, to be more precise. The pull effect of their trading partners, together with a more diversified export structure, helped the Asian LDCs both during and after the GFC (UNCTAD, 2011).

On the other hand, African LDCs' growth rate dropped sharply from 7.8% in 2008 to 4.5% in 2009, while their growth in 2010 picked up marginally to 5.2%. The composition of African LDCs' exports—more concentrated in commodities and less diversified than that of Asian LDCs—made them more vulnerable to external shocks. While the value of merchandise exports of LDCs as a group declined by around 28% in 2009, the slump in African LDCs' exports was − 33.6%, a much sharper fall than − 6.9% in the case of Asian LDCs. At the same time, the subsequent recovery was also much more subdued in the African LDCs. Despite experiencing a 20.2% increase in 2010, the merchandise exports of the African LDCs were still much lower than in 2008. In contrast, the growth of Asian LDCs' merchandise exports in 2010 was impressive at 29% (UNCTAD, 2011).

The global recession also affected FDI inflows to LDCs declining in 2009 and 2010. In 2010, FDI—US$26.39 billion—was around US$6 billion less than in 2008 (US$32.35 billion—or one-fifth smaller. Since the resource-rich African LDCs accounted for more than four-fifths of all inflows, they were more adversely affected than more diversified Asian LDCs.[1]

Second Decade (2011–2021): Boom-Bust Cycles and Exogenous Shocks

Growth in African structurally underdeveloped countries recovered to around 7.4% in 2012, but then decelerated to 3.7% in 2016 and 4.8% in 2017. In contrast, growth in Asian LDCs steadily increased to around 7% in 2017. This shows the vulnerabilities of the primarily commodity-dependent African LDCs to falling commodity prices. Crude oil prices plunged by − 47.2% in 2015, having previously fallen by − 7.5% in 2014. This was accompanied across the board by significant drops in prices of other commodities such as minerals, ores and metals and agricultural raw materials and food, confirming a downward trend in prices that started in 2012 (UNCTAD, 2016).

Oil and gas exporters contracted significantly in 2015 by − 4.5%, reflecting their strong exposure to the boom–bust price cycles. The other main commodity-specialised LDC groups (food and agricultural exporters and mineral exporters) experienced a decline in their growth rates to

[1] Three African LDCs—Angola, Equatorial Guinea and Sudan—accounting for 49% of all FDI inflows in 2010. The single largest recipient was Angola, with around 33% of the total for all LDCs (UNCTAD, 2011, op cit.).

less than – 4% in 2015. By contrast, LDCs that are mainly exporters of manufactures achieved the highest economic growth rate (6.2%) in 2015, higher than the rates (averaging 3.9%) recorded by other developing countries (UNCTAD, 2016).

African LDCs suffered also from other exogenous shocks, such as Ebola outbreaks in 2014. Three of them—Burundi, Sierra Leone and South Sudan experienced a contraction in their real GDP of – 3.9%, – 9.1%, – 20.6% and – 10.8%, respectively—while it stagnated in two others Angola (0.9%) and Liberia (0%) in 2015.

African countries that graduated out of the LDC category also experienced negative growth—Botswana – 1.7% and Equatorial Guinea – 9.1% in 2015. While Cabo Verde's growth was paltry 1% in 2015, Equatorial Guinea's negative growth continued (– 8.8% in 2016, – 5.7% in 2017, – 6.4% in 2018 and – 5.6% in 2019).

Ethiopia has been the best performer, growing at over 10% during 2011–2015 and recording the highest economic growth rate (10.4%) among all LDCs in 2015. It grew at 8.5% per annum in the subsequent period (2016–2019), before the country plunged into a civil war. The second-best performer during 2011–2015 was DRC (7.8%) followed by Djibouti (7.4%), Rwanda (7.3%) and Mozambique (7.2%). However, they diverged in the subsequent period (2016–2019), experiencing growth decelerations due to shocks such as drought and disease outbreaks.

The COVID-19 Pandemic

While Sub-Saharan Africa could avoid a catastrophic health scenario, the continent's economy suffered significantly as the average GDP growth dropped from around 3% in 2019 to about – 2% in 2020. Although, the continent's average GDP growth recovered to 4.8% in 2021, the continental average masks the country-level details. LDC graduated Cabo Verde was the worst hit country where GDP fell by 14.8%. The other two LDC-graduated countries also experienced severe contractions, GDP declining in Botswana by – 8.7% and in Equatorial Guinea by – 4.9%. Among the African LDCs that experienced the most GDP contractions during the pandemic were Lesotho (– 7.6), Madagascar (– 7.1), Angola (– 5.4), Sudan (– 3.6) and Rwanda (– 3.4).

Uncertain Growth Prospect

Being highly dependent on primary product exports, Africa's growth prospects remain uncertain. A number of factors exacerbate Africa's predicament. These include global economic slowdown due to overall tighter monetary and fiscal conditions in response to the COVID-19 pandemic and food, fuel and fertilizer crises caused by the Russia–Ukraine war. Many African economies faced significant inflationary pressures in 2023, largely because of high fuel and food prices. The overall weak trade performance globally has also weighed down on Africa's growth, due to a subdued demand from key export markets, notably China and commodity prices levelling off.

Several African currencies faced depreciation pressures due to weak export earnings and limited external financing inflows, while depreciation did not increase demand for their price-insensitive (inelastic) primary exports. Although CFA countries did not face such depreciation pressures, the institutionally pegged CFA Franc limits policy space, especially in times of crises. This situation has worsened their external debt, especially for those countries that borrowed from the global capital market, such as Eurobond, in the face of declining official development aid (ODA) and multilateral financing. Aid to Africa was in decline even before the pandemic (Harcourt, 2021). Aid to the African LDCs dropped by US$1.9 billion (– 4%), in real terms from US$45.2 billion in 2018 to $43.3 billion in 2019. In 2022 net bilateral ODA flows from Development Assistance Committee (DAC) countries of the OECD to Africa was US$34 billion, representing a drop of 7.4% in real terms compared to 2021. Within this total, net ODA to sub-Saharan Africa was US$29 billion, a fall of 7.8% in real terms (OECD, 2023).

High debt burden and exorbitant borrowing costs limit space for investment and growth. Debt sustainability challenges pose a significant headwind to Africa's growth prospects. According to the United Nations (2024), 18 countries in Africa recorded a debt-to-GDP ratio of over 70% per cent in 2023, with many of them facing debt distress. The United Nations (2024) also notes that borrowing costs for African countries are approximately 4 times higher than that for the developed countries. Access to, and high cost of, development financing remains a daunting challenge, with debt overhangs preventing many African countries from accessing funds at affordable rates from international capital markets.

Furthermore, as the United Nations (2024) observes, the effects of climate change continue to pose significant downward risks for Africa's economy. The rising frequency and impacts of climate-induced events and natural disasters are eroding African countries' economic potential. Climate financing flows to Africa fall far short of its needs—the estimated annual financing gap is about US$120 billion, and the continent receives only 2% of global clean energy finance flows (United Nations, 2024).

Domestic and geopolitical instability will continue to adversely impact Sub-Saharan African countries. IMF (2023) finds that if the world were split into two isolated trading blocs centred around China or the US and the European Union, Sub-Saharan African economies could experience a permanent decline of up to 4% of real GDP after 10 years—losses larger than what many countries experienced during the GFC.

Africa's Structural Transformation Failures

According to Albert Zeufack and James Cust (2023), the legacy of the boom and bust was one of missed opportunity and a failure to convert resource wealth into sustainable, diversified and inclusive prosperity. This highlights the critical role of policy space and institutions that are severely constrained due to neo-colonial arrangements and aid conditionality of the international financial institutions. Thus, ironically resource-rich African countries ended up with unsustainable growth paths and widening inequality with greater vulnerability to commodity price shocks and climate change crises.

As presented in Table 4.2, in a majority of African countries, the share of industry in gross domestic product (GDP) and employment declined while the sectoral composition of GDP has remained nearly unchanged since the 1960s (UNECA, 2020). Agriculture contributed about 18% to GDP in the post-independence planning period, and its GDP share remained at around 17% in the 2000s. The manufacturing sector, considered to be the most dynamic, declined; its contribution to GDP fell for nearly four decades reaching 12% in 2007.

Therefore, not only the process of structural transformation in Africa has been slower and the transfer of productive resources of higher productivity sectors has been sluggish, in the commodity-dependent African LDCs, the long commodity cycle of 2003–2011 has led to some degree

Table 4.2 Sectoral output shares (% GDP), 2000, 2010, 2020

Country name	*Agriculture, forestry, and fishing*			*Manufacturing*			*Services*		
	2000	*2010*	*2020*	*2000*	*2010*	*2020*	*2000*	*2010*	*2020*
Graduated African LDCs									
Botswana	2.8	2.5	2.2	5.6	6.4	5.7	42.7	52.7	66.2
Cabo Verde	12.9	8.0	4.9	9.3	5.4	7.3	65.4	61.2	58.9
Equatorial Guinea		1.1	2.9		21.0	20.1		24.7	51.5
Resource rich African LDCs									
Angola	5.7	6.2	9.1	2.9	4.5	6.9	22.2	41.9	45.1
Congo, Dem. Rep	32.0	21.4	20.9	9.9	16.2	19.0	44.5	35.4	35.7
Guinea	21.0	17.5	25.8	3.8	10.6	9.7	41.4	43.4	37.3
Mozambique	19.5	26.9	26.2	13.0	10.0	7.9	45.9	47.0	41.9
Niger	36.8	36.3	38.4	7.3	5.6	7.4	40.4	35.1	36.1
Tanzania	26.2	25.6	26.7	9.9	8.7	8.5	49.1	43.3	36.3
Zambia	16.1	9.4	3.0	9.5	7.6	7.7	49.0	52.8	53.6
Land locked African LDCs									
Burkina Faso	24.9	24.1	18.4	15.4	12.1	9.3	47.7	42.1	40.8
Burundi	44.1	38.4	28.6	10.9	9.2	9.4 (2016)	32.1	37.0	45.5

(continued)

Table 4.2 (continued)

Country name	*Agriculture, forestry, and fishing*			*Manufacturing*			*Services*		
	2000	*2010*	*2020*	*2000*	*2010*	*2020*	*2000*	*2010*	*2020*
Central African Republic		37.4	29.5		18.4	17.7		29.3	40.0
Chad	40.7	51.9	46.8	8.6	1.0	3.2	44.6	33.4	43.6
Ethiopia	44.7	41.4	35.6	5.6	4.0	5.3	37.4	41.8	36.8
Lesotho	7.8	4.8	4.8	13.6	12.9	14.4	51.3	54.6	49.3
Malawi	35.7	29.6	22.7	11.6	9.9	11.5 (2019)	38.4	47.9	52.6
Mali	32.9	33.0	36.2		3.1	6.8	37.3	35.5	34.4
Rwanda	37.2	24.2	26.6	11.6	8.3	8.7	44.3	49.9	46.6
South Sudan		5.3			2.3	3.5 (2015)		33.6	56.6 (2015)
Uganda	27.5	32.0	23.9	7.1	16.9	15.8	44.7	37.7	42.8
Coastal African LDCs									
Benin	23.5	25.8	27.1	14.0	11.7	9.7	35.3	44.5	47.9
Comoros	29.4	30.4	35.8				54.5	53.2	51.4
Djibouti			1.7			4.4		80.5 (2013)	77.3
Eritrea	12.6	14.1 (2009)		9.3	5.5 (2009)				
Gambia, The	24.5	35.2	21.2	6.8	4.6	2.6	60.6	49.2	54.0
Guinea-Bissau	41.7	45.1	30.9		11.3	9.1 (2018)	41.8	39.4	50.2
Liberia	76.1	44.8	41.1	2.5	2.6	1.7 (2019)	19.7	50.2	41.6

Country name	*Agriculture, forestry, and fishing*			*Manufacturing*			*Services*		
	2000	*2010*	*2020*	*2000*	*2010*	*2020*	*2000*	*2010*	*2020*
Madagascar	30.9	29.1	24.7		9.0	9.7	48.4	53.3	50.4
Mauritania	24.8	16.7	19.6	9.9	6.7	6.0	40.4	39.9	40.7
Sao Tome and Principe	10.4 (2001)	11.6	14.2	8.1 (2001)	8.5	5.7	69.8 (2001)	67.1	71.0
Senegal	16.9	15.8	16.2		15.5	14.3	50.8	52.8	50.3
Sierra Leone	55.0	52.9	59.5	3.3	2.2	1.9	12.5	35.3	31.0
Somalia									
Sudan	40.7	33.9	20.3	8.3	8.1	11.7 (2019)	35.7	44.5	36.2
Togo	30.6	28.7	18.8	7.5	7.2	14.4	53.5	56.3	49.3

World Bank, *World Development Indicators* (various issues)

of "re-primarisation".[2] These countries are finding it difficult to establish new drivers of growth and diversification after the end of the commodity boom. Even though manufacturing's GDP share rose to about 15% between 2007 and 2016, the sector's growth and transformation prospects remain uncertain. Thus, Africa's deindustrialisation trend is unlikely to be reversed as discussed later.

This is in contrast to the structural transformation experiences of Asian newly industrialising countries, such as Thailand, Indonesia, The Philippines and Vietnam, not to mention China, South Korea and Taiwan. These Asian countries witnessed rising shares of manufacturing in output and employment, specialisation in manufacturing exports and performing strongly in terms of labour productivity growth. The structural transformation process in the Asian LDC Bangladesh, and to some extent, Cambodia also roughly resembles a classical process of industrialisation.

Since the resources sector is more capital-intensive and does not absorb much labour, the majority of the labour force in structurally underdeveloped African countries remains concentrated in agriculture, where productivity growth has been very slow. Most of the people who left agriculture or rural economy and migrated to urban areas have been absorbed in low-productivity informal service sectors, rather than in manufacturing or knowledge-intensive services, both of which tend to have higher labour productivity. As a result, African LDCs recorded stagnant or slow productivity growth.

Since agriculture remains highly significant, employing a majority of the labour force (Table 4.3), structurally underdeveloped African countries have a high potential for productivity gains within agriculture (e.g., through modernisation and moving to high-value crops) while simultaneously transferring resources away from agriculture and ensuring food security. Therefore, structurally underdeveloped African countries face two concurrent challenges: they must strongly accelerate labour productivity growth in agriculture and generate substantial employment in other sectors for their rapidly growing populations. Moreover, these new jobs must be of a considerably higher productivity level than those in their respective agricultural sectors. This has been further discussed later in the section on Africa's structural transformation options.

[2] Dominance of primary commodities, mainly minerals, oil and gas.

Table 4.3 Sectoral Employment (% of total employment), 2000, 2010, 2020

Country name	*Agriculture*			*Industry*			*Services*		
	2000	*2010*	*2020*	*2000*	*2010*	*2020*	*2000*	*2010*	*2020*
Graduated African LDCs									
Botswana	20.0	24.6	20.4	21.2	18.2	18.1	58.9	57.1	61.5
Cabo Verde	22.9	16.2	11.1	18.7	22.2	22.1	58.4	61.5	66.8
Equatorial Guinea	51.5	41.7	42.5	13.6	22.9	18.5	34.9	35.4	38.9
Resource-rich African LDCs									
Angola	37.5	48.9	50.2	8.7	7.8	8.1	53.8	43.3	41.7
Congo, Dem. Rep	73.2	70.0	65.1	8.1	8.6	9.8	18.7	21.4	25.1
Guinea	71.2	67.5	61.3	5.5	5.3	6.2	23.3	27.2	32.5
Mozambique	81.9	76.4	69.9	3.0	5.3	8.6	15.1	18.3	21.5
Niger	77.9	77.1	74.8	8.6	7.5	7.2	13.5	15.4	18.0
Tanzania	83.0	70.4	64.9	2.8	5.8	6.8	14.2	23.8	28.3
Zambia	70.9	64.3	48.5	7.0	8.8	10.8	22.1	26.9	40.7
Land-locked African LDCs									
Burkina Faso	80.3	48.2	24.7	6.5	20.9	33.9	13.2	31.0	41.4
Burundi	92.2	92.1	92.0	2.1	1.8	1.4	5.7	6.1	6.5
Central African Republic	80.3	78.8	77.1	6.6	6.2	5.4	13.1	15.1	17.5
Chad	82.2	78.5	76.3	1.9	2.4	2.1	15.9	19.1	21.6
Ethiopia	76.7	74.0	65.6	6.6	8.0	10.4	16.7	18.0	24.0
Lesotho	16.1	11.3	8.4	41.1	42.4	41.9	42.9	46.3	49.6
Malawi	53.5	48.1	43.2	14.6	14.2	13.8	31.9	37.7	43.0
Mali	72.6	68.6	62.3	8.7	8.8	7.6	18.7	22.5	30.2
Rwanda	88.6	79.5	61.7	2.5	5.7	9.1	9.0	14.8	29.2
South Sudan	59.0	56.4	56.1	16.9	16.8	14.1	24.2	26.8	29.7
Uganda	70.1	66.8	72.4	7.7	7.8	6.6	22.2	25.4	20.9
Coastal African LDCs									
Benin	47.9	44.0	38.0	20.1	18.7	19.1	32.0	37.3	42.9
Comoros	56.6	53.7	49.9	14.8	13.7	13.0	28.6	32.6	37.0
Djibouti	44.9	40.7	32.4	12.2	11.5	13.3	42.9	47.8	54.3
Eritrea	65.5	64.7	60.8	10.5	9.1	8.5	23.9	26.3	30.7
Gambia, The	35.4	31.0	26.6	17.3	16.4	15.8	47.3	52.6	57.7
Guinea-Bissau	72.7	71.0	67.8	8.1	7.1	7.0	19.2	21.8	25.2
Liberia	51.3	47.3	43.0	11.3	10.8	10.1	37.4	41.9	46.9

(continued)

Table 4.3 (continued)

Country name	*Agriculture*			*Industry*			*Services*		
	2000	*2010*	*2020*	*2000*	*2010*	*2020*	*2000*	*2010*	*2020*
Madagascar	76.4	73.4	63.8	9.0	6.0	9.1	14.7	20.6	27.1
Mauritania	62.1	56.9	50.6	11.3	11.9	13.1	26.6	31.2	36.3
Sao Tome and Principe	30.8	24.3	18.7	19.0	17.8	18.5	50.2	57.9	62.9
Senegal	46.3	38.2	29.4	12.3	12.8	13.6	41.4	49.0	56.9
Sierra Leone	70.2	63.9	54.4	6.1	5.3	6.5	23.7	30.8	39.1
Somalia	84.5	83.8	83.0	4.8	4.1	3.5	10.8	12.1	13.4
Sudan	52.0	45.6	39.7	11.9	14.7	15.9	36.1	39.8	44.4
Togo	47.7	44.0	37.2	13.9	12.4	12.9	38.5	43.6	49.9

Same as Table 3.2
Note: Modelled ILO estimate

Africa's Premature Deindustrialisation

Disappointingly, the share of Africa's manufacturing sector in GDP has fallen since 2000 from 14 to 10%, and remained stagnant, while little progress has been made in producing more sophisticated goods. In 2017, manufacturing's share of Sub-Saharan Africa (SSA)'s total GDP was just under 10% (Signé, 2018). In terms of two other indicators of industrial development—manufacturing value added (MVA) and manufacturing exports—Africa lags far behind the rest of the world, even among developing countries. In 2017, SSA's MVA was only about US$145 billion, vis-à-vis around US$4000 billion for East Asia and the Pacific and close to US$7000 billion for the OECD (Signé, 2018).

Furthermore, much of Africa's industrial production remains centred on resource-based manufacturing. Resource-based manufacturing accounts for approximately half of total MVA and manufacturing exports. Moreover, manufacturing has also been uneven, with almost 70% of the continent's manufacturing activities concentrated in just four countries—South Africa, Egypt, Nigeria and Morocco (Signé, 2018). Thus, SSA's exports are dominated by a few products and a few market destinations as indicated by a high concentration index (Fig. 4.1). At the same time, the export diversification index for SSA remained high at around 0.6% between 1995 and 2022, implying that its export structure deviates significantly from the global pattern, vis-a-vis Europe's 0.178 and Asia's 0.189.

Diversification index is computed by measuring the absolute deviation of the trade structure of a country from the world structure. The diversification index takes values between 0 and 1. A value closer to 1 indicates greater divergence from the world pattern.

As illustrated in Chapter 3 (Fig. 3.1), the dynamics of the manufacturing sector typically follow a hump-shaped curve (or an inverted U-shaped) relationship for both employment and value added. That is, manufacturing's output and employment shares first rise and then decline when the shares of the high-productivity services pick up. In mature

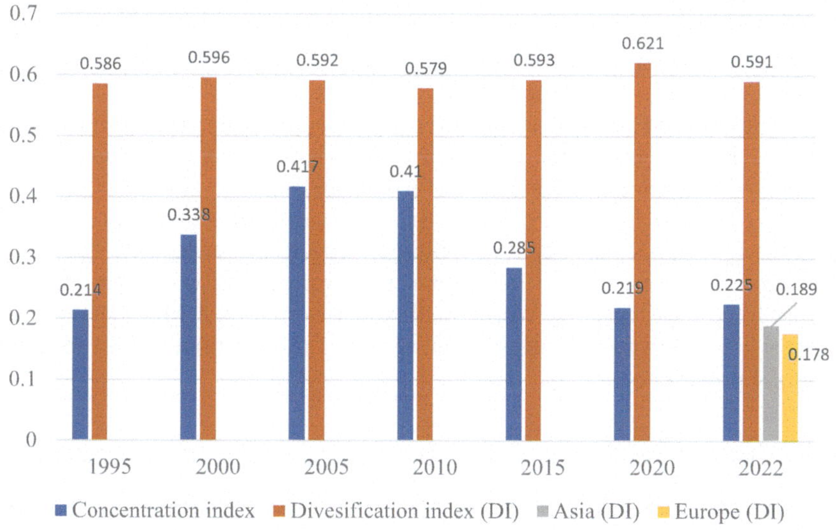

Fig. 4.1 Sub-Saharan Africa's export concentration index and diversification index. (*Source*: https://unctadstat.unctad.org/datacentre/dataviewer/US.ConcentDiversIndices. Note: *Concentration index*, also named Herfindahl–Hirschmann Index (Product HHI), is a measure of the degree of product concentration. The export concentration index measures, for each product, the degree of export market concentration by country of origin. It indicates if a large share of commodity exports is accounted for by a small number of countries or, on the contrary, if exports are well distributed among many countries. The index ranges from 0 to 1 with higher values indicating more market concentration)

developed countries, this turning point happened at a higher per capita income—estimated at around US$8000 for employment share and much higher for output share (Rodrik, 2016).

In the case of African countries, two distinct features are apparent: (i) despite lower initial industrialisation (i.e., lower initial shares of industry, particularly of manufacturing in employment and output) in Africa than in other regions, industry's shares in most structurally underdeveloped African countries have been growing very slowly; (ii) the turning point is a much lower per capita income when industry's (particularly manufacturing's) shares began declining than what was found in developed high-income or industrialised countries, such as Japan or Western Europe (Rodrik, 2016). This implies that African LDCs, LLDCs and SIDS are likely to run out of industrialisation expansion opportunities sooner rather than later and at a much lower level of industrialisation and per capita income than early industrialisers did. Many of them, thus, can become trapped even at low-income levels.

As highlighted in previous chapters, development is a path-dependent process. That is, the initial conditions play a critical role in determining a country's development and transformation trajectory. As discussed in the next section in greater detail, the root cause of Africa's premature deindustrialisation has been its colonial legacies, exacerbated by neo-colonial arrangements and neo-liberal policy prescriptions by the donor community, especially the World Bank and International Monetary Fund (IMF). This allowed continued exploitation of the continent by its former colonial powers.

Barriers to Africa's Structural Transformation

Mainstream Africa observers blame heterogenous factors for Africa's development failures. They include poor governance (e.g., corruption, democratic deficits), unfavourable demography (e.g., high dependency ratio), resource curse (e.g., resource-related conflict), ethnic conflict (e.g., the 1994 Rwandan genocide) and disadvantageous geography (e.g., extreme heat and desertification).

As we mentioned in Chapter 1, we reject the deterministic aspects of these explanations. Such explanations undermine the role of ideologically driven policies often imposed on countries by the donor community to serve their purpose. More importantly, they ignore initial conditions determined by centuries of colonial rules. However, besides

Walter Rodney's seminal 1972 book, a number of contemporary Africa observers, such as Joshua Settles (1996), Nathan Nunn (2007) and Francis Mahia (2016), linked Africa's current underdevelopment to its colonial past.

As we highlighted in Chapter 1, the root cause of ethnic conflicts, corruptions and democratic deficits can be traced to Africa's colonial past and continued exploitations through neo-colonial arrangements. This includes connivance of TNCs, Western governments, international financial institutions and local ruling elites as documented by investigative *The Financial Times* journalist, Tom Burgis (2015). Therefore, we focus on colonial legacies and neo-liberal policies as fundamental barriers to Africa's structural transformation.

Colonial Legacies and Neo-Colonial Fetters

Africa's borders were drawn up by European powers, especially following their 'Scramble for Africa' from the early 1880s (French, 2021a). Various culturally, linguistically and religiously different "ethnic" groups were forced together into colonies, to later become post-colonial "nations". Europeans came to Africa seeking slaves and minerals, later building colonial empires. The US attended the 1884 Berlin Congress, dividing Africa among European powers.

Colony-less "latecomer" Germany got Southwest Africa and Tanganyika, now Namibia and mainland Tanzania respectively (French, 2021b). When Namibia's Herero and Nama peoples revolted unsuccessfully against German occupation in 1904, General Lothar von Trotha ordered "every Herero ... shot" (quoted in Elling, 2020). Four-fifths of the Herero and half the Nama died! Communities were surrounded, with many killed. Others were held, with many dying in concentration camps, or driven into the desert to die of starvation. In 1984, the UN Whitaker Report concluded the atrocities were among the worst twentieth century genocides (Ochab, 2018). Although Germany lost its few colonies in Africa after losing the First World War, the influential West German *Die Welt* wondered wistfully in 1960, "Is Africa getting away from Europe?" (Lorenzini, 2022).

Belgian King Leopold II claimed the Congo River basin as his personal property. When Leopold's brutal atrocities and exploitation of his private Congo Free State domain, killing millions, could no longer be denied, other European powers forced Belgium to directly colonise the country!

The US was the first nation to recognise Belgian King Leopold II's personal claim to the Congo River basin in 1884. Since then, the US has shaped the Congo's destiny. The US has been keenly interested in its massive mineral resources. Congolese uranium, the richest in the world, was used in the Hiroshima and Nagasaki nuclear bombs (Williams, 2016). However, Washington would not allow Africans control their own strategic materials. Patrice Lumumba became the first elected prime minister of the Democratic Republic of the Congo (DRC). An advocate of pan-African economic independence, his wish for genuine independence and sovereign control of DRC resources threatened powerful interests. So, Lumumba was brutally humiliated, tortured and murdered in January 1961. The shameful assassination involved both US and Belgian governments which collaborated with Lumumba's Congolese rivals.[3]

Pan-Africanist leader Kwame Nkrumah wanted independent Ghana to chart an "anti-imperialist" path, staying non-aligned in the Cold War. He wanted hydroelectric dams to power Ghana's industrial progress, beginning by smelting its bauxite to develop an aluminium value chain (Miescher & Tsikata, 2009/2010). The US, the UK and the World Bank agreed to finance the Akosombo Dam, on the condition it provided cheap energy to a Kaiser Aluminium subsidiary to process alumina for export to Kaiser.[4] This arrangement was only rescinded decades later, early this century.

Ghana made technical cooperation agreements with the Czechs and Soviets to build two other dams (Miescher & Tsikata, 2009/2010). However, both were ended after Nkrumah was overthrown in a military coup abetted by Washington in February 1966 (Quits-Adade, 2021). Thus, Nkrumah's development ambitions for Ghana were killed (New Africa, 2018). A scaled-down Bui dam was finally built by Chinese contractors decades later. Nkrumah's 1965 book, *Neo-colonialism: The Last Stage of Imperialism*, was probably the final straw in embarrassing the West (Langan, 2017).

Elsewhere, Tanzania's Julius Nyerere's Ujamaa "African socialism" focused on developing villages and food security (James, 2014). Western

[3] USA/Africa: New Data on Murder of Lumumba, 08/01/02, https://www.africa.upenn.edu/Urgent_Action/apic080102.html (accessed 28/10/2023).

[4] Kaiser Aluminum and Chemicals Corporation of the USA, founded in 1946 by Henry J. Kaiser.

antagonism ensured Ujamaa's failure, while his efforts were harshly condemned to deter other Africans from trying to chart their own paths (Ibhawoh & Dibua, 2003). Meanwhile, Nyerere's pro-Western contemporaries were supported by the West. Such countries, e.g., neighbouring Kenya and Uganda, received much more Western aid although their development records have not been much better.

At independence, Zambia had no universities, with only 0.5% completing primary education. The country's copper mines were mostly in British hands. Most people survived on limited land for the villagers, without electricity and other amenities. Hemmed in by Western-supported racist states, President Kenneth Kaunda sought foreign help to bypass hostile South Africa and Rhodesia (now Zimbabwe) to change the landlocked nation's fate. After the US and World Bank refused to help, he reached out to the Soviet bloc and China. China built a US$500 million railway linking Zambia to the Indian Ocean through Tanzania.

Côte d'Ivoire has long been a major producer of cocoa and coffee. But three decades of misrule by its pro-Western founding father, Felix Houphouet-Boigny, ensured endemic poverty and stark inequalities, culminating in civil war. In 2020, almost 40% of its people lived in "extreme poverty". In 2019, the middle-income country's human development index score was as low 0.538, which dropped to 0.346, when adjusted for inequality.

Both Kaunda and Houphouet-Boigny later abandoned their early, more neo-colonial policies. Zambia nationalised copper mines, hoping to improve living conditions, instead of enriching foreign investors. Meanwhile, Ivorian cocoa was withheld to secure better prices. But both efforts failed, as copper and cocoa prices collapsed. Thus, both nations were severely punished for trying to better their fates.

Europe's post-Second World War recovery benefited immensely from their primary commodity-exporting colonies. After the wartime devastation, European imperial powers relied on colonial currency arrangements for precious foreign exchange. Imperial power also ensured captive colonial markets for uncompetitive post-war European manufacturers. Recovery and competition brought down commodity prices, especially after the Korean War boom. For well over a century, such prices have declined against those for manufactures.

France's Strangle-Hold

As decolonisation became inevitable, French politicians promoted the notion of "Eurafrica", mimicking the US Monroe Doctrine's claim to Latin America. French elite discourse insisted African independence should be defined by (asymmetric) "interdependence", not "sovereignty". For colonies to get "independence", France required membership of *Communauté Française d'Afrique* (CFA)—created in 1958, replacing Colonies with *Communauté*.

CFA countries are now in two currency unions. Benin, Burkina Faso, Côte d'Ivoire, Guinea-Bissau, Mali, Niger, Senegal and Togo belong to UEMOA, the French acronym for the West African Economic and Monetary Union. Its counterpart CEMAC is the Economic and Monetary Community of Central Africa, comprising—Cameroon, the Central African Republic, Chad, the Republic of the Congo, Gabon and Equatorial Guinea. Both UEMOA and CEMAC use the CFA franc (FCFA), effectively surrendering their monetary and exchange rate policy independence.

When the CFA was first created in 1945, the colonies deposited 100% of their foreign exchange reserves in a special French Treasury "operating account". This requirement was reduced to 65% from 1973 to 2005, and then to 50%, *plus* an additional 20% for daily foreign currency transactions or "financial liabilities". Thus, CFA states are still deprived of most of their foreign exchange earnings, retaining only 30%! Meanwhile, Banque de France holds 90% of CFA gold reserves (Gladstein, 2021), making it the world's fourth-largest holder of gold reserves (Banque de France, n.d.). William Dzekashu (2021) reviewed a large volume of literature to assess the impact of French hegemony over its former colonies and concluded that the continued use of CFA franc currency is exploitative, constraining their socio-economic progress. Eleven of the 14 former French West and Central African colonies remain LDCs, at the bottom of UNDP's Human Development Index (HDI).

Guinea was the first to leave the CFA in 1960. Before fellow Guineans, President Sékou Touré told President Charles de Gaulle, "We prefer poverty in freedom to wealth in slavery". It soon faced French destabilisation efforts. Counterfeit banknotes were printed and circulated for use in Guinea—with predictable consequences. This massive fraud brought down the Guinean economy. France withdrew more than 4000 civil servants, judges, teachers, doctors and technicians, telling them to sabotage everything left behind: "un divorce sans pension alimentaire"—a divorce without alimony. Ex-French espionage documentation service (SDECE) head Maurice Robert later acknowledged, "France launched a series of armed operations using local mercenaries, with the aim of developing a climate of insecurity and, if possible, overthrow Sékou Touré" (quoted in Diop, 2020, p. 87).

In 1962, French Prime Minister Georges Pompidou warned African colonies considering leaving the franc zone: "Let us allow the experience of Sékou Touré to unfold. Many Africans are beginning to feel that Guinean politics are suicidal and contrary to the interests of the whole of Africa" (quoted in Diop, 2020, p. 88). Togo independence leader, President Sylvanus Olympio was assassinated in front of the US embassy on 13 January 1963. This happened a month after he established a central bank, issuing the Togolese franc as legal tender. Of course, Togo remained in the CFA. Mali left the CFA in 1962, replacing the FCFA with the Malian franc. Then a 1968 coup removed its first president, radical independence leader Modibo Keita. Unsurprisingly, Mali later re-joined the CFA in 1984.

The eight UEMOA economies are all oil importers, exporting agricultural commodities, such as cotton and cocoa, besides gold. By contrast, the six CEMAC economies, except the Central African Republic, rely heavily on oil exports. CFA apologists claim pegging the FCFA to the French franc, and later, the euro has kept inflation low. But lower inflation has also meant "slower per capita growth and diminished poverty reduction" than in other African countries (Zafar, 2021). The CFA has "traded decreased inflation for fiscal restraint and limited macroeconomic options" (King, 2022). Unsurprisingly, CFA members' growth rates have been lower, on average, than in non-CFA countries (Zafar, 2021).

With one of Africa's highest incomes, petroleum producer Equatorial Guinea is the only CFA country to have "graduated" out of LDC status, in 2017, after only meeting the income "graduation" criterion. Its oil boom ensured growth averaging 23.4% annually during 2000–08. But growth has fallen sharply since, contracting by – 5% yearly during 2013–21! Its 2019 HDI of 0.592 ranked 145 of 189 countries, below the 0.631 mean for middle-ranking countries. With over 70% of its population poor, and over 40% in "extreme poverty", inequality is extremely high in Equatorial Guinea. The top 1% got over 17% of pre-tax national income in

2021, while the bottom half got 11.5%! Four of ten 6–12-year-old children in Equatorial Guinea were not in school in 2012, many more than in much poorer African countries. Half the children starting primary school did not finish, while less than a quarter went on to middle school.

CFA member Gabon, the fifth largest African oil producer, is an upper middle-income country. With petroleum making up 80% of exports, 45% of GDP and 60% of fiscal revenue, Gabon is very vulnerable to oil price volatility. One in three Gabonese lived in poverty, while one in ten were in extreme poverty in 2017. More than half of its rural residents were poor, with poverty three times more there than in urban areas.

Côte d'Ivoire, a non-LDC CFA member, enjoyed high growth, peaking at 10.8% in 2013. With lower cocoa prices and COVID-19, growth fell to 2% in 2020. About 46% of Ivorians lived on less than 750 FCFA (about $1.30) daily, with its HDI ranked 162 of 189 in 2019.

Clearly, the CFA "promotes inertia and underdevelopment among its member states" (Taylor, 2019). Worse, it also limits credit available for fiscal policy initiatives, including promoting industrialisation. Credit-GDP ratios in CFA countries have been low at 10–25%—against over 60% in other Sub-Saharan African countries! Low credit-GDP ratios also suggest poor finance and banking facilities, not effectively funding investments.

By surrendering exchange rate and monetary policy, CFA members have less policy flexibility and space for development initiatives. They also cannot cope well with commodity price and other challenges. The CFA's institutional requirements—especially keeping 70% of their foreign exchange with the French Treasury—limit members' ability to use their forex earnings for development. More recent fiscal rules limiting government deficits and debt—for UEMOA from 2000 and CEMAC in 2002—have also constrained policy space, particularly for public investment.

The CFA has also not promoted trade among members (Kangami & Akinkugbe, 2021). After six decades, trade among CEMAC and UEMOA members averaged 4.7% and 12% of their total commerce respectively (Yehoue, 2006). Worse, pegged exchange rates have exacerbated balance of payments volatility (Amin, 2000). Moreover, unrestricted transfers to France have enabled capital flight. The FCFA's unlimited euro convertibility is supposed to reduce foreign investment risk in the CFA. However, foreign investment is lower than in other developing countries (Signé, 2019). Total net capital outflows from CFA countries during 1970–2010 came to US$83.5 billion—117% of combined GDP! Capital flight from

CFA economies was much more than from other African countries during 1970–2015 (Ndikumana & Boyce, 2018, 2021).

On the other hand, France benefited almost unilaterally from the neo-colonial currency arrangements. Valéry Giscard d'Estaing, France's former President, complained about US dollar's "exorbitant privilege" when he was President de Gaulle's finance minister. But he ignored what a 1970 report by the French Socio-Economic Council said about CFA's "incontestable advantages for France".

First, France could pay its imports from CFA countries in its own currency, saving its foreign currency for other imports and repay its debt in a world where the US dollar is the main currency for international trade and finance. It was especially advantageous at times of weak and unstable French franc. Second, the French Treasury has often offered negative interest rates (in real terms) for African exchange reserves, meaning that the CFA countries have been losing money—it is as if they paid the French Treasury to keep their foreign reserves. Third, France profited from supplying CFA franc at a fixed rate depriving CFA countries of seigniorage—the difference between the cost of printing a paper note and its face value, or "the way in which the state acquires command over real resources through its ability to issue fiat money" (Buiter, 2007, p. 42). Since the introduction of Euro in 1999, the seigniorage from the CFA arrangement is reaped by the European Union. Fourth, French companies operating in the CFA zone benefit from large and stable outlets for trade. They also have the guaranteed freedom to repatriate their revenues and capitals without any foreign exchange risk.

Joseph Pouemi, in his *Monnaie, Servitude et Liberté*, aptly described the colonial legacy of the currency as "France is, indeed, the only country in the world to have achieved the extraordinary feat of circulating its currency, and nothing but its currency, in politically free countries". Thus, France enjoys a system of political control serving its own economic interests. On the few occasions that African countries have had foreign payment problems, France joined with the IMF to demand a currency devaluation, as in 1994, resulting in hardships from the inflation spike (King, 2022). On 18 June 2003, France's Foreign Minister Dominique de Villepin said at the French National Assembly, "Africa is a real opportunity for France. It broadens both our horizon and our ambition on the international scene. It is true in the diplomatic, economic and cultural context" (quoted in Touati, 2007).

CFA franc's benefits are not just for France; they extend to the African upper classes, whose appetite for imported luxuries explains their preference for an overvalued exchange rate. The CFA franc facilitates the transfer of financial resources by African elites, no matter how they were acquired. As long as they stay quiet on the issue, they have the backing of France—even when it had a socialist President Mitterrand—against political dissidents and their own people, allowing their authoritarian rule for decades. France deployed thousands of combat troops unilaterally on various missions, claiming its mission "legitimate" (Recchia, 2020), whenever France's monopoly of Africa came under threat (Touati, 2007). France is also alleged to have engineered coups and assassinations of prominent personalities opposed to France's interest.

Neo-Liberal Policy Disasters—Lost Decades of Development

Since embracing the market-oriented policy package of the World Bank's Berg Report of 1981 (World Bank, 1981), Africa's per capita income growth suffered disastrous secular or steady declines. Instead of accelerating growth as in the sub-title of the report, Africa's per capita income declined by − 1.2% in the 1980s. Output per capita continued to decline from 1990 to 1996 at a rate of 0.95 per year, and during 1985–96, per capita economic growth averaged − 0.6% per year (weighted by population) (Bloom & Sachs, 1998). While Easterly (2001) described this experience as "lost decades", to David Bloom and Jeffrey Sachs (1998, p. 208), "This record of growth is perhaps the greatest disappointment and surprise of recent African history".

The Berg Report and the IMF's structural adjustment programme (SAP) imposed through aid conditionality viewed the production of primary staples for export as the main engine of economic expansion in the continent. Both the Bank and the Fund were quick in blaming domestic policy inadequacies or errors, such as import substitution industrialisation (ISI), and general mismanagement by post-colonial governments for the economic stagnation and debt crisis that the continent faced in the early 1980s. The Berg report states explicitly that the continent's "disappointing economic performance" on its own "domestic policy inadequacies" and such other reasons as "geographic factors hostile to development" and rapidly growing population (p 4), exonerating developed countries' policies from any responsibility in that outcome (p 20).

Thandika Mkandawire (1998) exposed the flaws of the Berg Report—both its premises and policy recommendations, and concluded that it "had in many ways falsified economic performance during the preceding two decades". Thus, the Bank and the Fund ignored that much of the problems arose from external events in the previous decade (1970s). These included the breakdown of the Bretton Woods system of fixed exchange rate and dollar-gold convertibility in 1971,[5] followed by two oil price shocks in 1973 and 1979, recycling of dollar deposits of oil exporting countries as cheap loans to developing countries by the Western (mostly the US) commercial banks, stagflation in advanced countries and sudden sharp interest rate hikes in the late 1970s and early 1980s in advanced countries (mainly in the US and UK).

Since the implementation of the Berg report inspired SAP in the early 1980s, "the overall effective management of these [African] economies, in any meaningful sense of the term, has slipped out of the hands of sovereign governments and into the hands of western-dominated international agencies. The sector of the economy which suffered most because of this shift of decision-making power in economic management was manufacturing" (Saha, 1991, p. 2754). While the report recommended greater involvement and control of Africa's mining sector by multinational companies, industrialisation was accorded only a peripheral place, receiving a brief mention among other items in a chapter headed "Other Productive Sectors". Yet it went on to point out that industry in Africa has largely failed to play its "crucial role in long-term development" (World Bank, 1981, p. 91).

The manufacturing sector that developed in Africa with the Berg report inspired Bank-Fund framework was forced to fit on the margins of national economies whose main productive forces are geared to a Western-controlled mechanism of international commodity trade. Therefore, manufacturing in structurally underdeveloped African countries is

[5] Countries settled international balances in dollars, and US dollars were convertible to gold at a fixed exchange rate of $35 an ounce. In August 1971, President Nixon announced that the US would end on-demand convertibility of the dollar into gold for the central banks of other nations. So, the Bretton Woods system collapsed and gold traded freely on the world's markets.

better integrated with the global production and trading plans of multinational companies, instead of the national economies, thus lacking domestic backward and forward linkages.

One major casualty of such policy advice was public investment (Fig. 4.2). The restrictive budget targets, especially public debt, were achieved primarily by cutting public investment. African countries were told not to invest in food agriculture and to dismantle supportive arrangements. Thus, with trade liberalisation, food security suffered as Africa deindustrialised. Africa remains a net importer of food, although it has 60% of the world's uncultivated arable land (Plaizier, 2016).

Critiquing the Berg report's policy package Ranjit Sau (1983, p. 1899) wrote: "The so-called agriculture-based export-oriented development strategy and the associated package of policies as per the World Bank's agenda would reduce sub-Saharan Africa to a mere source of supply of minerals and beverages for West Europe and North America, and would make it totally dependent upon imports from abroad for food, clothing and everything else". No wonder, the predictions of critics came true unfortunately for the structurally underdeveloped African countries.

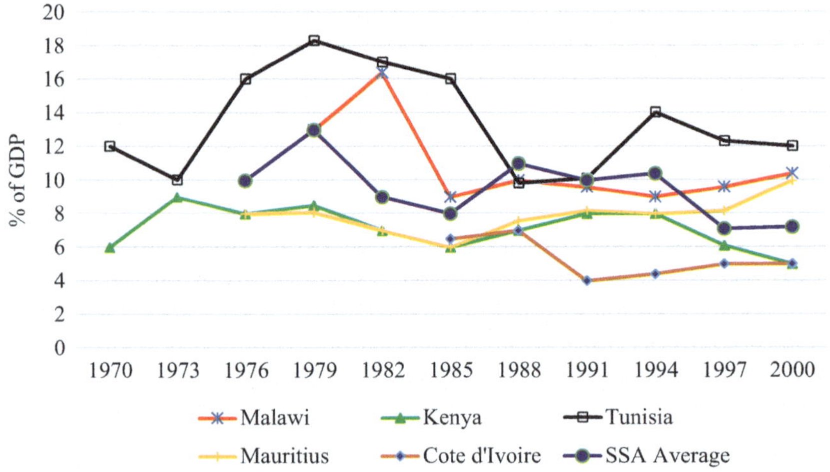

Fig. 4.2 Public investment in Africa during SAP. (*Source*: IMF (2004), "Public Investment and Fiscal Policy", Fiscal Affairs Department)

The New Partnership for Economic Development (NEPAD)—adopted at the African Union (AU)'s 37th session of the Assembly of Heads of State and Government in July 2001—has been touted as a home-grown policy framework—claiming that it aims full "domestic ownership and leadership". It was presented as fulfilling the need of "African Renaissance". However, many doubted it as "another false dawn for Africa" (Bostan, 2009).

The NEPAD did not break from the Bank-Fund's neo-liberal approach, giving the market the predominant role for economic governance (Schell-Kerr, 2009). There is a "land grab" underway in Africa. "Africa is for sale" is how some characterise the continent, while the World Bank notes euphemistically the "rising global interest in farmland". There is now ample evidence that large swathes of African farmland are being allocated to investors, usually on long-term leases, at a rate not seen for decades—indeed, not since the colonial period. "The fact that much of this land is being acquired to provide for the future food and fuel needs of foreign nations has, not surprisingly, led to allegations that a neo-colonial push by more wealthy and powerful nations is underway to annex the continent's key natural resources" (Hall, 2011, p. 1). A major concern is that "the land leased by African governments to foreign interests was previously occupied by poor local and indigenous populations who have little control over such land transfers" (Aryeetey & Lewis, 2010).

Thus, NEPAD has not been able to meet the structural transformation needs of the continent particularly because its development plans are designed and strung around exogenous influences (Nwakanma, 2016). It attaches great importance to so-called "productive partnerships" between Africa and its bilateral and multilateral partners. But this principle regulates the relationship between the donor and recipient countries and opens the door for the influence of Western donors who repeatedly failed to fulfil their various aid promises. For example, at the 2005 Gleneagles Summit, G7 leaders pledged to double their ODA by 2010, earmarking US$50 billion yearly for Africa. But actual aid delivery has been woefully short (Elliott, 2011), with little transparent reporting or accountability (Christiansen & Fagan, 2011).

Options for Structural Transformation

African LDCs' quest for development and industrialisation must not neglect other sectors. Agriculture will continue to play a critical role not only for Africa, but also for global food security as the continent has around 60% of the world's uncultivated arable land. Therefore, there should be commensurate agricultural and rural development as well as high-value services. Furthermore, as David Maimela (2013, p. 37) highlighted, "the twenty-first century Africa cannot afford a similar 'brown' European industrialisation process of the nineteenth century that has been harmful to the natural environment and human life".

The Role of Agriculture

Although the GDP and employment shares of agriculture have declined in many African LDCs, agriculture is still the largest employer, and poverty is concentrated in mainly rural areas. Therefore, the neglect of agriculture and rural development will lead to out migration, and hence increase pressure on unsustainable urbanisation, youth unemployment and informalisation. A lagging agriculture sector can hamper industrialisation as it can create shortages of food (wage goods) as well as raw materials for agro-based industries. Large low-productivity agricultural and informal sectors also constrain the ability to enhance tax revenues for structural transformation. All of these will seriously impair poverty reduction.

Structural change has been growth-enhancing in Asia because labour has transferred from low to higher productivity sectors, as manufacturing and agricultural sectors developed in tandem in contrast to the experiences in sub-Saharan Africa and Latin America. Neil Foster-McGregor and Bart Verspagen (2016) find that structural transformation largely depends on labour productivity and the rise in incomes. It is not necessary that agriculture sector needs to lose labour and resources in the process of structural transformation.

Therefore, policymakers should underpin the support for the agriculture sector with policies that support agroresearch and innovation. They also need to design "integrated sustainable rural development" strategies to foster sustainable rural agro-based industries. This is particularly important in light of rising hunger in Africa in recent years, which has prompted calls for a broad reckoning over what is wrong with food systems. Changing climate has added urgency to the crisis. Many experts warn that current agricultural practices are undermining the resource base—soil, water, seeds, climate—on which future food production depends.

Policymakers need to critically evaluate the Alliance for a Green Revolution in Africa (AGRA), launched in 2006 with the stated goals to double yields and incomes for 30 million farming households in 13 African countries by 2020 while halving food insecurity. As it reached the 2020 deadline, it is essential that AGRA, which had spent $1 billion, is objectively assessed.

Despite the investments, there are no signs of any productivity revolution in AGRA countries. As documented in *False Promises*,[6] yields for staple crops did not double (100%); increased by just 18% over 12 years. Even the heavy subsidies to maize produced paltry yield gains of just 29%. Incomes stagnated as well, and food insecurity worsened: there was a 30% increase in the number of undernourished people in AGRA countries.[7]

A growing number of farmers, scientists and development experts now advocate a shift from high-input, chemical-intensive agriculture to low-input ecological farming. They are supported by an impressive array of new research, documented in a new UN report from its High-Level Panel of Experts,[8] showing both the risks of continuing to follow current practices and the potential benefits of a transition to more sustainable farming practices informed by collaborations between farmers and scientists. These approaches are yielding far better results. Surveying nearly 300 large ecological agriculture projects across 57 poor countries, one University of Essex study documented an average 79% increase in productivity with decreasing costs and rising incomes (Pretty et al., 2006).

Policymakers also need to be cautious about opening up the agricultural sector to large-scale commercial farming, as advocated by many

6 https://pubs.acs.org/doi/epdf/10.1021/es051670d?ref=article_openPDF (accessed 12/02/2021).

7 AGRA carries out its activities in 16 countries, with a special emphasis on Ghana, Mali, Mozambique and Tanzania. AGRA also supports programs in Malawi, Zambia, Uganda, Kenya, Ethiopia, Rwanda, Nigeria, Niger and Burkina Faso, and it has recently ventured into three post-conflict locations: Sudan, Sierra Leone and Liberia.

8 http://www.fao.org/3/ca5602en/ca5602en.pdf, (accessed 12/02/2021).

international agencies, especially by the World Bank's *Enabling the Business of Agriculture* (EBA)[9] and *Investing Across Borders* (IAB) indicators,[10] which prioritise FDI, typically at the expense of SDGs. The World Bank claimed, "The indicators provide a tangible measure of progress and identify regulatory obstacles to market integration and entrepreneurship in agriculture", leading to a more modern commercial agriculture sector. However, the Bank does not explain how farmers, especially smallholder or peasant farmers, will benefit from the proposed reforms or from large-scale commercial agriculture. *Our Land; Our Business*[11] highlighted that the EBA will encourage corporate land grabs and undermine smallholder farmers who produce 80% of food consumed in the developing world. Critics claim that private agribusiness investors will be the main beneficiaries of its proposed land policies and environmental protection deregulation. They also fear that large-scale commercial farming will undermine food security.[12]

[9] The Bank's EBA indicators project is an extension of its Benchmarking the Business of Agriculture (BBA) programme, first launched in 2013. BBA, partly based on the DBR methodology, was created after the G8 asked the Bank in 2012 to develop such an index for the G8's controversial New Alliance for Food Security and Nutrition programme.

[10] The Bank's International Finance Corporation (IFC) introduced its IAB indicators in 2010. Heavily influenced by Hernando de Soto, the IAB indicators were designed to complement the Bank's DB indicators. The IAB indicators claim to help accelerate economic growth by giving primacy to FDI as a driver for job creation, technology transfer, upgrading skills, fostering competition and fiscal consolidation. In fact, IAB indicators encourage frameworks that limit benefits for host countries besides enhancing the harmful effects of cross-border investment deals. The indicators also violate the letter and spirit of the IFC's Performance Standards for Environmental and Social Sustainability; Principles for Responsible Agricultural Investment respecting rights, livelihoods and resources; Voluntary Guidelines on the Responsible Governance of Tenure of Land, Fisheries and Forests; and various other international instruments. https://papers.ssrn.com/sol3/papers.cfm?abstract_id=2167410 (accessed 22/01/2021).

[11] Http://ourlandourbusiness.org/ (accessed 22/01/2021).

[12] In January 2017, over 158 organisations and academics from around the world denounced the EBA, demanding its immediate end. In response, the Bank made some cosmetic changes and dropped its controversial land indicator. However, its latest (2019) EBA still reflects its strong bias for commercial agricultural inputs and mono-cropping, undermining food security, sustainability as well as customary land holdings. https://cagj.org/2017/01/why-do-the-world-banks-new-indicators-enabling-the-business-of-agriculture-pose-a-threat-to-african-agriculture/ (accessed 22/01/2021).

The Role of the Service Sector

"Servicification" also offers an avenue to prosperity, as a complementary tool to industrialising strategy. In an era when the production process is broken up and involves multiple locations, services connecting complementary processes and locations play an important role. Fostering pre- and post-manufacturing services presents structurally underdeveloped African countries, especially those with smaller labour force, a better chance to plug themselves into transnational production networks and make progress with industrialisation. These manufacturing related services require relatively less labour input, and hence fit better with small population size, whereas transportation logistics may also enhance the benefit of some landlocked position as a land in-between globally large manufacturing bases, such as South Africa.

In most of the African structurally underdeveloped countries, the service sector is significant, accounting for 40–50% of their GDP—in the case of Cabo Verde, it is over 60%. But the service sector is comprised of mostly low productivity informal activities. In resource-rich and tourism-dependent African structurally underdeveloped countries, this large share could be due to a relatively large share of services to foreign population and tourists, and not all services are equally related to manufacturing. In many countries, services sector is dominated by wholesale and retail, mostly small-scale and local market-oriented, and are therefore less relevant for manufacturing. On the other hand, the GDP shares of transport, finance and real estate, which can be regarded as more relevant to manufacturing, are very low.

UNCTAD (2022) argued in favour of catalytic role of business and financial services and trade in services to diversify economic activities into new and potentially transformative sectors. UNCTAD (2022) noted that there were about 50 million formal microenterprises and small and medium-sized enterprises in Africa, with an unmet financing need of US$416 billion every year. Exporting firms, particularly new entrants and small-scale exporting firms, need to secure external financing to cover the high costs of entering into export markets. Governments need to address these export-oriented micro, small and medium enterprises' credit constraints and facilitate their access to the financial technology and affordable complementary financing. This is critical for the growth and competitiveness of micro, small and medium-sized businesses, which represent the bulk of private enterprises in Africa.

Box 1: Servicification

The twenty-first century's industrialisation is closely interlinked with so-called "servicification", in which factories and facilities (including goods, know-how, ideas, capital, investment and people) are unbundled with the support of information and communication technology (ICT) in order to trade in raw materials, final goods and services through disintegrated production processes, which constitutes a strong trade, investment and services nexus.

While the intermediate input of services (e.g., accounting, professional business consulting) into the manufacturing production processes have been growing, the service elements of intra-firm activities add more weight. The value added by the manufacturing industry in the developed countries has shifted either to "upstream" business activities (e.g., R&D, product design) or to "downstream" business activities (e.g., marketing, after-sales service). Modern servicification in the manufacturing industry is closely related to these developments.

Value added from the service sector is more important in manufacturing output than it was in the past. Furthermore, it is not surprising that aside from production and trade, existing services are more elaborate through the use of new technology such as ICT as the service economy advances. Value added created at pre- and post-manufacturing process has increased significantly since 1990s.

Source: Baldwin, Ito and Sato (2014).

The Way Forward: Pan-Africanism

Moving forward Africa has to turn its "extraordinarily disadvantageous geography" into a strategic asset as being in the middle of the globe. Africa's demography is no longer "unfavourable" as other regions are ageing while its young workforce growing. Instead of being "ethically fractionalised", Africa can be a beacon of "unity in diversity".

Resurgence in Pan-Africanism offers hope that the expectations of early Pan-Africanists for complementary development, respecting the continent's cultural, religious and ethnic diversities can finally be achieved. The new generation of assertive African leaders does not want to see their continent continue to occupy a peripheral position. Being at the centre of the globe, Africa can be a global hub for production, trade and services for other continents—Americas, Europe and Asia. While other regions are ageing, Africa's relatively young population places it in an advantageous position in the global production and supply chains.

As there is a new "twenty-first century scramble for Africa", African leaders are increasingly using Africa's geopolitically strategic position and natural resources to redefine Africa's relations with their former colonial powers as they balance their relations with emerging powers, such as Russia, China and India. Margaret Lee (2007, pp. 324–325) emphasised "... it has become evident that additional official development assistance will not help Africa from sliding into abyss. If they are serious, the Western powers need to (i) map out a strategy for forgiving Africa's debt; (ii) remove protectionist barriers against African exports; (iii) eliminate welfare payments to their farmers that have resulted in the destruction of African economic sectors; (v) ensure that a significant percentage of the profits arising from exploitation of Africa's natural resources are used to enhance Africa's development".

Pan-Africanism is a liberation consciousness, which hinges on social mobilisation and the organic unity and solidarity of the black race. Pan-Africanism arose as political and social movements of resistance aimed at the dignity and emancipation of the black race and the African continent. The idea was floated in the Americas in reaction to the realities of slavery and its aftermaths in the US and the West Indies in the early twentieth century. Marcus Garvey, W.E. Dubois, George Padmore, Paul Robeson and Maya Angelou were some of the leading advocates. They associated the continent of Africa with freedom.

The pioneering thinkers helped Africans—home and abroad—see their commonalities as victims of racism. The partitioning of Africa at the Berlin Conference created pseudo-nation-states out of what was an undivided continent. Pan-Africanism provided an ideology for rallying Africans at home and abroad against colonialism, and the creation of nation-states did not erase the idea of a united Africa. As different African nations gained political independence, they took it upon themselves to support those countries fighting for their independence. As Mark Malisa and Phillippa Nhengeze (2018) pointed out, Pan-Africanism meant that as long as one African nation was not free, the continent could not be viewed as free.

Thus, Pan-Africanism spread far and wide, assuming the theology for Africa's political liberation. Soon Kwame Nkrumah, Amilcar Cabral, Sékou Touré, Leopold Senghor, Julius Nyerere and Nnamdi Azikwe, among others, became the torchbearers of Pan-Africanism and African liberation struggles. There was heated debate at the dawn of independence in Africa heated. The issue was, what course should Africa take? On the one hand, there were those who wanted a united Africa (the Casablanca Group) right from the 1960s, and on the other hand, there were the incrementalists (the Monrovia Group) who would not give up their newly won sovereignty to any supranational organisation. Emperor Haile Selassie's incredible mediating skills broke the deadlock, leading to the formation of the Organisation of African Unity (OAU).

The transition from the OAU to the AU in 2002 and the on-going discourse on the formation of a continental union government indicate that the Pan-African path remains a viable course for the future of Africa. Writing for *New African*, Said Adejumobi (2013) observed, "The Pan-African struggle remains an enduring political project; it is a struggle for equality, justice, human dignity, integrity and progress in a lopsided world, in which Africa and its people loom at the periphery. The notion of collective action and a drive towards self-reliance are the guiding principles of an emancipatory Pan-African project".

The new Pan-Africanism is underpinned by a stronger AU promoted by Kwame Nkrumah and Muammar Gaddafi. It is also buttressed by more engagement of the AU with African citizens as Rwanda's President Paul Kagame recommended for the proposed reform of the AU (Kagame, 2017). Samuel Oloruntoba (2023) believes that through the reformed AU, Pan-Africanism can contribute to the reimagination of the political, social and economic structures in Africa, away from the political legacy of the imperial logic that shaped the current structures. That is, reinvigorated Pan-Africanism with the engagement of the old and new generations of Africans at home and in the diasporas can serve as an ideological force for resistance against the subordination of Africa. It would require paying conscious attention to the unresolved political question that continues to undermine its unity, collaboration and collective action.

As David Maimela (2013, p. 35) pointed out, "The advancement of a pan-African agenda will depend on two cardinal realisations: that we need to reclaim, revive and reassert pan-Africanism and defeat neo-colonialism; secondly, that no society has ever made history or progress without relying on its own resources—financial, human, technological, ideational or leadership". He warned, "whereas there are signs of great potential for the regeneration and restoration of the continent, new forms of domination and exclusion exert enormous pressure in a continuous struggle between hope and despair, restoration and marginalisation" (p. 36).

The growth surge at the advent of the twenty-first century led to the "Africa rising narrative", buoyed by the decade-long commodities boom and some progress in human development indicators such as per capita incomes. However, David Maimela emphasised, "The positive trend of an improving human development index cannot be built upon through aid. Rather, it will require that African economies be built on innovation and new foundations that accord with the realities of the twenty-first centuries, and are better to enable sustainable development and growth. These can only be achieved if systemic changes are effected in the economic structures of the continent, including the manner in which the African economy relates with the global economic structures" (p. 37).

"Africa rising" narrative can be misleading; as this chapter has highlighted, most African economies, especially the African LDCs, have failed to achieve any meaningful structural transformation. Rick Rowden (2013) pointed out that even if an African country like Malawi achieves higher GDP growth rates and increased trade volumes, this does not mean that the GDP or employment shares of manufacturing and high value added services have increased over time. Malawi may have earned higher export earnings for tea, tobacco and coffee on world markets and increased exports, but it is still largely a primary agricultural economy with little movement towards the increased manufacturing or labour-intensive job creation that is needed for Africa to "rise".

African development and the integration of the continent in the global economy should translate into shared prosperity between nations and within countries as well as progress in human development. Following Amartya Sen's *Development as Freedom*, Africa's transformation should mean not only the development of productive capacity of the economy but also social development in the form of education, health and other social infrastructure to ultimately expand Africans' choice and capabilities.

Challenges

The resurgent Pan-Africanism is not without challenges. Recent surge in internal conflicts, such as that in DRC, Ethiopia, Somalia and Sudan as well as diplomatic tensions between Ethiopia and Somalia, is quite a blow to African unity. Such events provide colonial powers to intervene as seen in the wake of recent uprisings in North Africa. Fortunately, the French-inspired threat of military action against Mali's junta by the Economic

Community of West African States (ECOWAS) did not materialise and economic sanctions were lifted.

Nevertheless, surges in coups and democratic slides, as narrated in Chapter 3, are worrying for several reasons. As highlighted in Chapter 1 and Chapter 8, democratic accountability is critical to undo the existing neo-colonial arrangements which the late Prime Minister of Ethiopia Meles Zenawi aptly described in the following words:

> "[T]he underlying fact is that African states are systems of patronage and are closely associated with rent-seeking activities. Their external relationship is designed to generate funds that oil this network of patronage. Their trading system is designed to collect revenue to oil the system. Much of productive activity is mired in a system of irrational licenses and protection that is designed to augment the possibilities of rent collection"[13]

Much of the resurgence in Pan-Africanism is state-led. This runs the risks of being derailed by former colonial power-inspired coups and counter coups as historical evidence tells. Therefore, Mammo Muchie, Adam Habib and Vishnu Padayachee (2006) argued for a shift from a "statist Pan-Africanism" to a "democratisation of African integration". They held:

> "[T]he advantage of civil society participation is bringing integration and its potential benefits down to grassroots. In the process there will be public education, public debate, public participation and open and transparent process that lead to accountability and legitimacy of the African project of integration".

Democracy's "instrumental values", such as accountability and participation are discussed in greater details in the next chapter on South and Southeast Asian LDCs' structural transformation. In the end, the Pan-African project is aimed at uniting the African people, economies and states. Therefore, emphasis must be placed on the role of the people and the twenty-first century accelerated tempo for African unity must come from below.

Interestingly, support for democracy among the people of Africa remains stable despite the persistence of deprivations and the recent resurgence of authoritarianism, according to the most recent nationally

[13] As quoted in Mbeki (2013, p. 18).

representative survey by Afrobarometer (Isbell, 2023). Around two in three say that democracy is preferable to any other form of government while a substantial majority (~80%) routinely reject one-man rule and one-party rule with some variations across countries. "Regardless, the key take away is that across the continent ordinary citizens feel that they are not getting what they want or expect from 'democracy'" (Isbell, 2023, p. 2).

Africa is a youthful continent; its youth bulge is an economic challenge—to find productive and meaningful jobs for a fast-growing working-age population, Youth bulge is also a political time-bomb—failure to absorb them in productive and decent jobs can trigger political and social unrests. Young people are the continent's biggest drivers of change, including democratisation.

Nonetheless, governments cannot escape their responsibilities. As *The* Economist (2023) emphasised, "African governments that claim to be democratic will have to govern better, by curbing corruption, fostering growth and resisting the temptation to hogtie the opposition". They must progressively deliver and fulfil their obligations under the United Nations Declaration on Right to Development. If they fail, support for democracy will drop, and the continent's future will remain in peril.

Appendix

Classifications of African LDCs

Landlocked Economies—
Botswana, Burkina Faso, Burundi, Central African Republic, Chad, Ethiopia, Lesotho,
Malawi, Mali, Niger, South Sudan, Rwanda, Uganda, Zambia.
Coastal Economies—
Benin, Cabo Verde, Comoros, Democratic Republic of Congo, Djibouti, Eritrea, Gambia,
Liberia, Madagascar, Mauritania, Mozambique, São Tomé and Príncipe, Senegal, Sierra Leone, Somalia, Sudan, Tanzania and Togo.
Resource-Rich Economies—
Angola, Democratic Republic of Congo, Ghana, Guinea, Mozambique, Niger, Tanzania and Zambia.

Graduated African LDCs

Botswana (resource-rich landlocked), Cabo Verde (Small Island Developing State) and Equatorial Guinea (resource-rich, coastal).

Regional Economic Blocks in Africa

The Economic Community of West African States ECOWAS is a regional political and economic union of fifteen countries located in West Africa. The union was established on 28 May 1975, with the signing of the Treaty of Lagos, with its stated mission to promote economic integration across the region. A revised version of the treaty was agreed and signed on 24 July 1993 in Cotonou. Considered one of the pillar regional blocs of the continent-wide African Economic Community (AEC), the stated goal of ECOWAS is to achieve "collective self-sufficiency" for its member states by creating a single large trade bloc by building a full economic and trading union.

The West African Economic and Monetary Union (WAEMU) is an organisation of eight, mainly French-speaking, states within the ECOWAS which share a customs union and currency union, established in 1994. The currency they all use is the CFA franc, which is pegged to the euro.

Economic and Monetary Community of Central Africa (CEMAC) within the ECOWAS aims to promote the entire process of sub-regional integration through the forming of a monetary union with the Central Africa CFA franc as a common currency. CEMAC currently operates a customs union and monetary union. The common market is in place, but many exceptions to the tariff-free regime still exist.

The East African Community (EAC) is a regional intergovernmental organisation of 6 Partner States: The Republics of Burundi, Kenya, Rwanda, South Sudan, the United Republic of Tanzania and the Republic of Uganda, with its headquarters in Arusha, Tanzania. Through the Customs Union Protocol, EAC aims to enhance trade within the EAC region while the common market guides the free movement of goods, people, labour, services and capital among Partner States. The East African Monetary Union Protocol provides for the attainment of a single currency for daily transactions within the Common Market.

References

Adejumobi, S. (2013). Rekindling Pan-Africanism. *New African*, 3 May, https://newafricanmagazine.com/3731/ (accessed 6/01/2024).

Amin, A. (2000). *Long-term growth in the CFA Franc Zone Countries*. UNU-WIDER Reserch in Progress, August https://www.wider.unu.edu/sites/default/files/rip25.pdf (accessed 28/10/2023).

Areetey, E., & Zenia, L. (2010). African land grabbing: Whose interests are served? *Bookings Commentary*, 25 June, https://www.brookings.edu/articles/african-land-grabbing-whose-interests-are-served/ (accessed 03/01/2021).

Baldwin, R., Tadashi, I., & Hitoshi, S. (2014). The smile curve: Evolving sources of value added in manufacturing. *Joint Research Program Series*, IDE-JETRO. https://www.uniba.it/ricerca/dipartimenti/dse/e.g.i/egi2014-papers/ito (accessed 22/01/2021).

Bloom, D., & Sachs, J. (1998). Geography, demography, and economic growth in Africa. *Brookings Papers on Economic Activity, 2*, 207–295.

Bostan, Z. (2009). Another false dawn for Africa?' An assessment of NEPAD. *E-International Relations*, 19 July, https://www.e-ir.info/pdf/10726 (accessed 28/10/2023).

Buiter, W. (2007). Seigniorage. *National Bureau of Economic Research (NBER) Working Paper* # 12919.

Burgis, T. (2015). *The looting machine: Warlords, oligarchs, corporations, smugglers, and the theft of Africa's wealth*. Harper Colins.

Christiansen, K., & Craig, F. (2011). Why the G8 should open its books. *The Guardian* (Australian edition), 20 May.

de France B. (n.d). *Custody and management of gold*. https://www.banque-france.fr/en/custody-and-management-gold (accessed 18/02/2023).

Diop, M. D. (2020). *French monetary neo-colonialism: The CFA franc, Master's Degree dissertation*. Università Ca' Foscari Venezia.

Dzekashu, W. (2021). French economic and monetary policies in Francophone Africa: A barrier to economic development in the Central and West African monetary zones. *Archives of Business Research, 9*(11), 51.

Easterly, W. (2001). The lost decades: Developing countries' stagnation in spite of policy reform 1980–1998. *Journal of Economic Growth, 6*(2), 135–157.

Economist. (2023). Why Africans are losing faith in democracy: The alternatives will undoubtedly be worse. *The Economist*, 5 October.

Elling, T. (2020). *Explore Berlin: A short history of the German capital in 81 curious episodes*, XinXii (eBook).

Elliott, L. (2011). Western countries fail to meet Gleneagles aid pledges. *The Guardian* (Australian edition), 6 April.

Foster-McGregor, N., & Bart, V. (2016). The role of structural transformation in the potential of Asian economic growth. *Asian Development Bank Economics*

Working Paper Series No. 479 (March), https://www.adb.org/sites/default/files/publication/182277/ewp-479.pdf (accessed 22/01/2021).

French, H. (2021a). Africa's 'big states crisis' has deep historical roots. *World Political Review*, 7 July, https://www.worldpoliticsreview.com/in-africa-borders-are-part-of-a-bigger-problem/ (accessed 28/10/2023).

French, H. (2021b). Germany's—and the West's—Insufficient Reckoning With the Herero Genocide. *World Political Review*, 2 June, https://www.worldpoliticsreview.com/germany-s-and-the-west-s-insufficient-reckoning-with-the-herero-genocide/ (accessed 28/10/2023).

Gladstein, A. (2021). France still uses monetary colonialism to exploit 15 African nations: Could Bitcoin be a way out? *Fighting Monetary Colonialism with Open-Source Code*, June, https://bitcoinmagazine.com/culture/bitcoin-a-currency-of-decolonization (accessed 18/02/2023).

Hall, R. (2011). Land grabbing in Africa and the new politics of food. *Future Agricultures Policy Brief* 4, June, https://www.yumpu.com/en/document/read/41291123/land-grabbing-in-africa-and-the-new-politics-of-food-future- (accessed 28/10/2023).

Harcourt, S. (2021). Aid to Africa was in decline even before the pandemic, 4 February 2021, https://www.one.org/stories/africa-aid-declines-before-covid/ (accessed 8/03/2024).

Ibhawoh, B., & Jeremiah, D. (2003). Deconstructing Ujamaa: The legacy of Julius Nyerere in the quest for social and economic development in Africa. *African Journal Political Science, 8*(1), 59–83.

IMF. (2004). Public investment and fiscal policy. *Fiscal Affairs Department*, 12 March, https://www.imf.org/external/np/fad/2004/pifp/eng/pifp.pdf (accessed 22/01/2021).

IMF. (2023). *Geoeconomic Fragmentation: Sub-Saharan Africa Caught Between the Fault Lines: April 2023 Regional Economic Outlook: Sub-Saharan Africa Analytical Note*. The IMF.

Isbell, T. (2023). The supply and demand of democracy in Africa today. *German Institute of Development and Sustainability* (IDOS), 20 November, https://www.idos-research.de/en/the-current-column/article/the-supply-and-demand-of-democracy-in-africa-today/ (23/05/2024).

James, S. (2014). What we can learn from Tanzania's hidden socialist history. *The Guardian*, 11 December.

Kagame, P. (2017). *Report on the Reform of the African Union. The Imperative to Strengthen Our Union: Report on the Proposed Recommendations of the Institutional Reforms of the African Union*. African Union.

Kangami, D., & Oluyele, A. (2021). Common currency and intra-regional trade in the Central African Monetary Community (CEMAC). *Journal of African Trade, 8*(1), 13–22.

King, I. (2022). True sovereignty? The CFA Franc and French influence in West and Central Africa. *Harvard International Review*, 18 March, https://hir.harvard.edu/true-sovereignty-the-cfa-franc-and-french-influence-in-west-and-central-africa/ (accessed 18/02/2023).

Langan, M. (2017). Let's talk about neo-colonialism in Africa. *LSE Blog*, 15 November, https://blogs.lse.ac.uk/africaatlse/2017/11/15/lets-talk-about-neo-colonialism-in-africa/ (accessed 28/10/2023).

Lee, M. (2007). The 21st Century scramble for Africa. *Journal of Contemporary African Studies, 24*(3), 303–330.

Lorenzini, S. (2022). *Global development: A cold war history*. Princeton University Press.

Mahia, F. (2016). *The African state and the legacy of colonialism*. https://papers.ssrn.com/sol3/papers.cfm?abstract_id=2771151 (11/05/2024).

Maimela, D. (2013). Pan-Africanism of the 21st century: Challenges and prospects. *The Journal of the Helen Suzman Foundation, 71*(November), 34–39.

Malisa, M., & Phillippa, N. (2018). Pan-Africanism: A quest for liberation and the pursuit of a united Africa. *Genealogy, 2*(28), 1–15.

Mbeki, T. (2013). Africa must unite! An imperative of our time. *The Thinker, 51*(May), 12–18.

Miescher, S., & Dzodzi, T. (2009/2010). Hydro-power and the promise of modernity and development in Ghana: Comparing the Akosombo and Bui dam projects. *Ghana Studies 12*(13), 15–53.

Mkandawire, T. (1998). Thinking about developmental states in Africa. In Paper presented at *Public Forum: African Development in the 21st Century*, The United Nations University Headquarters, Tokyo, Japan, 16 October. https://archive.unu.edu/hq/academic/Pg_area4/Mkandawire.html (2/05/2024).

Muchie, M., Adam, H., & Vishnu, P. (2006). African integration and civil society: The case of the African Union. *Transformation: Critical Perspectives on Southern Africa, 61*(1), 3–23.

Ndikumana, L., & James, B. (2018). Capital flight from Africa: Updated methodology and new estimates. In *Political Economy Research Institute* (PERI), University of Massachusetts-Amherst, June, https://peri.umass.edu/publication/item/1083-capital-flight-from-africa-updated-methodology-and-new-estimates (accessed 18/02/2023).

Ndikumana, L., & James, B. (2021). Capital flight from Africa 1970–2018: New estimates with updated trade misinvoicing methodology. *Political Economy Research Institute* (PERI), University of Massachusetts-Amherst, Research Report.

New Africa. (2018). *The Volta River project: How Kwame Nkrumah's dream project was frustrated*. 8 February, https://newafricanmagazine.com/16321/ (accessed 28/10/2023).

Nkrumah, K. (1963). *Africa Must Unite*. Frederick A. Praeger Inc., Publisher.

Nunn, N. (2007). Historical legacies: A model linking Africa's past to its current underdevelopment. *Journal of Development Economics, 83*(1), 157–175.

Nwakanma, E. (2016). NEPAD and Africa's development: A critical analysis. *Pan African Social Science Review, 13*(December), 92–110.

Ochab, E. (2018). The Herero-Nama genocide: The story of a recognized crime, apologies issued and silence ever since. *Forbes*, 24 May, https://www.forbes.com/sites/ewelinaochab/2018/05/24/the-herero-nama-genocide-the-story-of-a-recognized-crime-apologies-issued-and-silence-ever-since/ (accessed 28/10/2023).

OECD. (2023). *ODA Levels in 2022—Preliminary data Detailed summary note*. 12 April, https://www.oecd.org/dac/financing-sustainable-development/ODA-2022-summary.pdf (accessed 8/03/2024).

Oloruntoba, S. (2023). (Re)negotiating existence: Pan-Africanism and the role of African Union in a changing global order. *Global Studies Quarterly, 3*(3), C–10.

Plaizier, W. (2016). 2 truths about Africa's agriculture. *World Economic Forum Blog*, 22 January, https://www.weforum.org/agenda/2016/01/how-africa-can-feed-the-world/ (accessed 28/10/2023).

Pouemi, J. T. (1980). *Monnaie, Servitude et Liberte: La Repression Monetaire de l'Afrique*. Menaibuc.

Pretty, J. N., Noble, A. D., Bossio, D., Dixon, J., Hine, R. E., Penning de Vries, F. W. T., & Morison, J. I. L. (2006). Resource-conserving agriculture increases yields in developing countries. *Environmental Science & Technology, 40*(4), 1114–1119.

Quist-Adade, C. (2021). How did a fateful CIA coup—executed 55 years ago this February 24—doom much of sub-Saharan Africa? *Monthly Review Online*, 25 February, https://mronline.org/2021/02/25/how-did-a-fateful-cia-coup-executed-55-years-ago-this-february-24-doom-much-of-sub-saharan-africa/ (accessed 28/10/2023).

Recchia, S. (2020). A legitimate sphere of influence: Understanding France's turn to multilateralism in Africa. *Journal of Strategic Studies, 43*(4), 508–533.

Rodney, W. (1972 [2018]). *How Europe Underdeveloped Africa*, London: Verso.

Rodrik. (2016). Premature deindustrialization. *Journal of Economic Growth, 21*(1), 1–33.

Rowden, R. (2013). The myth of Africa's rise. *Foreign Policy*, 20 August.

Saha, S. (1991). Role of industrialisation in development of Sub-Saharan Africa: A critique of World Bank's approach. *Economic and Political Weekly, 26*(48), 2753–2762.

Sau, R. (1983). Africa's options in development strategy. *Economic and Political Weekly, XVIII*(44), 1897–1903.

Schell-Kerr, L. (2009). Global governance initiative: A critique of the New Partnership for Africa's Development (NEPAD). *Federal Governance, 6*(1), 1–17.

Settles, J. D. (1996). *The impact of colonialism on African economic development*. Chancellor's Honors Program Projects. University of Tennessee.

Signé, L. (2018). *The potential of manufacturing and industrialization in Africa: Trends, opportunities, and strategies*. The Brookings Institution.

Signé, L. (2019). How the France-backed African CFA franc works as an enabler and barrier to development. *Brookings Op-ed*, 7 December, https://www.brookings.edu/opinions/how-the-france-backed-african-cfa-franc-works-as-an-enabler-and-barrier-to-development/ (accessed 18/02/2023).

Taylor, I. (2019). France à fric: The CFA zone in Africa and neocolonialism. *Third World Quarterly, 40*(6), 1064–1088.

Touati, S. (2007). French foreign policy in Africa: Between pré carré and multilateralism. *Chatham House Africa Note Programme Briefing*, February, https://www.chathamhouse.org/sites/default/files/public/Research/Africa/bnafrica0207.pdf (accessed 28/10/2023).

UNCTAD. (2010). *The Least Developed Countries Report, 2010: Towards a New International Development Architecture for LDCs*, https://unctad.org/system/files/official-document/ldc2010_en.pdf (accessed 29/12/2023).

UNCTAD. (2011). *The Least Developed Countries Report, 2011: The Potential Role of South-South Cooperation for Inclusive and Sustainable Development*, https://unctad.org/system/files/official-document/ldc2011_en.pdf (accessed 29/12/2023).

UNCTAD. (2014). *The Developed Countries Report 2014: Growth with Structural Transformation: A post-2015 Development Agenda*, (accessed 29/12/2023).

UNCTAD. (2016). *The Least Developed Countries Report 2016: The Path to Graduation and Beyond: Making the Most of the Process*, https://unctad.org/system/files/official-document/ldc2016_en.pdf (accessed 29/12/2023).

UNCTAD. (2017). *Commodities and Development Report 2017: Commodity Markets, Economic Growth and Development*, https://unctad.org/system/files/official-document/suc2017d1_en.pdf (accessed 29/12/2020).

UNCTAD. (2022). *Economic Development in Africa Report 2022: Rethinking the Foundations of Export Diversification in Africa—The Catalytic Role of Business and Financial Services*. New York & Geneva: UNCTAD.

UNECA. (2020). *Aggregate demand and structural transformation in Africa*. UNECA Occasional Paper, https://archive.uneca.org/sites/default/files/PublicationFiles/en_occasional_paper_series_aggregate_demand_and_structural_transformation_in_africa_0.pdf (accessed 18/02/2023).

United Nations. (2024). *World Economic Situation and Prospects, 2024*, New York & Geneva, The United Nations.

Williams, S. (2016). The link between uranium from the Congo and Hiroshima: A story of twin tragedies. *The Conversation*, 24 August, https://theconversation.com/the-link-between-uranium-from-the-congo-and-hiroshima-a-story-of-twin-tragedies-64329

World Bank. (1981). *Accelerated Development in Sub-Saharan Africa: An Agenda for Action (Berg Report)*. World Bank.

Yehoue, É. (2006). The CFA arrangements: More than just an aid substitute? *Dans Économie Internationale, 3*(107), 107–133.

Zafar, A. (2021). CFA franc zone: Economic development and the post-COVID recovery. *Brookings Op-ed*, 5 August, https://www.brookings.edu/blog/africa-in-focus/2021/08/05/cfa-franc-zone-economic-development-and-the-post-covid-recovery/ (accessed 18/02/2023).

Zeufack, A., & James, C. (2023). *The Legacy and Lessons of Africa's Commodity Price Boom and Bust*. World Bank.

CHAPTER 5

South and Southeast Asia's LDCs: Geopolitics and Authoritarianism

"In the Asian context, the pace of structural transformation has differed widely across countries ... This suggests that in spite of a successful record of economic growth, Asian countries has not done equally well in structural transformation" (Kunal Sen, 2016, p. 1).

South, East and Southeast Asia are generally seen as more successful sub-regions than Africa in achieving sustained growth and poverty reduction. The World Bank data reveal that while in 1990 about 14% of the world's extreme poor lived in Sub-Saharan Africa, by 2019, the Sub-Saharan Africa's share of global extreme poverty increased to 59%.[1] In 2019, the estimated proportion of the continent's population living in extreme poverty was 35% in Sub-Saharan Africa (Kofi et al., 2023). During the same period, South Asia's share of global extreme poverty declined from 28 to 24%; and that of East Asia and the Pacific dropped dramatically from 53 to 4%. The estimated proportions of population living in extreme poverty in 2019 were 1% in East Asia and the Pacific and 9% in South Asia (Kofi et al., 2023).

[1] Based on the World Bank data and measure of international poverty line, currently set at $2.15 per day.

A. Chowdhury et al., *Structural Transformations as Developing Africa, Asia, and the Pacific*, https://doi.org/10.1007/978-981-97-9092-0_5

Some of the economies of South, East and Southeast Asia have also undergone rapid and profound structural transformation. There is a large body of literature discussing structural transformation in newly industrialised countries of East and Southeast Asia and large developing countries in South Asia, such as India, Pakistan or Bangladesh (see, for example, Aggarwal, 2021; Bathla, D'Souza & Joshi, 2019; Chowdhury & Islam, 1993; Felipe, 2010; Jha & Afrin, 2021; Mujeri & Mujeri, 2021; Nayyar, 2019; Sen, 2016; World Bank, 1993). Structural transformation of China also features prominently in the literature, and often its experience is compared with that of India.

While different explanations are provided for their varied experiences, it is generally believed that these countries followed a "flying-geese" pattern of "product cycle" theory that sees more standardised and labour-intensive activities being passed on from one country to another as they upgrade and move up the ladder of development and structural transformation.[2] Japan was the first to industrialise, followed by Singapore, Taiwan, Hong Kong and South Korea, and then by Malaysia, Thailand, Indonesia and the Philippines. Behind them followed China, Vietnam, Bangladesh and India in a "flying-geese" formation, see Kojima (2000) for a comprehensive discussion.

The flying-geese model implies international division of labour and gives greater emphasis on the role of the market forces (see, for example, Balassa, 1981, 1983; Radelet, Sachs and Lee, 1997; Lim, 1994; Hughes, 1988; Little, 1979, 1981). That is, these countries followed their natural comparative advantage due to abundance of labour. The newly industrialised countries of East Asia began with labour-intensive manufacturing for export as matured industrialised countries shifted their standardised (mature) labour-intensive activities to these labour-abundant countries when they exhausted low-skilled labour and wages rose with full employment. The first tier of newly industrialised East Asian countries gradually moved up the technology and skill ladder and, in turn, shifted low-skilled labour-intensive activities to the next tier Southeast Asian countries.

The East and Southeast Asian development experience is also thought to have followed the 2-sector model of Arthur Lewis (see, for example, Manning & Posso, 2008). As the labour-intensive manufacturing

[2] The flying-geese model of development was first proposed by Kaname Akamatsu (1961). Raymond Vernon (1966) developed the Product Life cycle theory.

expanded for exports, it drew surplus labour from the rural or agricultural sector, thereby raising agricultural labour productivity and income, which helped industrialisation via two channels. First, higher agricultural income generated demand for manufactured products. Second, higher agricultural productivity kept the price of wage goods (food in particular) low even when demand for industrial labour was rising. Thus, a "virtuous circle" between manufacturing and agriculture propelled structural transformation in these countries along the line hypothesised by Lewis in his 2-sector model.

However, there is considerable debate about the role of the State (government) vis-à-vis the role of the market in these countries' structural transformation. Leading economists such as Bala Balassa, Helen Hughes, Ian Little, Anne Krueger, Peter Bauer, T.N. Srinivasan, Jagdish Bhagwati believe that market forces played a greater role. On the other hand, Robert Wade, Alice Amsden, Ha-Joon Chang, Peter Evans, Stephan Haggard and Chalmers Johnson emphasise the role of the government, in particular of industrial policy, in shaping and guiding the structural transformation of these economies. Others, such as Peter Berger, Hsin-Huang Michael Hsiao, Adrian Chan, Frederic Deyo and Gary Hamilton also highlighted the role of culture and institutions; see Chu (2016), Gong and Jang (1998), Quibria (2002) for good overviews of the debate.

This chapter looks at structural transformation experiences and challenges in a sub-set of Asian countries which are categorised as least developed countries (LDCs). They are Afghanistan, Bangladesh, Bhutan and Nepal in South Asia and Cambodia, Laos and Myanmar in Southeast Asia. Among the South Asian LDCs, Afghanistan is a post-conflict fragile and landlocked country, while Bhutan and Nepal are landlocked. All three Southeast Asian LDCs are transition economies—having followed the Soviet-style State-guided planned model of development, they have introduced market reforms at varied paces since the late 1990s.

South and Southeast Asia's Growth Fragility and Uncertainty

As can be seen from Table 5.1 all South and Southeast Asian LDCs achieved decent growth rates since the beginning of this millennium until the COVID-19 pandemic hit. Even the war-torn Afghanistan's economy grew at 10% annually during the first decade, perhaps due to high aid flows and military expenditures by the occupying forces. However, the

Table 5.1 South and Southeast Asian LDCs: Annual GDP growth (%, 1971–2022)

Country name	*1971–1980*	*1981–1990*	*1991–1999*	*GDP growth (annual %)*				
				2000–2010	*2011–2019*	*2020*	*2021*	*2022*
Afghanistan				10.0	4.7	– 2.4	– 20.7	– 2.4
Bangladesh	1.0	4.0	4.6	5.6	6.6	3.4	6.9	7.1
Bhutan		10.1	4.8	8.4	6.1	– 10.0	4.1	4.6
Nepal	2.1	4.8	4.9	4.1	5.0	– 2.4	4.8	5.6
Cambodia			0.4	8.2	7.1	– 3.1	3.0	5.2
Lao PDR		4.6	6.2	7.0	7.2	0.5	2.5	2.7
Myanmar	4.5	1.6	6.0	12.2	6.8	3.2	– 17.9	3.0

Source: World Bank online database

pandemic exposed these economies' fragility as growth declined in almost all of them.

South Asia

War and conflict since the late 1970s made Afghanistan a fragile state. As Peter Marsden and Emma Samman (2000) observed, Afghanistan closely conforms to the model of a war-torn society in almost every respect and exhibits all the expected features of macroeconomic decline, following the near-collapse of its political system. One IMF study (Barrett, 2018) estimated that the Afghan government lost around US$3 billion revenues during 2005–2016 due to conflict.

Thus, the country remains highly dependent on external aid. Its structural fragility became clear during the pandemic when its economy shrank by about 2.5% in 2020 and by about 25% during 2021–2022 (World Bank, 2023a). Economic downturn affected all sectors of the Afghan economy. The services sector, accounting for up to 45% of the country's GDP, shrank by 6.5% in 2022, following a staggering 30% drop in 2021. The agriculture sector, which makes up for 36% of GDP, declined by 6.6% in 2022 due to unfavourable weather conditions and farmers' lack of resources to cope. The industrial sector also saw a contraction of 5.7% in 2022, as businesses faced closures due to limited access to resources and financial challenges.

Bhutan, too, recorded impressive growth during the first decade of the new millennium; but failed to keep the momentum in the following decade. It also suffered significantly in 2020 due to COVID closure which affected its tourism sector heavily, exposing its vulnerability. The re-opening of its border in September 2022 helped the economy to grow by 4.6% during 2022–2023. More importantly, Bhutan's growth prospects remain uncertain due to a lack of diversification. Besides tourism, Bhutan's economy is highly dependent on public investment in hydropower, while its agriculture, like all other countries, is affected by the vagaries of nature.

Nepal's economy is very similar to that of Bhutan—both highly dependent on tourism, hydropower and agriculture—with the exception that Nepal is a significant recipient of remittances. Nepal also has a much larger population (around 30 million) than Bhutan's 777, 486 to drive its domestic demand. Thus, Nepal suffered significantly less during COVID lockdowns, the economy shrinking by 2.4% in 2020 as opposed to Bhutan's contraction by10%.

The decadal growth averages can be misleading as they are affected by occasional extreme values or unusually high growth performances in some years. Figure 5.1 shows that Nepal's economic growth has remained erratic, exceeding 6% only occasionally and trending down. Though less fluctuating, Bhutan, like Nepal, experienced a falling growth trend. Bangladesh is the only country that could maintain its growth momentum, raising its average annual GDP growth rate from 5.6% during 2000–2010 to 6.6% in the following decade.

Bangladesh's average annual GDP growth rate reached around 7% during 2021–2022. The World Bank's country office observed, "A robust demographic dividend, strong ready-made garment (RMG) exports, resilient remittance inflows, and stable macroeconomic conditions have supported rapid economic growth over the past two decades" (World Bank, 2023b). However, debt-financed large-scale infrastructure investment has been the main driving force in recent years. This has caused concerns about Bangladesh's debt sustainability, especially when corruption is rampant in the country and the project selection process is not transparent, prompting the country's leading English Newspaper *The Daily Star* (14 August 2020) titling one of its editorial, "When corruption eats the infrastructure development". The critiques and sceptics are proven right as the country sought support from the International Monetary Fund (IMF) in the face of falling foreign exchange reserves.

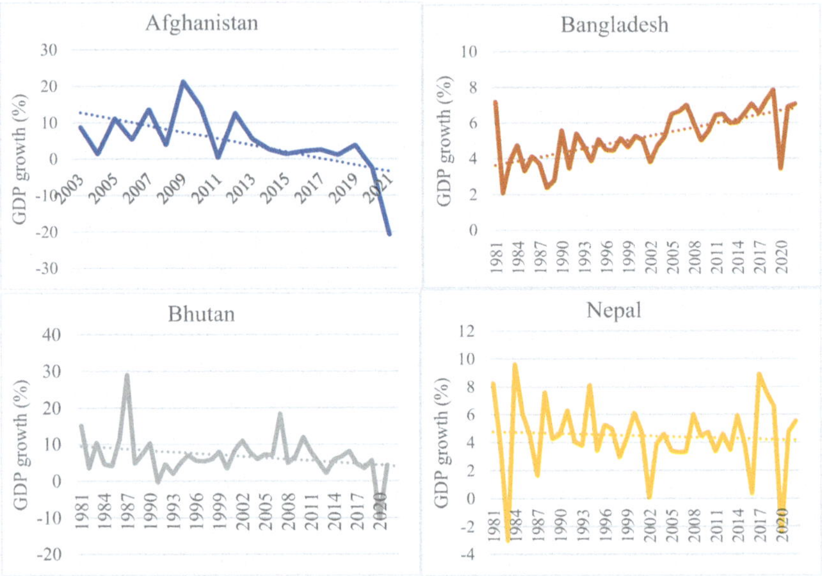

Fig. 5.1 Annual GDP growth of South Asian LDCs (1981–2022). *Source*: World Bank online database

Bangladesh's progress has been truly remarkable. It was one of the world's poorest countries at birth in late 1971. Faced with the daunting challenge of re-building a war-devasted country in adverse external circumstances following the break down of the Bretton Woods system in 1971 and oil price shock in 1973 as well as natural calamities, Henry Kissinger dubbed Bangladesh as an "international basket case" (Tripathi, 2021). Two World Bank economists, Just Faaland and John Parkinson (1976, p. 5), described Bangladesh as "the test case of development", meaning if development succeeds in Bangladesh, it can succeed anywhere else. Looking at Bangladesh in mid-1975, Kevin Rafferty of *The Financial Times* (6 June 1975) judged it as "the end of the great development dream".

Proving the sceptics wrong, Bangladesh forged ahead. Thus, one leading economic development textbook observed, "And without question, from the viewpoint of the broader meaning of development,

Bangladesh seemed to be forging ahead in the early years of the twenty-first century. As a result, there are good reasons to expect Bangladesh to soon move into the lead in income as well" (Todaro and Smith, p. 89). Observing Bangladesh's progress, the UNDP's 2000 *Bangladesh Human development Report* (p. 3) concluded, "It was like a re-birth for Bangladesh, having moved from the status of being at the margin of history in the whirlpool of history, from the status of a mere testing site to that of a learning site...".

Southeast Asia

Among the Southeast Asian LDCs, Myanmar has the largest population—about 54 million, followed by Cambodia (about 16.6 million), while Lao PDR has only 7.5 million people spread over a vast land of 236,800 km^2. All three Southeast Asian economies are endowed with a significant variety of natural resources, such as oil, natural gas, timber, minerals, hydropower and arable land and posted impressive growth during the first two decades of the new millennium until they were hit by the pandemic in 2020. Cambodia is more open and export-dependent than both Laos and Myanmar.

The extent of pandemic shock and the nature of recovery reveal structural weaknesses which could be masked by the decadal averages. For example, Cambodia, being more dependent on tourism and exports than both Laos and Myanmar, was more severely affected by the COVID lockdowns, experiencing around a 3% decline in its GDP in 2020, but being more diversified recovered robustly. On the other hand, less open Laos and Myanmar economies could weather the pandemic; but their recovery was tepid. Myanmar's slow recovery was derailed by a military coup d'état that toppled the democratically elected government of Aung San Suu Kyi. Thus, the Myanmar economy shrank by 18% in 2021.

As can be seen from Fig. 5.2, Laos has been slowing since 2012, while Myanmar experienced secular growth slowdowns since 2003 despite a brief recovery in 2012–2013, revealing their structural weaknesses. On the other hand, Cambodia maintained an average annual growth rate of around 7% since its recovery in 2010 after experiencing growth slowdowns during 2006–2009 due to global recession.

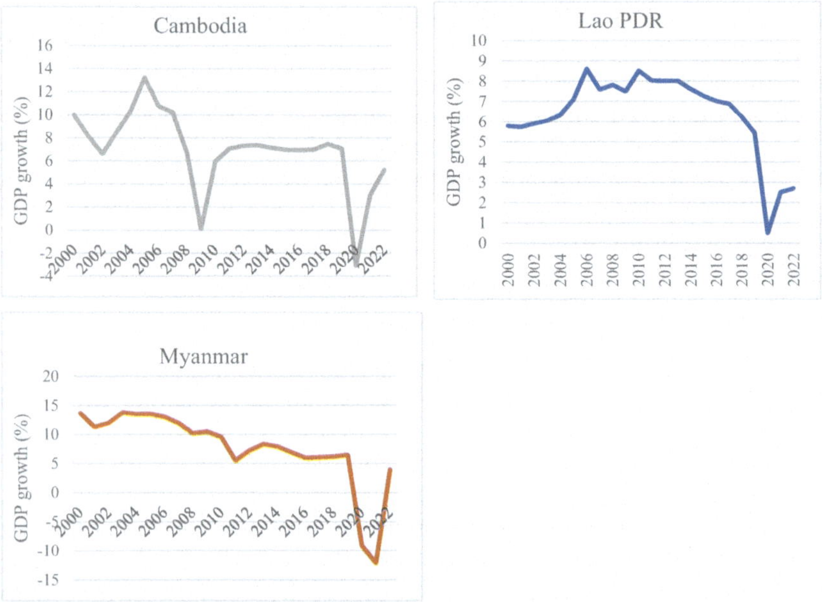

Fig. 5.2 Annual GDP growth of Southeast Asian LDCs (2000–2022). *Source*: World Bank online database

Cambodia has successfully transformed itself "from battlefield to marketplace".[3] In just 20 years, Cambodia has transited from a post-conflict, aid-dependent, LDC to one of the fastest growing economies in Southeast Asia. Cambodia's sustained growth in the decade prior to the pandemic translated into rapid gains in poverty reduction with the poverty rate in Cambodia declining to 18% in 2020, thus 1.2 million fewer Cambodians living on US$2.70 a day or less, according to the World Bank.[4]

However, still, about half of the Cambodians live on only US$4.15 or less a day, while its growth remains below the pre-pandemic level.

[3] https://knowledge.wharton.upenn.edu/article/cambodia-from-battlefield-to-global-marketplace/ (14/09/2020).

[4] https://blogs.worldbank.org/en/eastasiapacific/cambodia-2030-economic-slowdown-offers-opportunity-speed-reforms#:~:text=This%20means%201.2%20million%20fewer,%244.15%20or%20less%20a%20day (23/05/2024).

Being more open, Cambodia's growth slowdown has to do with a challenging global environment. However, while the external environment contributed to a cyclical slowdown, the pandemic has also exposed structural challenges in the domestic economy. World Bank economists Sebastian Eckardt and Faya Hayati (2023) claim that these challenges predate the pandemic, but were masked by rapid capital inflows that fuelled the pre-pandemic construction boom. According to them, Cambodia's structural challenge is mainly due to negative total factor productivity growth—a measure of the efficiency of resource allocation and innovation in the economy. Cambodia's aggregate labour productivity level remains well below Vietnam and Thailand, which are three and five times higher, respectively.

The growth experience of South and Southeast Asian LDCs can be best summarised by the findings of the study by Nyingtob Norbu, Yusuke Tateno and Andrzej Bolesta (2021). They found that the main source of growth in these countries has been increasing the output of existing products, with limited diversification. They also found that the indirect transmission links from productivity growth to economy-wide growth and job creation are weak in these countries as their production network structure is characterised by low levels of network density that have only evolved incrementally over time.

Therefore, it follows that the growth uncertainty and fragility of South and Southeast Asian LDCs are the reflections of their inability to achieve dynamic structural transformation. The next section examines the extent and nature of structural changes in the South and Southeast Asian LDCs.

South and Southeast Asia's Mixed Structural Transformation

Tables 4.2 and 4.3 present snap-shots of changing economic structure of South and Southeast Asian LDCs during 2000–2020. As can be seen from Table 5.2, the share of agriculture has declined in all countries except in Afghanistan. During the same period, the GDP shares of services increased in all countries, except in Myanmar, where the services sector shrank and in Bangladesh where it remained stable at around 50%. In both Bangladesh and Myanmar, the manufacturing sector gained—manufacturing's GDP share rising from 14 to 22% in Bangladesh and from 7.6 to 24.8% in Myanmar. In short, the changes in the sectoral GDP shares

Table 5.2 South and Southeast Asian LDCs: Sectoral GDP shares (%)

Country name	*Agriculture, forestry and fishing*			*Manufacturing*			*Services*		
	2000	*2010*	*2022*	*2000*	*2010*	*2022*	*2000*	*2010*	*2022*
Afghanistan	38.6 (2002)	26.2	44.4 (2021)	18.8 (2002)	12.5	9.1 (2021)	36.1 (2002)	48.9	46.5 (2021)
Bangladesh	22.7	17.0	11.2	14.0	16.1	21.8	50.6	53.5	51.0
Bhutan	24.3	14.8	19.2 (2021)	8.5	8.9	5.9 (2021)	37.1	37.3	44.0 (2021)
Nepal	38.2	33.2	21.1	8.8	5.9	4.9	34.7	46.4	52.3
Cambodia	35.9	33.9	21.9	16.0	14.7	18.1	37.1	38.3	33.7
Lao PDR	33.6	22.6	14.6	8.7	11.1	8.7	42.2	43.6	41.2
Myanmar	57.1 (2001)	37.4	20.3 (2019)	7.6 (2001)	19.0	24.8 (2019)	50.5 (2001)	37.0	38.6 (2019)

Source: World Bank online database

are not fully consistent with the stylised facts observed in the historical experiences of the now-developed countries.

However, as can be seen from Table 5.3, the changes in sectoral employment shares followed the historical patterns. That is, all South and Southeast LDCs experienced declines in the employment shares of agriculture and commensurate increases in the employment shares of industry and services sectors, albeit at different rates. This is true of even Afghanistan where the GDP share of agriculture rose, and yet its employment shares declined. Thus, in the case of Afghanistan, it should mean significantly increased efficiency or labour productivity in the agricultural sector, which is perplexing.

For other countries, except Myanmar, the declines in agriculture's employment shares are larger than the declines in its GDP shares. This also should mean increases in labour productivity in the agriculture sector. In that case, following the historical patterns of the East Asian newly industrialising economies or Lewis' 2-sector model, the manufacturing sector should have expanded. However, as highlighted earlier, in most South and Southeast Asian LDCs, the manufacturing sector's relative position shrank. Therefore, these countries failed to achieve structural transformation that is dynamic to propel them onto a path of sustained growth. This is reflected in the fluctuations and declining trends in their GDP growth rates.

Table 5.3 South and Southeast Asia: Sectoral employment shares (%)

Country name	*Agriculture*			*Industry*			*Services*		
	2000	*2010*	*2021*	*2000*	*2010*	*2021*	*2000*	*2010*	*2021*
Afghanistan	65.5	53.8	46.0 (2020)	8.6	15.2	18.5 (2020)	25.9	31.0	35.5 (2020)
Bangladesh	60.8	47.3	37.1	10.0	17.6	21.7	29.2	35.1	41.2
Bhutan	70.0	54.7	56.0	7.1	6.1	10.1	22.9	39.2	33.9
Nepal	72.6	67.9	62.3	13.5	14.2	16.1	13.9	17.9	21.6
Cambodia	73.5	54.8	38.9	8.5	16.0	25.4	18.0	29.2	35.7
Lao PDR	81.9	71.5	58.1	4.7	8.3	10.8	13.4	20.2	31.1
Myanmar	61.5	52.3	46.5 (2020)	12.8	17.6	18.6 (2020)	25.7	30.0	35.0 (2020)

Source: World Bank online database

In the case of Myanmar, the decline in agriculture's employment share is far less than the decline in its GDP share, implying that labour productivity in Myanmar's agriculture should be very low. Thus, Myanmar does not display the pattern of successful countries and it failed to follow the path outlined by Arthur Lewis in his 2-sector model.

In sum, structural transformation in South Asian and Southeast Asian LDCs is consistent with the first phase observed in successful countries experiencing declines in agriculture's employment share; but is not consistent with the second phase of expansion of manufacturing's employment share. Instead, labour is moving towards construction (classified under industry) and services, while manufacturing's employment share stagnates in most South and Southeast Asian LDCs. This is because the manufacturing sector is dominated by micro enterprises with limited job opportunities.

South Asia

As can be seen, the GDP share of agriculture declined in all South Asian LDCs, except Afghanistan, where it increased after declining during 2000–2010. These declines in agriculture's share in GDP were not followed by a commensurate increase in manufacturing sector's GDP share, except in Bangladesh. In all other South Asian LDCs, the manufacturing sector experienced declines in its GDP share (Fig. 5.3). In the case of Bhutan and Nepal, this deindustrialisation happened even before any meaningful development of the manufacturing sector, accounting for less than 10% of GDP.

It seems conflict and war had a toll on Afghanistan's manufacturing, its GDP share declining from around 19% in 2002 to 3.5% in 2017. Afghanistan's manufacturing has recovered in 2018 to raise its GDP share to 9.1% in 2022; however, uncertainty remains with continued political instability that may discourage investment, especially in critical infrastructure, such as the energy sector.

Nepal's manufacturing showed some promise since the mid-1980s until the 1990s, raising its GDP share from 5.4% in 1985 to around 9% in 1998; but since 2000 it contracted to reach the 1960s level in 2021. Bhutan's manufacturing mimicked that of Nepal. Manufacturing's GDP share rose from around 3% in 1980 to around 12% in 1997. Since then, it declined to reach around 5% in 2020. There was a brief recovery between

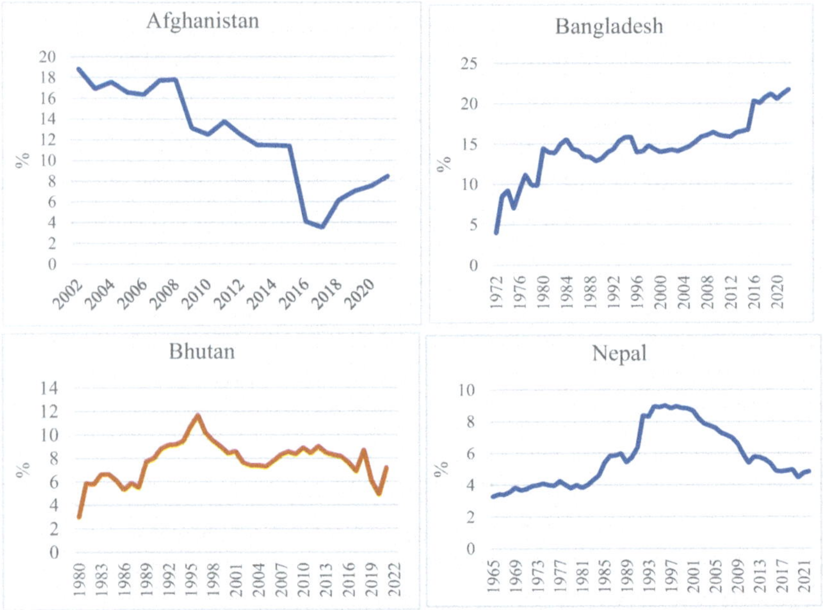

Fig. 5.3 GDP share of manufacturing (%): South Asian LDCs. *Source*: World Bank online database

2005 and 2012, but Bhutan could not sustain its manufacturing revival. Manufacturing in Bhutan accounted for around 6% of GDP in 2022.

Bangladesh made impressive progress in manufacturing and diversifying its economy away from agriculture. The share of manufacturing in GDP increased from less than 10% in the 1970s to nearly 22% in 2021. The growth of Bangladesh's manufacturing sector began in the late 1970s, driven by labour-intensive ready-made garments (RMG) for exports, taking advantage of the end of preferential market access to the US and Europe of the East Asian first tier newly industrialising countries, in particular South Korea.

However, after three decades, Bangladesh's manufacturing remains dominated by the RMG sector, accounting for some 80% of the country's total export earnings. A World Bank report (World Bank, 2021) finds that microenterprises, with fewer than 10 workers, account for 90% of all manufacturing enterprises in the country. The food- and beverage-manufacturing establishments generate only 14% of the manufacturing value added. On the other hand, minerals and metal establishments have a share of 17%, but contribute about 22% to the manufacturing value added.

The World Bank report points out that manufacturing in Bangladesh is still of a basic nature, and productive capabilities have not developed significantly despite the success of the RMG subsector. In other words, the manufacturing sector including RMG remains focused on low-productivity activities involving limited technological complexities that require only basic skills. Therefore, not unsurprisingly, annualised manufacturing sector productivity growth in Bangladesh during 2010–16 was only 2.2% on an average (World Bank, 2021).

Moreover, despite the textile sector's dominance in the Bangladesh economy, its linkages are weaker than sectors such as construction (Norbu, Tateno & Bolesta, 2021). There has been little or no change in the network structure for the textile and garment sector, suggesting that while the sector has seen significant output growth, there has been limited dissemination of productivity gains to other sectors of the economy. That is, Bangladesh has not been able to "develop strong internal and external linkages that would enable a more diversified productive transformation, including insertion in global production chains" (Mercer-Blackman, Foronda & Mariasingham, 2017, p. 1).

Because of the dominance of low-tech RMG sector, Bangladesh scores poorly in terms of "economic complexity index" (ECI), developed by

Cesar Hidalgo and Ricardo Hausmann.[5] ECI, is a measure of an economy's productive capacity, inferred from data connecting locations (e.g., countries) to the production activities in them (countries). In particular, ECI seeks to explain the knowledge accumulated in a population as expressed in economic activities in a country. In 2021, ECI of Bangladesh's merchandise trade was – 0.85, ranked 101 out of 131 countries; and ECI of Bangladesh's technology was – 1.35, ranked 86 among 96 countries.

Economic development requires the accumulation of productive knowledge and its use in both more and more complex industries. The manufacturing sector in the South Asian LDCs is still very rudimentary, engaged in low-tech, labour-intensive activities. The South Asian LDCs have not experienced a truly sustained episode of convergence towards the structural characteristics of the advanced countries in terms of their manufacturing capabilities. Mujeri and Mujeri (2021, p. 46) observed that the South Asian LDCs suffer from "arrested or incomplete industrialization". This points to the challenge for the South Asian LDCs to alter the sectoral share pattern towards a greater share of high value added manufacturing, in view of the existing un- and under-realised productivity potential in manufacturing and the prospects of achieving higher employment growth in manufacturing.

Southeast Asia

The growth momentum of Southeast Asia's LDCs seen in the first decade of the new millennium stalled in the second decade. Besides experiencing fluctuating economic growth, the changes in sectoral GDP shares in these economies did not accompany commensurate declines in sectoral employment shares, indicating low-level productivity. Additionally, the rise in industry's GDP share was not driven by manufacturing, implying a failure to inject dynamism into the economy (Fig. 5.4). Lao PDR was unable to sustain the manufacturing spurt seen in the 1990s when manufacturing's GDP share rose from 3.8% in 1989 to 15.6% in 1997. Since then, manufacturing declined; its GDP share falling to 8.8% in 2022. Although in figures, both Cambodia and Myanmar seem to be industrialising, a closer look at the manufacturing sector reveals a different picture.

[5] The ECI data are available from *The Observatory of Economic Complexity*, https://oec.world/en/profile/country/bgd.

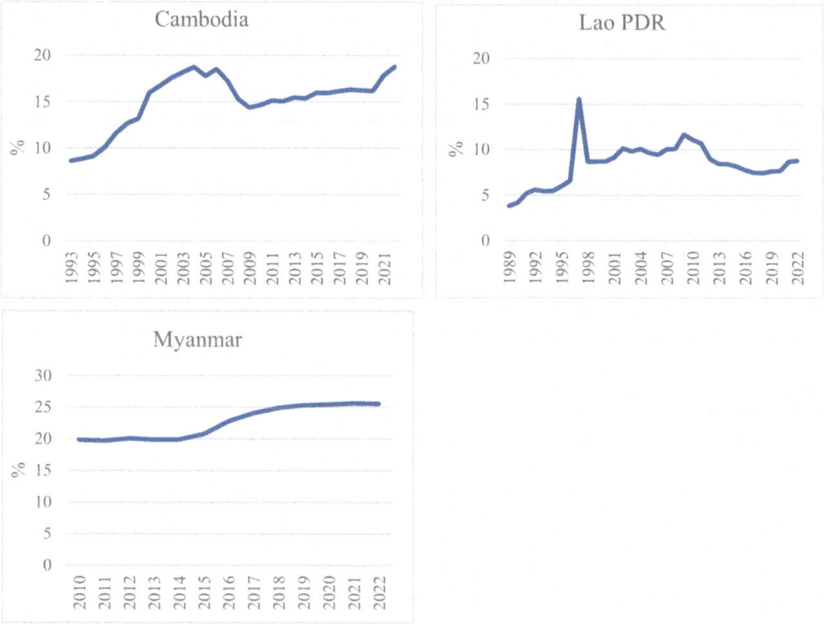

Fig. 5.4 GDP share of manufacturing (%): Southeast Asian LDCs. *Source*: World Bank online database

Cambodia's economic structure has shifted only marginally during 2000–2022. While the share of agriculture in GDP declined from around 36% in 2020 to 22% in 2022, the GDP share of manufacturing remained stagnant at around 17%. Furthermore, Cambodia's manufacturing sector remains very narrow, dominated by ready-made garments (RMG), textiles and footwear, accounting for about 75% of the country's total manufacturing output, and 70% of total merchandise exports in 2018 (World Bank, 2019). Garment manufacturing alone constitutes more than half of total manufacturing output, while agricultural processing industries and household goods manufacturing remain low-key.

Most of Cambodia's industrial/ manufacturing establishments are SMEs. In 2011, almost 91% of industrial enterprises were micro-establishments and only 1.5% were medium or large accounting for 35% of industrial employment (Chhair & Ung, 2016). A further issue is low productivity. The level of productivity of Cambodian workers is lower by around 20% than that of workers in Vietnam (World Bank, 2019). Moreover, activities within the manufacturing sector, particularly in garments, are not well diversified. For example, although the top five garment products exported in 1997 represented 57% of total garment exports declined to 36% in 2017, the composition of Cambodia's top garment exports has not changed significantly since then—four of the top five garment products in 2017 were also the top five garment products exported in 2000 (World Bank, 2019).

Cambodia's prospects for diversification and upgrading are challenging because of its over-dependence on a few markets. According to the ADB (2014b), Cambodia's export concentration is the third highest in the ASEAN, as measured by the Herfindahl–Hirschmann Index. Despite an impressive growth performance in recent decades, Cambodia's exports remained heavily dependent on the EU (39%, 2018) and the US (31%, 2018) markets, making the sector vulnerable to the external environment. While Cambodia has been able to attract a few pioneer producers of bicycles, electrical appliances (e.g., Minibea) and auto parts (e.g., Denso, Sumi Wiring System), it has so far been unable to form industrial clusters in these value chains and export diversification remains limited.

Lao PDR made little progress in structural transformation despite having a decade (2004–2014) of rapid growth. Even though the GDP share of agriculture declined while that of services and industry increased, there had been little impact on the composition of employment. Agriculture, which accounted for about 15% of GDP in 2022, accounted for close to 60% of total employment, implying low productivity in agriculture. The service sector's GDP share hovered around 41%, while its employment share rose from around 13% in 2000 to about 31% in 2021. This too implies low productivity in the service sector.

With about 31% of GDP share, the industry sector remains dominated by resource-based products (mining and electricity) accounting for more than 50% of sector's activities. Unable to provide job opportunities, the industry sector's share in total employment increased only to around 11% in 2021. Moreover, manufacturing's GDP share remained stagnant at around 8% after briefly rising to 11% in 2010 from 11.7% in 2009 to 7.5% in 2019—the period when the GDP growth fell continuously. Lao PDR displays the classic case of "Dutch disease"—the share of non-resource industries in industry value added declining from over 70% in 2000 to around 45% in 2019.

Furthermore, Lao PDR's manufacturing sector is dominated by small and micro enterprises, accounting for nearly 90% of total manufacturing enterprises. Thus, their technology intensity is also very low, and they are generally composed of unorganised businesses, whose competitiveness is rather low (Keola, 2015). Low-technology beverages, food, furniture and wood products, and garments and textiles account for more than half of the manufacturing value added (MVA). The Lao PDR's exports are highly concentrated on low value added products. The resource exports have dominated the country's exports, while private investment has not been expanded potentially limiting the scope for expansion in the productive capacity of the economy.

Most of the Lao PDR's workers have low levels of education and lack the skills needed to produce high value added and diverse products. The computations based on the Lao PDR Expenditure and Consumption Survey 2012–2013 show that 44% of the population did not complete primary school, and 88% of the population did not finish secondary school at the national level. The low level of education and poor quality of human capital stock are also manifested in low labour productivity (Chowdhury, 2021).

Like Lao PDR, Myanmar's structural transformation was distorted by natural resource dominance, even though the GDP share of manufacturing more than trebled between 2001 and 2019. As acknowledged by the government, Myanmar's current industry is highly focused on limited sectors such as agriculture, natural resources and some labour-intensive manufacturing industries.[6] Agricultural activities still remain the largest occupation, though the share of the working-age population working in agriculture dropped from more than 66% in 1991 to 42% in 2013, while the manufacturing share of employment remains low, increasing marginally from 7.1% in 1991 to just over 10% in 2013 (Gelb, Calabrese & Tang, 2017). The large divergence between sectoral output and employment shares indicates economy-wide low productivity. Thus, their ECI is very low (Cambodia: − 0.36, Laos: − 0.43; Myanmar: − 0.38;) compared to other Southeast Asian economies, such as Thailand (1.14) and Vietnam (0.5) (Chowdhury, 2021).

[6] Ministry of Industry, The Republic of the Union of Myanmar, Strategic Directions for Industrial Development Summary of Industrial Development Strategy 2017, p. 4.

https://www.charltonsmyanmar.com/myanmar-economy/smes-in-myanmar/ (10/09/2020).

Moreover, the majority of manufacturing is labour-intensive, low-technology industries engaged in relatively low value added activities like textiles/garments.[7] Approximately 99.4% of all businesses in Myanmar are classified as SMEs, accounting for nearly 95% of employment and about 53% of GDP.[8] The manufacturing sector is dominated by micro and small enterprises, lacking dynamism and significant backward and forward linkages. The 2016 World Bank Economic Survey revealed that 38% of registered SMEs were small and low-growth firms, with 5–19 employees and growth rates between 0 and 10% per annum (Totten, Lwin & van Roosmalen, 2019). These figures are roughly similar to UNESCAP's, 2014 Business Survey, which found only about 7% of firms were large with 250 or more employees (UNESCAP, 2014). As the ADB (2014a, p. 88) observed, "SMEs in Myanmar tend to be technologically backward and their productivity and quality standards are low. They use obsolete machines and equipment for production, some dating back to the colonial period, which badly constrains productivity enhancement and quality upgrading".

In sum, Southeast Asian LDCs' GDP growth was not propelled by factors—such as progressive shifts of resources (particularly labour) from low-productivity sectors (e.g., agriculture) to higher productivity sectors (e.g., manufacturing) and upgrading of activities within each sector to lift sectoral productivity—seen historically in labour surplus countries, especially in newly industrialising economies in East Asia. Based on stylised facts, Rodrik (2008) concluded that economic development requires diversification; growth accelerations are associated with structural changes in the direction of manufacturing; and rapidly growing countries are those with large manufacturing sectors. All three Southeast Asian LDCs are characterised by the absence of product diversification, a limited range of manufacturing activities and dominance of micro and small enterprises implying serious deficits in their productive capacity.

[7] Ministry of Industry, op cit., p. 4.

[8] https://www.charltonsmyanmar.com/myanmar-economy/smes-in-myanmar/ (accessed 10/09/2020).

Barriers to South and Southeast Asian LDCs' Structural Transformation

Like other LDCs, South and Southeast Asian LDCs face the same constraints to development, such as lack of capital, deficits in skilled labour force and inadequate institutional or State capabilities, which together manifest themselves in low productive capacity. The LDCs also suffer from high economic vulnerability and bear disproportionate impacts of climate change-related extreme weather conditions. These common barriers to structural transformation and development are highlighted and elaborated in Chapters 1 and 3. The previous chapter (4) expounded barriers to transformative development that are more specific to African LDCs. This chapter draws attention to geopolitical factors and democratic deficits that are more relevant for the South and Southeast Asian LDCs.

Geopolitics and Trust Deficits

Afghanistan is a classic example of geopolitical rivalries scuttling development and structural transformation. After decades of relative stability, the Soviet Union wanted to transform Afghanistan into a socialist republic and supported the overthrow of Daoud Khan in 1978 in a coup d'état. The subsequent invasion by Soviet forces in 1979 marked the beginning of a prolonged period of conflict. By the time the Soviet Union left in 1989, 7–9% of the Afghan population were killed, with the death count rising to a staggering one in five for working-age males, and before the US invasion in 2001, the war in Afghanistan had already killed, wounded or displaced half of the population (Goepner, 2018). Between October 2001 and August 2021, 46,319 Afghan civilians died as a direct result of the US-led war.[9] This figure does not include deaths caused by disease, loss of access to food, water, infrastructure and/or other indirect consequences of this war.

As the *Britannica* notes, "many thousands were killed as a direct result of factional fighting; hundreds or thousands of prisoners and civilians were executed by tribal, ethnic, or religious rivals; ... and tens of thousands

[9] The Costs of War project, Watson Institute for International and Public Affairs, Brown University, https://watson.brown.edu/costsofwar/figures/2021/human-and-budgetary-costs-date-us-war-afghanistan-2001-2022 (accessed 1/1/2024).

died of starvation or of a variety of diseases, many of which in less-troubled times could have been easily treated, and hundreds of thousands were killed or injured by the numerous land mines in the country".[10] By the end of the twentieth century, Afghanistan was one of the most heavily mined countries in the world,[11] and vast quantities of unexploded ordnance littered the countryside.

According to Oxfam (2009), by 2008, more than 870,000 Afghans were killed, three million were maimed or wounded, a million were internally displaced and over five million were forced to flee the country. The number of Afghan refugees living abroad reached a peak of some six million people in the late 1980s.

Based on interviews, Oxfam (2009) reported that properties were destroyed for approximately two in five (43%) individuals, a quarter (25%) of land destroyed, one in three (34%) people were robbed, one in five (21%) people were tortured. Oxfam (2009) also reported that three in four (76%) people were forced to leave their homes at some point during the conflict. Of these, 41% were internally displaced, 42% were externally displaced and 17% were both internally and externally displaced. Many individuals were displaced multiple times, moving from one place to another in search of security, only to be forced to flee once again months or years later or after having returned home again.

Such devastations had serious setbacks for Afghanistan's development as a whole generation grew up never having experienced peace and many Afghans had to struggle to cope with the psychological, economic, social and physical ramifications of the conflicts. Around 52% of the population live in multidimensional poverty, around one-third of the population is regularly food insecure, while only around 36% of the population uses safely managed drinking water and 41% use safely managed sanitation services (UNDP, 2020).

Conflict can affect a country's development through various channels, including the loss of physical and human capital, the disruption of production processes, and the undermining of markets (Blattman & Miguel 2010). Virgilio Galdo, Gladys Lopez-Acevedo and Martin Rama (2020) found that conflict had led to a rise in the informal activities in Afghanistan, which is consistent with an earlier study (Ciarli,

[10] https://www.britannica.com/event/Afghan-War (accessed 1/1/2024).

[11] https://www.britannica.com/technology/land-mine (accessed 1/1/2024).

Kofol and Menon, 2015) that households were more likely to engage in subsistence agriculture or self-employment, whereas firms were small and had low capital intensity. Illicit activities, including drug production and commercialisation, were common (Stepanova, 2012). During the Soviet occupation of Afghanistan, much of the irrigation infrastructure in rural areas was destroyed, making it more economical to grow drought-resistant poppies—the plant that produces opium paste—than food staples. Thus, Afghanistan's booming population slowly became more dependent on imported foodstuffs. Lind, Moene and Willumsen (2014) noted that conflict increased the perception of lawlessness while destroying infrastructure that is crucial to the production of alternative crops. In interviews conducted by Keohler and Zuercher (2007), Afghan farmers confirmed that opium poppy was one of the few available cash crops.

Post-conflict failed recovery and development regress are not a foregone conclusion as the experience of Vietnam shows. Vietnam also endured about two decades of US-led war and conflict, but made significant strides in transforming its economy since it comprehensively defeated the US. It even repaired its relations with its former enemy, the US, following a pragmatic approach, keeping its national interests protected. However, sadly Afghanistan's future does not appear certain even after the humiliating defeat of the US and its Western allies. Goepner (2018) noted that 40 years of war have fundamentally changed Afghan society and made it more polarised and fragmented along tribal and other cleavages, thus making the country more prone to conflict and war.

Reactions of the international community, especially of the US and Western nations, to the humiliating defeat of the US-led coalition and the Taliban take-over, such as freezing of Afghanistan's US$7 billion reserves and cuts in aid, have crippled the Afghan economy and sank the country deeper into crisis as Afghanistan resists Western-imposed transformation of Afghan society. The US imposed sanctions on the Taliban since 1999, with the severity and breadth of sanctions designations rising markedly since 2001 as part of the response to the 9/11 attacks. Mark Weisbrot of Center for Economic and Policy Research warned, "Unless those sanctions are soon reversed, it is estimated that more people will die from the economic impact of sanctions over the next year than the number who died in 20 years of war" (Weisbrot, 2022).

Geopolitical rivalries between regional powers, China and India, severely impact the development prospects of landlocked Bhutan and

Nepal—both historically dependent on India, especially for their access to sea. Nepal is predominantly a Hindu State with cultural and religious ties with India. A treaty was signed between Nepal and India in July 1950 obligating both governments "to inform each other of any serious friction or misunderstanding with any neighbouring state likely to cause any breach in the friendly relations subsisting between the two governments". Letters were also exchanged at the time providing that: "Neither Government shall tolerate any threat to the security of the other by a foreign aggressor. To deal with any such threat, the two Governments shall consult with each other and devise effective counter-measures".

On the other hand, Bhutan is a predominantly a Buddhist State; its Buddhism basically came from Tibet. Since China's annexation of Tibet, Bhutan sees China as a threat to its sovereignty, especially when Bhutan's border with Tibet has never been officially recognised, much less demarcated, and China officially maintains a territorial claim on parts of Bhutan. Thus, Bhutan developed strong economic and military ties with India, while having no diplomatic relations with China. Under a treaty signed in 1949, India gained a formal right to guide Bhutan's foreign policy in exchange for free trade and security guarantees. The foreign policy provision was scrapped in 2007, but India remained Bhutan's most important diplomatic and economic partner.

Like America's Monroe doctrine which treats the South American continent as exclusive to its sphere of influence, India regards Nepal and Bhutan from the perspective of its strategic heritage passed on to it by British India, which held that the defensive frontiers of India lay in the mountain fortress of the Himalayas (Garver, 1991). On the other hand, China treats its relations with these two countries from the perspective of its strategic interest linked to Tibet which it annexed in 1951. It is also influenced by its objections to the China–India border drawn by the British and claims that part of Himalayan Indian Ladakh and India's Arunachal Province historically belong to China.

In 1989, when India and Nepal disputed about trade and transit agreements between them, India imposed almost a complete economic blockade of Nepal, closing 13 out of 15 transit points for trade. India also banned the entry of all essential items like coal, cooking oil and petrol into Nepal and obstructed Nepal's imports from third countries (Shakoor, 1989). As Barbara Crossette of *The New York Times* reported, "It is almost universally believed in Katmandu that the trade dispute was only a pretext for New Delhi to vent its displeasure with Nepal for an accumulation of grievances. Growing Nepalese–Chinese cooperation, culminating in Katmandu's purchase in August 1988 of Chinese antiaircraft guns, is a major factor" (Crossette, 1989).

India imposed an undeclared crippling economic blockade again in September 2015, lasting about four and a half months. Although the closer was only at point stopping all essential supply trucks and oil tankers heading to Nepal, it triggered an economic and humanitarian crisis when the country was still suffering from the April 2015 earthquake (Karki, 2022). Nepal accused India of imposing a blockade to punish it for changes to the Nepali constitution and its increasing cooperation with China. Karki (2022) termed India's undeclared blockade as a "political black-mailing".

Despite long-running border disputes, the Bhutan–China relations experienced some thaws. In 1998, the two countries signed a peace and tranquillity agreement, although border disputes remained. China reaffirmed its respect for Bhutan's sovereignty and territorial integrity in the agreement. The two sides also proposed the Five Principles of Peaceful Coexistence. In June 2012, then-Chinese Premier Wen Jiabao met with Bhutanese Prime Minister Jigme Thinley, which was the first meeting between the two countries heads of government. Bhutan–China relations improved following China's Belt and Road Initiative (BRI) in 2013, and on 14 October 2021, Chinese Assistant Foreign Minister Wu Jianghao and Bhutanese Foreign Minister Thandit Dorji signed a Memorandum of Understanding on the "Three-Step Roadmap" for accelerating the Sino-Bhutan border negotiations.

Bhutan seeks balance with its larger neighbours China and India in order to avoid dependency on either country. It does not want to face a situation like that of Nepal under constant threats of transit closures by India. Bhutan's apprehension is not unfounded. India used coercive economic tools when differences arose between India and the first democratically elected prime minister of Bhutan, Jigme Yoser Thinley (2008–13) on foreign policy issues (Mitra & Thaliyakkattil, 2018). To punish Bhutan for its cosying up to China, India withdrew its subsidy of kerosene and liquefied petroleum gas (LPG) supplies to Bhutan in July 2013, resulting in a doubling of prices. This was done deliberately in the middle of Bhutan's second democratic election in order to influence its outcome.

India's withdrawal of fuel subsidies came against the backdrop of (and was exacerbated by) another economic crisis also brought about by Bhutan's excessive economic dependency on India. As Mitra and Thaliyakkattil (2018, p. 255) noted, "In 2012 a shortage of Indian currency in Bhutan led to an increase in the price of goods, impeded economic growth, and adversely affected the general public". Therefore, it became clear to Bhutan that excessive dependence on India was harmful to the country's independence and security.

The visit of Bhutan's Foreign Minister to China in October 2023—the first ever by a Bhutanese Foreign Minister—was unprecedented as Bhutan and China do not maintain diplomatic relations. In his meeting, Mr Wang said China was ready to complete the border talks as soon as possible and to establish formal ties with Bhutan, describing it as a "historic opportunity". Bhutan's Prime Minister, Lotay Tshering, suggested to an Indian newspaper earlier in October 2023 that a possible land swap involving Doklam had been proposed.

According to *The Economist* (2023), "That has caused India to worry about its own territory and a loss of influence" in countries it considered its backyard. India's biggest concern is Bhutan could cede land to China that is close to the Doklam area which connects North-Eastern India to the rest of the country. There was already a military standoff between Chinese and Indian troops in 2017 as a result of road construction by Chinese troops in the Doklam area of the disputed boundary between Bhutan and China.

Unsurprisingly, Marcus Andreopoulos of the influential US opinion maker, *Foreign Policy*, sounded alarm, "A resolution between the CCP and the government of Bhutan would reverberate throughout India, threatening peace in the region and escalating the crisis along the Sino-Indian border. The issue requires close attention from New Delhi as well as the Quadrilateral Security Dialogue—the Indo-Pacific partnership that includes Australia, India, Japan, and the United States".

Getting entangled in wider regional geopolitics will certainly complicate Bhutan's development path. As Economist Intelligent Unit (2023) notes, "China will continue to woo Bhutan with financial, technical and security assistance, keeping India on its toes to block the former's attempts at making inroads".

Unfortunately, unlike Southeast Asia, South Asia does not have an effective forum for peace to mediate conflicting views and interests. The South Asia Association for Regional Cooperation (SAARC), established in 1985, to promote economic growth and democracy across South Asia has hardly any influence and has in recent years stopped meeting regularly. The elephant in the room is India. As V.V. Desai (2010, p. 26) in an ADB working paper noted, "An extreme imbalance of power among member states has given rise to fears over security resulting from domination by India, and fostered an environment of suspicion and mistrust". Pratiksha Chaturvedi, Zaki Hussain & Biswajit Nag (2017, p. 78) concurred, "India's evident dominant position in the group [is] a cause for insecurity among other members" of SAARC. When the power balance among members is highly asymmetric, anxiety about the hegemonic designs of the most powerful member State is felt by other member States, creating substantial "trust deficits" among members vis-à-vis the most powerful State (Desai, 2010).

Rendering SAARC ineffective, India has been pushing for the Bay of Bengal Initiative for Multi-Sectoral Technical and Economic Cooperation (BIMSTEC)[12]—established in 1997—as an alternative to SAARC. During his first tenure, Indian Prime Minister Modi seemed to have a preference for SAARC, as can be inferred from his invitation to the heads of States of all SAARC member countries at his swearing-in ceremony. In order to explore new opportunities for dialogue with Pakistan, he made a surprise visit to Islamabad; but relations between the two countries deteriorated in the years following. At the start of his second term, PM Modi's preferences had shifted when he invited the heads of BIMSTEC member countries for his swearing-in.

Like SAARC, BIMSTEC faces lots of challenges as its member states (Bangladesh, Bhutan, India, Myanmar, Nepal, Sri Lanka and Thailand) are the least integrated in terms of trade, connectivity and cooperation and their progress is usually at a snail's pace. BIMSTEC took 17 years to establish a Permanent Secretariat (located in Dhaka) and failed to come up with a BIMSTEC Charter for two decades.[13]

[12] Following the inclusion of Myanmar on 22 December 1997 during a special Ministerial Meeting in Bangkok, the Group was renamed 'BIMST-EC' (Bangladesh, India, Myanmar, Sri Lanka and Thailand Economic Cooperation). In 1998, Nepal became an observer. In February 2004, Nepal and Bhutan became full members.

On 31 July 2004, in the first Summit the grouping was renamed as BIMSTEC or the Bay of Bengal Initiative for Multi-Sectoral Technical and Economic Cooperation.

[13] The BIMSTEC Charter was signed and adopted during the Fifth BIMSTEC Summit held in a virtual format in Colombo, Sri Lanka, on 30 March 2022.

Geopolitics is also a critical factor in the case of Southeast Asia. Here China is the elephant in the room. China–Japan and China–Vietnam rivalries, especially China's territorial claims in the South China Sea, are causes of significant regional tension, compounded by the attempts of the US and its allies (Australia and Japan) to contain China. Seeking access to the Bay of Bengal through Myanmar for its landlocked North-eastern regions, China aligned with Myanmar's military regimes in the on-going ethnic conflicts that have been a serious barrier to Myanmar's development and transformation prospects. Myanmar's rich mineral resources are also an attraction for China as well as its rivals, notably the US and Japan. China is also a staunch ally of Cambodia in its dispute with Vietnam. While both Cambodia and Myanmar are firmly in China's orbit, Lao PDR has maintained friendly and cooperative relations with both neighbours—China and Vietnam. Writing for *The Diplomat*, To Minh Son noted, "In playing a balancing game between its bigger socialist brothers, Laos seeks to benefit from China's ascendant economy and Belt and Road Initiative (BRI) infrastructure push, while remaining committed to the security interests of Vietnam, its longstanding ally".

However, regional fora, such as the Association of South East Asian Nations (ASEAN), ASEAN *plus* 3 (China, Japan, South Korea) and Asia–Pacific Economic Cooperation (APEC), have so far successfully managed regional tensions as they regularly meet at the Summit level, allowing dialogues at the highest level. Indonesia, the largest and militarily most powerful country among the founding ASEAN members played a significant role in creating mutual trust, by signing a peace treaty to end *Konfrontasi*, an "undeclared war", with Malaysia on 11 August 1966. The end of the *Konfrontasi* led to the formation of ASEAN in 1967. Writing for *The Diplomat*, Adam Leong Kok Wey (2016) observed, "ASEAN has served remarkably well to quell regional competition and suspicions among its members, even though most of its members are still entangled in border and territorial disputes with each other. ASEAN has also done well in managing to integrate its regional economy and cooperate in natural disaster response and management". Nevertheless, a significant risk of regional armed conflict arose due to China's more assertive role since President Xi became China's supreme leader and increased Sino-US tensions with President Trump's election victory.

Democratic Deficits

All South and Southeast Asian LDCs suffer from democratic deficits of various degrees, while Afghanistan, Myanmar and Bangladesh experienced the largest declines in democracy during 2012–2023, according to the Freedom House's *Freedom in the World 2023* report. The Report listed Afghanistan and Myanmar among the "worst of the worst" performers. The Report reminds "the devastating costs that authoritarian rule can impose on entire populations. In the absence of any meaningful constraints on political power and the use of force, a growing number of regimes around the world have engaged in wholesale persecution of women or ethnic minority groups, in some cases drawing accusations of genocide" (p. 4).

The Freedom House classified Afghanistan, Cambodia, Lao PDR and Myanmar as "Not Free" and Bangladesh, Bhutan and Nepal as "Partly Free". Table 5.4 shows that South and Southeast Asian LDCs are among the lowest ranking countries in terms of "quality of democracy", Afghanistan is placed at the bottom of the list by the Economist Intelligence Unit and the V-Dem Institute (the University of Gothenburg).

Ironically, countries, such as Bangladesh and Cambodia, which experienced democratic regress, insist that they are "democratic", even though they brutally suppressed opposition and seriously compromised fair and free elections. They claim that "some" suppressions of civic and political rights are necessary for accelerating development, implying that there is

Table 5.4 Ranking of South and Southeast Asian LDCs by quality of democracy

Country	*Economist Intelligence Unit (167 countries, 2022)*	*V-Dem (Liberal democracy index, 179 countries, 2023)*
Afghanistan	167	175
Bangladesh	73	146
Bhutan	84	71
Cambodia	121	162
Lao PDR	159	148
Myanmar	166	177
Nepal	101	56

Note: A higher number means lower quality

a trade-off. They draw inspiration from the rapid transformation experiences of authoritarian China since the 1990s and East Asia's newly industrialised countries—South Korea, Singapore and Taiwan since the late 1960s—as well as Malaysia under Mahathir.

Singapore's founding father late Prime Minister Lee Kuan Yew gave legitimacy to such a claim by promoting the idea of choice between two D's—democracy and discipline (a code word for suppression)—for achieving the third D—development. Lee claims that this view is more congruent with the so-called "Asian values" rooted in Confucian traditions that respect social authority.

However, Carl Knutsen's (2010) empirical study, based on panel data analysis on more than 20 Asian countries, did not support the hypothesis that dictatorship increases economic growth in Asia. Asian dictatorships did invest a larger fraction of their GDP than democracies, but they were worse at generating high enrolment ratios in education after primary school. Similarly, rigorous econometric study by Michael Rock (2009) rejected the Lee hypothesis that democracy slows the growth and revealed that democracy caused growth and investment to rise. Russell Dalton and Nhu-Ngoct Ong (2005) also refuted the Lee hypothesis based on their survey of six East Asian and four Western democracies. The growth experiences of the 7 South and Southeast Asian LDCs presented in Figs. 4.1 and 4.2 also do not support the claim that authoritarian regimes deliver better results; only Bangladesh recorded increases in growth rate albeit fluctuating.

The so-called "Lee hypothesis" implies a "u-shaped" relationship between development and democracy that democracy initially declines and then improves with development. This presupposes that countries at a low level of development are not fit for democracy. Nobel Laureate Amartya Sen (1999, p. 4) reminded "A country does not have to be deemed fit for democracy; rather, it has to become fit through democracy".

However, it is not always clear that an authoritarian regime cannot provide the framework for rapid growth and transformation. The authoritarian regimes of Chiang Kai-shek in Taiwan and Park Chung-hee in South Korea provided a reasonably predictable and durable contractual environment for private businesses to thrive. So, was the case for the semi-democracies of Lee Kuan Yew's Singapore or Mahathir Mohamad's Malaysia. One can also cite President Soeharto's Indonesia before it imploded in the 1997–98 financial crisis. Pakistan also produced spectacular growth in the 1960s under the authoritarian rule of Field Marshal Ayub Khan before the country broke up in a violent war of liberation that gave birth to Bangladesh.

However, these are very selective examples of a few success cases. In fact, looking for a "benevolent" authoritarian ruler, like the ones cited above, is risky. The probability of finding another Lee Kuan Yew or Park Chung-hee is extremely low; but there are many despots, like Mobuto of the Democratic Republic of Congo, Marcos of the Philippines or Idi Amin of Uganda, and countries can be stuck in poor governance setting back development for decades under despotic rules.

Moreover, the so-called benevolent authoritarian regime's growth can collapse suddenly as evidenced during the 1997–1998 Asian financial crisis (AFC). The worst hit country was Indonesia where the economy contracted by about 14% and the recovery took longer than any other AFC hit country. The country also broke as East Timor (Timor-Leste) seceded. On the other hand, South Korea which successfully democratised its polity towards the end of the 1980s was the least affected country and had the fastest recovery. Mahathir's semi-democratic Malaysia also experienced a sharp fall in GDP and the political instability that ensued hampered its recovery. Since then, Malaysia has been trapped in a so-called "middle-income trap", whereas having consolidated its multi-party democracy, Indonesia has maintained both political stability and economic growth, aspiring to join the rich country club, the Organisation for Economic Co-operation and Development (OECD).

One of the weaknesses of an authoritarian regime is its inability to resolve disagreements or conflicts between "winners" and "losers" from structural transformation in a peaceful manner. For example, the authoritarian Bangladesh government faced workers demanding higher minimum wage and better working conditions with brutal police force, causing deaths of at least one worker[14]; and the police filed criminal cases against some 18,000 workers.[15] Such violent suppression of labour rights may attract sanctions from democratic Western countries which are important export destinations.

[14] https://www.reuters.com/world/asia-pacific/one-killed-garment-workers-clash-with-police-bangladesh-over-pay-rise-police-2023-11-08/ (accessed 5/01/2024).

[15] https://www.theguardian.com/global-development/2023/nov/15/bangladesh-garment-workers-fighting-for-pay-face-brutal-violence-and-threats (accessed 5/01/2024).

The European Union (EU), for instance, decided in February 2020 to partially withdraw the duty-free quota-free access under the "Everything But Arms" (EBA) from Cambodia scheme due to its "serious and systematic concerns related to human rights".[16] In December 2019, the IMF warned that the withdrawal of the EU's trade preferences under the EBA scheme from Cambodia would cause a decline of exports to the EU of about 13%, and a 3 per centage point decline in GDP growth, without prejudice to other indirect effects.[17] According to the European Institute for Asian Studies, 43% of garment workers (nearly 225,000 people) plus 20% of workers in footwear factories (more than 20,000 people) would become unemployed (Cao, 2018).

The failure to resolve social discontent without violence makes authoritarian regimes vulnerable to political instability and civil/social unrests that are detrimental not only to economic growth but also to national security. In the case of Indonesia, for example, the authoritarian Soeharto regime failed to mediate inter-regional discontents, thus faced separatist insurgencies in a number of provinces such as resource-rich Aceh and resource-poor East Timor as well as in Irian Jaya (West Papua) (Tadjoeddin, 2011).

Authoritarian regimes can be good at igniting rapid growth at an early phase when growth predominantly "factor driven"—to use Michael Porter's (Porter, 1990) terminology, mainly engaged in standardised production activities using unskilled labour and simple technology. This requires a disciplined labour force who can be trained in "how to do" various stages in assembly-line industrial production. To use Paul Krugman's (Krugman, 1994) terminology, growth at this stage is due to "perspiration". However, as the surplus labour is absorbed and the

[16] According to the EU, "(t)he withdrawal of preferential access to the EU market concerns approximately 20% of Cambodia's exports to the EU. Cambodia may still export those products to the EU but they will be subject to general tariffs applicable to any other member of the WTO. The remaining 80% of Cambodia's exports continue to enjoy preferential (duty-free, quota-free) access to the EU market. The Commission, together with the European External Action Service (EEAS), will continue its enhanced engagement with Cambodia. The EU will keep on monitoring the situation in the country, with a particular focus on current restrictions in the areas of freedom of expression and civil and political rights, as well as land disputes and labour rights in the context of the ongoing reforms." https://ec.europa.eu/commission/presscorner/detail/en/IP_20_1469 (20/09/2020).

[17] IMF, Cambodia Article IV Consultation, *IMF Country Report* No. 19/387 (December 2019).

investment-GDP ratio peaks, countries need to proceed to the next stage that is "innovation driven" *a la* Porter or "inspiration driven" in Krugman's framework. At this "why" becomes more critical than "how" in the production process. Democratic regimes do better here; due to freedom of expression, people are not afraid of asking "why' and experimentation without fear or prejudice. In general, the authoritarian systems are good in imitating, but not in innovating; thus, lose dynamism and unable to sustain growth.

One of the channels through which autocratic regimes create vulnerability is the rise in inequality—both vertical (inter-personal) and horizontal (e.g., inter-region or inter-ethnicity) because of the lack of citizen's participation or voice in the decision process and the suppression of labour's bargaining power or attenuation of labour rights. For example, Field Marshal Ayub Khan's authoritarian Pakistan was a star performer in the 1960s, being one of the few countries that achieved the 5% growth target of the First United Nations Development Decade (1961–1970). Pakistan was presented as a role model of development by the leading development economists of Harvard University, such as Gustav Papanek, for Indonesia, South Korea and the Philippines which were regarded as bulwarks for the US against communism in the region. The rapid growth phase of Pakistan also widened inter-regional disparities that led to the break-up of Pakistan within a few years of its celebration of the Decade of Development.

Inequality also rises in authoritarian regimes through corruption due to lack of accountability. Besides creating social discontents, the corruptly acquired wealth and money are likely to leave the country due to the increased risk of political instability that inequality creates in an authoritarian regime. For example, Bangladesh, the only LDC in the region recording rising growth rates, is labelled as one of the most corrupt countries by the Transparency International and witnessed the highest rise in its ultra-wealthy population that surpassed any other country in the world, according to the 2018 report of Wealth-X.[18] It also topped the list of LDCs for illicit transfer of funds during 1990–2008, according to a

[18] https://www.thedailystar.net/opinion/more-just-facts/news/the-rise-the-super-rich-1636018 (accessed 5/01/2024).

2010 UNDP report.[19] Thus, Mujeri and Mujeri (2021) regard the rise in inequality as the biggest threat to Bangladesh's progress and challenge to its structural transformation. Bangladesh's rapid growth phase has in fact hit roadblocks from depleting foreign reserves and rising debt (domestic and external), forcing the country to seek financial support from the IMF in 2023. Faltering growth and economic crisis may likely undermine the political legitimacy of the regime, further slowing Bangladesh's structural transformation.

Options for Structural Transformation

In light of the disappointing experiences of manufacturing, these LDCs should be seriously considering whether they can follow the historical pattern of structural transformation from agriculture to manufacturing and then to the high-value services sector. Alternatively, is the 2-sector surplus labour model of Lewis relevant for landlocked LDCs like Nepal, Bhutan or Lao PDR?

A quick and rough answer can be found from the labour force size of these countries vis-à-vis selected countries in the region where the Lewis model seems to have worked (Fig. 5.5). Only Bangladesh can be described as a truly labour-abundant country, and clearly, Bhutan and Lao PDR do not fulfil the requirements for the Lewis model. Afghanistan, Cambodia and Nepal are likely to exhaust the labour-intensive manufacturing phase quickly, while Myanmar may have some prospects for emulating the historical pattern.

As mentioned earlier, Bangladesh seems to have hit the roadblocks. Industrial unrest is on the rise as garment workers are asking for higher minimum wages and better working conditions. A total of 593 labour unrests took place in different industrial sectors of the country in 2020.[20] The garment sector's four million workers went on a protest campaign for 12 days (between the last week of October and the first week of

[19] https://financialtransparency.org/undp-commissioned-report-from-global-financial-integrity-illicit-financial-flows-from-the-least-developed-countries-1990-2008-now-available/ (accessed 5/01/2024).

[20] https://thefinancialexpress.com.bd/trade/bangladesh-industries-saw-rise-in-labour-unrest-in-2020-amid-layoffs-1610251088 (accessed 5/01/2024).

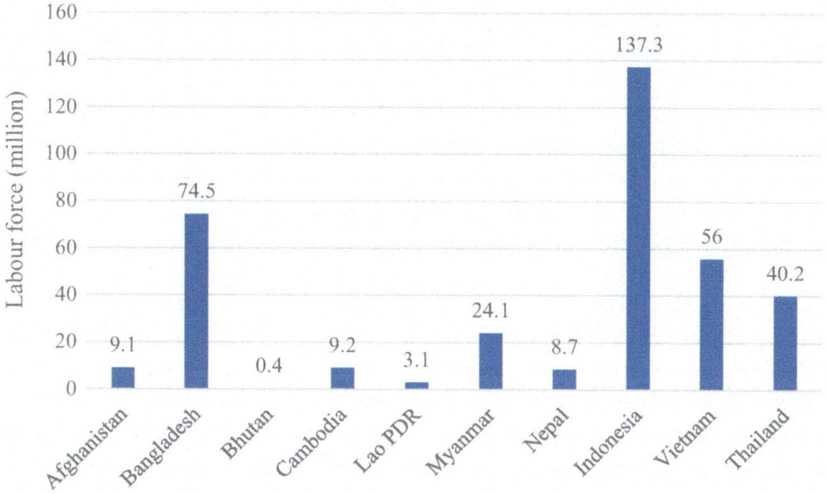

Fig. 5.5 Labour force size of South and Southeast Asian LDCs (2022). *Source*: World Bank online database. Note: Indonesia, Vietnam and Thailand are included for comparison

November 2023) for a minimum wage of at least Tk 20,000, causing the suspension of production in as many as 500 factories.[21]

Instead of trying to suppress wages and working conditions heavy-handed by using lethal police actions, Bangladesh needs to take steps to move to the next phase of higher value added manufacturing that is more skill-intensive. As the experience of Singapore's industrial restructuring in the 1980s shows, better working conditions and higher wages act as an incentive for the factory owners to invest in technology upgrading and encourage workers to invest in skill upgrading. Higher wages also create domestic demand, making the country less vulnerable to external factors.

Myanmar, Afghanistan, Cambodia and Nepal may begin with labour-intensive standardised manufacturing, knowing that this phase will be short-lived. They are also likely to face more intense competition for low-end labour-intensive manufacturing than the first-generation newly industrialising East and Southeast Asia countries from other low-cost

[21] https://www.thedailystar.net/business/news/unrest-bearing-fragile-economy-3463381 (accessed 5/01/2024).

countries in a more globalised world. The standalone factories producing garments in the low-technology cut-make-trim stage and selling them through the GSP route may not survive an open market regime, while those that restructure should thrive. Therefore, these countries have to leap-frog from low-end labour-intensive manufacturing, creating competitive advantage in high value added niche products. This will require urgent investment in education, skill formation and healthcare, as well as implementing integrated industry and trade policies. Singapore, South Korea and Taiwan offer them examples (see Chowdhury & Islam, 1993). These countries followed complementary industry, trade, wages and human resource development policies in the 1980s to accelerate the transformation of their manufacturing into high-valued activities.

Bhutan and Lao PDR with a very small labour force are special cases and simply do not have much prospects of succeeding in labour-intensive manufacturing. Therefore, they cannot follow the diversification path of early industrialisers in the region, which were largely labour surplus economies. In this regard, the transformation experience of Switzerland, a landlocked European country with a relatively smaller labour force may offer some lessons.

Unable to compete with the UK, the home of the industrial revolution, and larger European countries, for example, Germany and France, during its early stage of development, Switzerland began industrialisation with textile-related activities, such as printing textiles with colourful patterns, silk production and embroidery along with niche activities—watch-making and the mechanised production of chocolate. Contrary to popular belief, Switzerland did not entirely follow laissez-faire policies. While tariffs were gradually reduced, the State invested in education and training as well as in transport (railway) and energy (hydro) infrastructures. Switzerland enacted laws to protect labour rights and followed a "social partnership" model that maintained industrial harmony. The State also intervened in economic developments via the currency policy of the Swiss National Bank and through economic support measures. The Swiss State actively promoted economic development, for instance by concluding international agreements to create favourable basic conditions for the Swiss export industry.

As highlighted for some smaller African LDCs in Chapter 4, "servicification" may offer an avenue to prosperity for Bhutan and Lao PDR. In an era when the production process is broken up and involves multiple locations, services connecting complementary processes and locations play an important role. Fostering pre- and post-manufacturing services presents these two smaller landlocked LDCs a better chance to plug itself into transnational production networks and make progress with industrialisation. These manufacturing related services require relatively less labour input and hence fit better with smaller labour force size of Bhutan and Laos. Developments in information and communications technologies (ICTs) as well as in artificial intelligence (AI) also offer opportunities to these smaller landlocked LDCs to develop niche ICT and AI-related activities. These would require urgent investment in education and training.

Both Bhutan and Laos as well as Nepal are rich in hydropower. Therefore, these countries can also capitalise on the world's quest for cheap clean energy sources to tackle global warming. In this respect fast-growing large neighbours—China, India, Thailand and Bangladesh—offer market opportunities for their hydropower.

Finally, none of these countries can ignore the role of agriculture which remains a significant source of employment. As the findings of Nyingtob Norbu, Yusuke Tateno and Andrzej Bolesta (2021) revealed, agriculture continues to create more jobs for one additional unit of final demand in agriculture than other sectors. That is, agriculture has the highest employment multiplier in South and Southeast Asian LDCs. Because of its employment creation capacity, growth in the agriculture sector also has a large impact—i.e., growth elasticity—on poverty reduction.

Therefore, these countries should focus on raising agricultural productivity. If the increases in agricultural productivity can be accompanied by stronger production linkages with other sectors, the impact of structural transformation on job creation and poverty reduction would be greater. Rural modernisation and the expansion of agro-based industries are critical for dynamic structural transformation as seen in more successful countries.

The Way Forward

The South and Southeast Asian LDCs will have to tackle the common barriers to their structural transformation, especially low levels of productive capacity. In addition, the landlocked ones will have to address their connectivity bottlenecks and infrastructure shortages. These will require not only state capability but also large-scale investment. They can turn their geopolitical barriers into an advantage to meet their investment needs and enhance productive capacity. This is possible by not taking a side and maintaining friendly relations with all.

To counter China's BRI, launched in 2013, Japan initiated "Free and Open Indo-Pacific" (FOIP) strategy in August 2016. Liqin Wang (2023) has shown that Japan-led Asian Development Bank (ADB) and the China-led Asian Infrastructure Bank (AIIB) can cooperate at the institutional level. Zhao Hong (2018) concluded that China–Japan competition in Southeast Asian infrastructure could be constructive since this competition can contain the two countries' respective behaviour and prompt them to improve their investment approaches.

Japan and India announced their intention to undertake third-country cooperation in 2020 to undertake projects in countries across the Bay of Bengal region. South Asian and Southeast Asian LDCs can maximise their national interests from these initiatives by maintaining non-alignment in China–Japan and China–India rivalries. The expanding commitments of China, India and Japan are an opportunity to inject new energy into the transformation efforts of South and Southeast Asian LDCs.

Both China and India have shown that they can rise above their geopolitical interests to support their neighbours during the COVID-19 pandemic. India led from the front in hosting the first SAARC meeting, four years after it had declined to meet in Islamabad in 2016, citing cross-border terrorism. As the US dragged its feet, China offered help to India to deal with the pandemic and establish a COVID-19 "emergency supplies reserve" for South Asian countries.[22]

Afghanistan and Myanmar can leverage their natural resources to attract foreign direct investment beyond extractive activities, especially when the demand for "rare minerals" is rising. They can also find innovative ways of raising revenues, such as profit-sharing, from natural resource-related activities. This would require a sound and reasonable legal framework to clarify all areas of activity and investment. However, natural resources are the major cause of conflicts as highlighted in the case of African LDCs. Therefore, one of the issues that deserve a good deal of attention is the re-distribution of revenues generated in the extractive sector.

Given the concerns over the potential for horizontal conflicts emanating from geographical or regional distribution of resources across

[22] https://edition.cnn.com/2021/04/28/china/china-india-covid-relief-mic-intl-hnk/index.html (accessed 5/01/2024).

the country, it is important to understand what the people think as fair shares and the appropriate uses of natural resource revenues. Creation of a sovereign fund with natural resource revenues, managed by independent professionals and earmarking of certain percentages of natural resource revenues for social spending can serve to mitigate natural resource-related social discontents. Such arrangements can also avoid macroeconomic imbalances, such as exchange rate appreciations.

None of these countries can afford to ignore their agriculture and rural economy. Agriculture plays a crucial role in driving industrialisation by supplying wage goods (food) and inputs. The rural economy is also a vital source of domestic demand for manufactured products. Strengthening the linkage between agro-rural economy and domestic manufacturing is critically important for balanced and stable job-rich growth and structural transformation. Such development strategies have the maximum impact on sustained poverty reduction and food security and assume particular significance in light of heightened uncertainty in the global economy.

Finally, South and Southeast Asian LDCs have to address their democratic deficits. These countries are not what the leading public choice theorist James Buchanan (1954) defined as "government by discussion". In such a polity, there is a lack of interest in the acceptability of the principle of "agreeing to disagree" or "distributive fiscal systems" for compensating the losers in the structural transformation process.

Thus, South and Southeast Asian LDCs lack what Amartya Sen (1999) calls the "constructive" role for which democracy is valued in the first place. The absence of democracy's constructive role denies citizens an opportunity of what the leading philosopher John Rawls (1971) calls "the exercise of public reason". That is, their citizens cannot participate in political discussions to be in a position to influence public choice. Nor can they learn from one another and help society to form its values and priorities. In other words, instead of inclusionary and participatory, the South and Southeast Asian LDCs have become exclusionary and plutocracy, or in the extreme, "mafiacracy". Therefore, their citizens' demand for economic needs and justice go unheard or unmet when elites and mafia linked to the ruling party amass wealth through pillage and coercion. These are serious impediments for inclusive prosperity, sustainable development and growth-enhancing transformation.

References

ADB. (2014a). *Myanmar: Unlocking the Potential, Country Diagnostic Study*, https://www.adb.org/sites/default/files/publication/42870/myanmar-unlocking-potential.pdf (accessed 12/09/2020).

ADB. (2014b). *Cambodia: Diversifying Beyond Garments and Tourism – Country Diagnostic Study*, www.adb.org/sites/default/files/publication/149852/cambodia-diversifying-country-diagnostic-study.pdf (accessed 12/09/2020).

Aggarwal, R. (2021). Comparative analysis of structural transformation process of selected Asian developing economies. *Journal of Asian Economic Integration, 3*(1), 7–24.

Akamatsu, K. (1961). A theory of unbalanced growth in the world economy. *Weltwirtschaftliches Archiv, 86*(2), 196–217.

Amsden, A. (1989). *Asia's Next Giant: South Korea and Late Industrialization.* Oxford University Press.

Andreopoulos, M. (2023). China's border talks with Bhutan are aimed at India: The disputed Doklam plateau is a pressure point for both regional powers. Beijing is moving in. *Foreign Policy*, 18 July.

Balassa, B. (Ed.). (1981). *The Newly Industrializing Countries in the World Economy*. Pergamon Press.

Balassa, B. (1983). Outward versus inward orientation once again. *The World Economy, 6*(2), 215–218.

Barrett, P. (2018). The fiscal cost of conflict: Evidence from Afghanistan 2005–2016. *IMF Working Paper*, WP/18/204.

Bathla, S., D'Souza, A., & Pramod, J. (2019). Structural transformation in Southeast Asian countries and key drivers. *IFPRI Discussion Paper* 1856 (August).

Bauer, P. (1984). *Reality and Rhetoric: Studies in the Economics of Development*. Weidenfeld & Nicholson.

Berger, P. (1983). Secularity: East and West. In *Cultural Identity and Modernization in Asian Countries*, Proceedings of Kokugakuin University Centennial Symposium, Tokyo: Kokugakuin University Press.

Berger, P., & Hsin-Huang, H. (Eds.). (1988). *In Search of an East Asian Development Model*. Transaction Press.

Bhagwati, J. (1988). Export-promoting trade strategy: Issues and evidence. *World Bank Research Observer, 3*(1), 27–37.

Blattman, C., & Edward, M. (2010). Civil War. *Journal of Economic Literature, 48*(1), 3–57.

Buchanan, J. (1954). Social choice, democracy, and free markets. *Journal of Political Economy, 62*(2), 114–123.

Cao, C. (2018). EU trade sanctions on Cambodia: An ethical debate. https://www.eias.org/wp-content/uploads/2016/03/EU_Asia_at_a_Glance_Cambodia-Oct2018-V2.pdf (accessed 5/01/2024).

Chan, A. (1996). Confucianism and development in East Asia. *Journal of Contemporary Asia, 26*(1), 28–45.

Chang, H.-J. (1996). *Political economy of industrial policy*. St. Martin's Press.

Chaturvedi, P., Zaki, H., & Biswajit, N. (2017). SAARC geopolitics and trade: Missing intra-regional connectivity a hindrance to further economic integration. *South Asian Survey, 22*(1), 78–106.

Chhair, S., & Luyna, U. (2016). Cambodia's path to industrial development: policies, lessons, and opportunities. In Carol Newman and others (eds). *Manufacturing Transformation: Comparative Studies of Industrial Development in Africa and Emerging Asia*. Helsinki: UNU-WIDER.

Chowdhury, A. (2021). Structural transformation, LDC graduation and the Coronavirus disease 2019 pandemic: Policy options for Cambodia, Lao People's Democratic Republic and Myanmar. *UN-ESCAP Working Paper*, No. ESCAP/1-WP/7, https://www.unescap.org/sites/default/d8files/knowledge-products/Working%20Paper%20CLM.pdf (accessed 27/12/2023).

Chowdhury, A., & Iyanatul, I. (1993). *The newly industrialising economies of East Asia*. Routledge.

Chu, Y. (Ed.). (2016). *The Asian developmental state*. Palgrave Macmillan.

Ciarli, T., Chiara, K., & Carlo, M. (2015). *Business as unusual. An explanation of the increase of private economic activity in high-conflict areas in Afghanistan*. SERC Discussion Papers 0182, Spatial Economics Research Centre, https://eprints.lse.ac.uk/65015/ (accessed 03/01/2024).

Crossette, B. (1989). Nepal's economy is gasping as India, a huge neighbor, squeezes it hard. *The New York Times*, 11 April.

Dalton, R., & Nhu-Ngoct, O. (2005). Authority orientations and democratic attitudes: A test of the 'Asian Values' hypothesis. *Japanese Journal of Political Science, 6*(2), 1–21.

Desai, V. V. (2010). The political economy of regional cooperation in South Asia. *ADB Working Paper Series on Regional Economic Integration* No. 54 (July).

Deyo, F. (Ed.). (1987). *The Political Economy of the New Asian Industrialism*. Cornell University Press.

Eckardt, S., & Faya, H. (2023). Cambodia 2030: Economic slowdown offers opportunity to speed up reforms. *World Bank Blogs*, 13 December, https://blogs.worldbank.org/eastasiapacific/cambodia-2030-economic-slowdown-offers-opportunity-speed-reforms (accessed 24/12/2023).

Economist Intelligent Unit. (2023). *China's overtures to Bhutan will make India edgy*. 30 October, https://www.eiu.com/n/chinas-overtures-to-bhutan-will-make-india-edgy/ (accessed 3/01/2024).

Economist. (2023), China and Bhutan aim to resolve a long-running border dispute. *The Economist*, 2 November.

Evans, P. (1982). Reinventing the bourgeoisie: State entrepreneurship and class formation in dependent capitalist development. *American Journal of Sociology, 88*(s), s210–s247.

Faaland, J., & Parkinson, J. R. (1976). *Bangladesh: The Test Case of Development*. C. Hurst.

Felipe, J. (2010). *In inclusive growth, full employment, and structural change: Implications and policies for developing Asia*. Anthem Press.

Galdo, V., Gladys, L. -A., & Martin, R. (2020). Conflict and the composition of economic activity in Afghanistan. *IZA Policy Paper* No. 153 (March).

Garver, J. (1991). China–India rivalry in Nepal: The clash over Chinese arms sales. *Asian Survey, 31*(10), 956–975.

Gelb, S., Linda, C., & Xiaoyang, T. (2017). *Foreign Direct Investment and Economic Transformation in Myanmar*. Overseas Development Institute (ODI) & UK-Aid, https://set.odi.org/foreign-direct-investment-economic-transformation-myanmar/ (accessed 28/12/2023).

Goepner, E. (2018). War State, trauma State: Why Afghanistan remains stuck in conflict. *CATO Institute Policy Analysis*, 19 June (No. 844).

Gong, Y., & Wonho, J. (1998). Culture and development: Reassessing cultural explanations on Asian economic development. *Development and Society, 27*(1), 77–97.

Haggard, S. (1990). *Pathways from the Periphery: The Politics of Growth in the Newly Industrializing Countries*. Cornell University Press.

Hamilton, G., & Nicole, W. B. (1988). Market, culture, and authority: A comparative analysis of management and organization in the Far East. *American Journal of Sociology, 94*(1), 52–94.

Hughes, H. (Ed.). (1988). *Achieving industrialization in East Asia*. Cambridge University Press.

Jha, R., & Sadia, A. (2021). Structural transformation in South Asia: Does the pattern ensure growth momentum? *South Asia Economic Journal, 22*(1), 7–28.

Johnson, C. (1982). *MITI and the Japanese Miracle*. Stanford University Press.

Karki, T. (2022). *Political blackmailing: A Case Study of India's unofficial blockade on Nepal*. Available at SSRN: https://ssrn.com/abstract=4197326 or https://doi.org/10.2139/ssrn.4197326 (accessed 03/01/2024).

Keola, S. (2015). *Upgrading and diversification of industrial structure in Lao PDR: Prospect and challenges*. https://www.researchgate.net/publication/265036332_CHAPTER_7_UPGRADING_AND_DIVERSIFICATION_OF_INDUSTRIAL_STRUCTURE_IN_LAO_PDR_PROSPECT_AND_CHALLENGES (accessed /09/2020).

Knutsen, C. (2010). Investigating the Lee thesis: How bad is democracy for Asian economies? *European Political Science Review, 2*(3), 451–473.

Koehler, J., & Christoph, Z. (2007). State building, conflict and narcotics in Afghanistan: The view from below. *International Peacekeeping, 14*(1), 62–74.

Kofi, S., Tetteh, B., Dean, J., Christoph, L., & Daniel, M. (2023). Where in the world do the poor live? It depends on how poverty is defined. *World Bank Blog*, 2 August, https://datatopics.worldbank.org/world-development-indicators/stories/where-do-the-poor-live.html (accessed 9/11/2023).

Kojima, K. (2000). The 'flying geese' model of Asian economic development: Origin, theoretical extensions, and regional policy implications. *Journal of Asian Economics, 11*(4), 375–401.

Krueger, A. (1978). *Foreign trade regimes and economic development: Liberalization attempts and consequences*. National Bureau of Economic Research.

Krugman, P. (1994). The myth of Asia's Miracle. *Foreign Affairs, 73*(6), 62–78.

Leong Kok Wey, A. (2016). The war that gave birth to ASEAN. *The Diplomat*, 9 September.

Lim, D. (1994). Explaining the growth performances of Asian developing economies. *Economic Development and Cultural Change, 42*(4), 829–844.

Lind, J., Karl, M., & Fredrik, W. (2014). Opium for th masses? Conflict-induced narcotics production in Afghanistan. *Review of Economics and Statistics, 96*(5), 949–966.

Little, I. (1979). An economic reconnaissance. In W. Galenson (Ed.), *Economic growth and structural change in Taiwan*. Cornell University Press.

Little, I. (1981). The experiences and causes of rapid labour-intensive development in Korea, Taiwan Province, Hong Kong and Singapore and the possibilities of emulation. In E. Lee (Ed.), *Export-led industrialisation and development*. ILO.

Manning, C., & Alberto, P. (2008). Manufacturing growth, trade and labour market outcomes in East Asia: Why did the NIEs forge so far ahead? *The Australian National University Working Papers in Trade and Development* No. 2008/23 (November).

Marsden, P., & Emma, S. (2000). Afghanistan: The economic and social impact of conflict. In F. Stewart & V. Fitzgerald (Eds.), *War and underdevelopment*. Oxford University Press.

Mercer-Blackman, V., Amador, F., & Joseph, M. (2017). Using input-output analysis framework to explain economic diversification and structural transformation in Bangladesh. *ADB Economics Working Paper Series* No. 513 (May).

Mitra, S. K., & Srikanth, T. (2018). Bhutan and Sino-Indian rivalry: The price of proximity. *Asian Survey, 58*(2), 240–260.

Mujeri, M., & Neaz, M. (2021). *Structural Transformation of Bangladesh Economy: A South Asian Perspective*. Springer.

Nayyar, D. (2019). *Resurgent Asia: Diversity in Development*. Oxford: Oxford University Press for United Nations University World Institute for Development Economics Research UNU-WIDER).

Norbu, N., Yusuke, T., & Andrzej, B. (2021). Structural transformation and production linkages in Asia–Pacific least developed countries: An input-output analysis. *Structural Change and Economic Dynamics., 59*(October), 510–524.

Oxfam. (2009). *The Cost of War: Afghan Experiences of Conflict, 1978–2009*, https://www-cdn.oxfam.org/s3fs-public/file_attachments/afghanistan-the-cost-of-war_14.pdf (accessed 31/12/2023).

Porter, M. (1990). *The competitive advantage of the nations*. MacMillan Press Ltd.

Quibria, M. G. (2002). Growth and poverty: Lessons from the East Asian miracle revisited. *ADB Institute Research Paper Series* No. 33 (February).

Radelet, S., Jeffrey, S., & Jong-Wha, L. (1997). *Economic growth in Asia*. Harvard Institute for International Development.

Rawls, J. (1971). *A theory of justice*. Harvard University Press.

Rock, M. (2009). Has democracy slowed growth in Asia? *World Development, 37*(5), 941–952.

Rodrik, D. (2008). Industrial development: Stylized facts and policies. In D. O'Connor & M. Kjollerstrom (Eds.), *Industrial development for the 21st century*. Zed Books in association with UN-DESA.

Sen, K. (2016). The determinants of structural transformation in Asia: A review of the literature. *ADB Economics Working Paper Series* No. 478 (March).

Sen, A. (1999). Democracy as a universal value. *Journal of Democracy, 10*(3), 3–17.

Shakoor, F. (1989). Indo-Nepal dispute. *Pakistan Horizon, 42*(3/4), 68–80.

Srinivasan, T. N. (1985). Neoclassical political economy, the State and economic development. *Asian Development Review, 3*(2), 38–58.

Stepanova, E. (2012). Illicit drugs and insurgency in Afghanistan. *Perspectives on Terrorism, 6*(2), 4–18.

Tadjoeddin, M. Z. (2011). The economic origins of Indonesia's secessionist conflicts. *Civil Wars, 13*(3), 312–332.

To Minh S. (2022). Navigating Socialism, Security, and China in Laos-Vietnam Relations. *The Diplomat*, 7 October.

Totten, D., Grace Pyone Mya Moe, L., & van Roosmalen M. (2019). *Myanmar: Entrepreneurial Ecosystem Assessment, #ClosingTheGap Mekong Country Report*, https://cdn.ymaws.com/www.andeglobal.org/resource/resmgr/research_library/researchlibrary2/ctg-countryreport-myanmar-fi.pdf (accessed 11/09/2020).

Tripathi, S. (2021). Bangladesh's long journey from 'basket case' to rising star. *Foreign Policy*, 10 April, https://foreignpolicy.com/2021/04/10/ban

gladesh-independence-anniversary-basket-case-rising-star/ (accessed 21/12/2023).

UNDP. (2020). *Pitfalls and Promise: Minerals Extraction in Afghanistan*. Afghanistan Human Development Report 2020.

UNESCAP. (2014). *Myanmar Business Survey 2014*, https://www.unescap.org/sites/default/files/MBS_Survey_Results.pdf (accessed 11/09/2020).

Vernon, R. (1966). International trade in the product cycle. *Quarterly Journal of Economics, 80*(May), 190–207.

Wade, R. (1990). *Governing the market: Economic theory and the role of government in East Asian industrialization*. Princeton University Press.

Wang, L. (2023). China–Japan competition in infrastructure investment in Southeast Asia: A two-level analysis. *Chinese Political Science Review, 8*, 527–552.

Weisbrot, M. (2022). *Biden's sanctions on Afghanistan threaten to kill more civilians than two decades of war*. https://cepr.net/bidens-sanctions-on-afghanistan-threaten-to-kill-more-civilians-than-two-decades-of-war/ (accessed 03/01/2024).

World Bank. (2019). *Cambodia Economic Update: Upgrading Cambodia in Global Value Chains*, November, http://documents1.worldbank.org/curated/en/707971575947227090/pdf/Cambodia-Economic-Update-Upgrading-Cambodia-in-Global-Value-Chains.pdf (accessed 17/09/2020).

World Bank. (1993). *The East Asian Miracle: Economic Growth and Public Policy*. Oxford University Press.

World Bank. (2021). *Creating Markets in Bangladesh: Unleashing the Private Sector to Sustain Development Success*. World Bank.

World Bank. (2023a). *South Asia Development Update: Toward Faster, Cleaner Growth*. World Bank.

World Bank. (2023b). *The World Bank In Bangladesh*. https://www.worldbank.org/en/country/bangladesh/overview (accessed 21/12/2023).

Zhao, H. (2018). Chinese and Japanese infrastructure investment in Southeast Asia: from rivalry to cooperation? *Institute of Developing Economies (IDE) Discussion Paper* No, 689 (February), https://core.ac.uk/download/pdf/288468979.pdf (accessed 5/01/2024).

CHAPTER 6

Landlocked Central Asia: The Peril of Transition

"The regional organisations in Central Asia have been fragmented and weak, unable to tackle the sources of interstate tensions, and with at best limited resources and mandates to address key regional infrastructure needs." (Johannes Linn, 2012, p. 114)

The Central Asian countries came into existence only after the final dissolution of the Soviet Union in 1991. These vast territories, equalling the size of continental Europe gradually came under the rule of the Russian Empire in the eighteenth and nineteenth centuries, and then were part of the USSR until its collapse. While major changes to the century-old traditional nomadic system were introduced with permanent settlements in the fertile lowlands during the Tsarist Russia, the Soviet era was responsible for large-scale infrastructures and industrialisation as part of Soviet Union's industrialisation and modernisation drive.

The sudden dissolution of the Union of Soviet Socialist Republics (USSR) not only created political vacuum, but also a complete collapse of Central Asian economies. As Pauline Luong (2004) noted, society at large as well as governance and administrative structures had to adapt to a completely new situation characterised by simultaneous breakdown of both political and economic systems. The local political elites—mostly former leaders of the Soviet Communist Party—grasped the opportunity to fill the political vacuum and establish new authoritarian regimes

A. Chowdhury et al., *Structural Transformations as Developing Africa, Asia, and the Pacific*, https://doi.org/10.1007/978-981-97-9092-0_6

replacing communist ideology with nationalist ideologies (Batsaikhan & Dabrowski, 2017; Pomfret, 2021).

On the economic side, the dissolution of the USSR meant the end of an economic union wherein the landlocked Central Asian economies were linked with the economies of other Soviet republics. This, together with the collapse of support mechanisms—in particular for the industrial and agricultural sectors—and the discontinuation of infrastructure projects caused almost a decade of total decline, with productivity in all sectors nearly coming to a complete halt.

The struggle for mere survival caused many families to revert to subsistence farming, with little agricultural knowledge and experience and few tools. Declines and chaos in public service sectors, e.g., health and education resulted in increased poverty and declines in life expectancy (Batsaikhan & Dabrowski, 2017). On the other hand, mass-scale privatisation provided opportunities for the people connected with the ruling elites to acquire state assets at fire-sale prices resulting in a skewed wealth concentration (Pomfret, 2021).

The repatriation of former Soviet inhabitants to their home country, Russia, added to the loss of both know-how and do-how. As the region was emerging from the transition, it was hit by the further negative shock of the 1998 Russian rubble crisis and debt default. The resource-rich Central Asia countries got a reprieve only in the late 1990s and early 2000s with commodity prices booms.

However, even when the situation improved, the Central Asian countries, except Uzbekistan, deindustrialised. The share of manufacturing in GDP declined from around 20% to less than 10%, and these countries became extremely dependent on natural resource rents, a phenomenon described by Vladimir Popov (2009) as "re-primarisation". As Richard Pomfret (2021) noted, only after the commodity price boom ended in 2014, the Central Asian governments recognised the need for economic diversification.

This chapter reviews the transition experiences and structural transformation challenges of five Central Asian countries—Kazakhstan, Kyrgyzstan, Tajikistan, Turkmenistan, Uzbekistan—and Azerbaijan. Although not classified as a Central Asian country, Azerbaijan shares a common history and geography, including natural resource endowments with the five Central Asian economies. The rest of this chapter proceeds as follows. In "Central Asia: Common Geography and History" Section introduces Central Asia as a region emanating from the ashes of the

USSR. In "Transition Challenges and Lessons" Section discusses their transition from centrally planned economies to market economy and the crises that followed. In "Growth and Structural Changes" Section assesses growth and structural changes since their independence in the early1990s. In "Challenges of Structural Transformation" Section discusses unique development challenges faced by Central Asian countries. The last section concludes.

Central Asia: Common Geography and History

The five Central Asia's transition economies and Azerbaijan are characterised by a unique geographical challenge of being landlocked. While Kazakhstan, Kyrgyzstan, Tajikistan, Turkmenistan and Uzbekistan are within a continuous land area, Azerbaijan, is located across the Caspian Sea from Kazakhstan and Turkmenistan. Although these three countries share the coasts of the world's largest inland body of water, often described as the world's largest lake, they have no access to an open sea for international trade routes, and hence should still be categorised as landlocked. The Caspian Sea gives them waterway access only to countries along the lake's shore: Russia and Iran. Uzbekistan is double landlocked—it borders other landlocked countries, with limited transportation connections inside and outside the region. To outsiders, the history of the Central Asian region is primarily associated with the great Silk Road, which once stretched from the edges of the Roman Empire to the gates of China.

Their common history tied them to the former Soviet Union (USSR—Union of Soviet Socialist Republics). Being part of a larger economic union, these countries overcame the disadvantages of landlockedness. These republics, like other former Soviet republics, traded very intensively both between themselves and with the other members of the USSR, although had a meagre volume of trade with the rest of the world. They inherited not only a socialist economy, but also an industrial base as well as an integrated economy facilitated by Soviet central planning. While the bold Soviet experiment enabled rapid industrialisation and urbanisation of these Central Asian countries, they too faced the problem of stagnation and declining productivity since the mid-1970s that led to the collapse of the USSR (Popov, 2007).

In retrospect, the Soviet Union era with its central planning economic system is particularly important, as it determined the nature of these

Central Asian states or the path dependence of their transformation challenges and prospects. One important feature was the collectivisation of agriculture or the expropriation of peasants and nomads and their concentration in state-controlled collective farms in the 1930s to support the ambition of the Former Premier Josef Stalin for rapid industrialisation of the Soviet Union (Kamp and Pianciola, 2022). The labour and produce of Central Asian herders and farmers were used to back Soviet industry and the industrial labour force. In short, the six Central Asian Soviet Republics were the hinterlands.

In the second half of the twentieth century the Kremlin treated Central Asia as a "developing" region that needed investment, technology and expertise from the more developed part of the Union (Kalinovsky, 2022). This made Central Asia as an integrated economy based on the resource complementarities of the Soviet republics. The region supported the USSR's drive towards rapid industrialisation in three significant ways. The first was energy in the forms of hydropower in Tajikistan and Kyrgyzstan, and oil and gas in Azerbaijan, Kazakhstan, Uzbekistan and Turkmenistan.

The second and third resource complementarities for Soviet industrialisation were related to region's demography, i.e., relatively younger population, due to rapid population growth in the Central Asian republics in the post-war period. Thus, these countries were the source of "excess" labour to be reallocated from low-productivity nomadic pastoral and agriculture sector for industrialisation as postulated in the Lewis model, supplying cheap industrial labour in the labour-shortage European republics of the USSR. The exponential expansion of higher education in the post-war era of Central Asia for the growing youths supported new industries or upgrading which required engineers, architects and other professionals.

The Soviet economy was characterised by a high degree of self-sufficiency combined with a high degree of regional specialisation (Pomfret, 1995). For example, Uzbekistan, Tajikistan and Turkmenistan were assigned the role of cotton production for the socialist economy and investment was directed towards irrigating land to make the mission possible. This created a high degree of complementarity among the Soviet Central Asian republics and with the rest of the Soviet Union.

As the result of economic integration and regional specialisation, an industrial base was developed in the region, although much more limited than in other parts of USSR. This was in addition to the role of the region as a supplier of natural resources that naturally characterised them. For example, Kyrgyzstan specialised in producing washing machines supplying the rest of USSR. Azerbaijan produced more than 70% of the equipment used in oil and gas industry, 100% of air conditioners, 100% of electronics (radio and transistor), and 4.5% of all canned food during the Soviet era (Chowdhury, 2018). The capital of Uzbekistan, Tashkent, was the dominant industrial complex in Central Asia, and the country had steel and aircraft industries. In Kazakhstan, the most important industrial sectors were in mining and energy; in 1989 the country produced 19% of coal, 10% of iron ore and 4% of oil in the USSR (IMF et al., 1991). Major hydroelectricity projects in Tajikistan, completed in the 1970s and 1980s, supplied about three quarters of the country's power demand. Half of the country's electricity output were consumed by the Tursunzade aluminium plant as the most modern aluminium smelter in the Soviet Union accounting for 15% of the USSR aluminium capacity (Pomfret, 1995). In the early 1990s, the manufacturing shares of these economies varied between 20 and 35%, but then have continuously declined (Pomfret, 1995).

In sum, under the Soviet Union planned economy, Central Asia was an integral part of the empire's division of labour. Major Central Asian transportation routes built during the Soviet era crossed and recrossed the borders of Soviet republics. However, despite rapid and forcible industrialisation, Central Asia was a hinterland and a periphery within the Soviet Union, lagging behind the other parts of the empire. Nevertheless, the region was able to maintain a higher level of development than its productivity would have supported. This was largely due to the fact that the region was fully integrated to the empire, highly subsidised by the central government, and received artificial price supports (Batsaikhan & Dabrowski, 2017). In fact, within the Soviet Union, Central Asian republics were the primary recipients of large net transfers of fund from the central government (Orlowski, 1995).

Transition Challenges and Lessons

The way the disintegration of the USSR affected Central Asia, including Azerbaijan was spatial as well as systemic (UNDP, 2005). The spatial nature was the disintegration of what was a unified economic space with an integrated economic and social infrastructure unobstructed by borders to become independent countries (Linn, 2004). As Uuriintuya Batsaikhan and Marek Dabrowski (2017) observed, the transformation of formerly intra-Soviet administrative borders into borders between newly independent Central Asian states, with border and custom controls and, quite frequently, visa requirements, created an enormous challenge to intra-regional trade and to the domestic movement of people and goods within individual countries, especially in the densely populated Fergana Valley shared between Kyrgyzstan, Tajikistan and Uzbekistan.

Thus, the territorial disintegration has made these countries "economically landlocked", resulting in drastic falls in trade between the former Soviet republics during their transition in the 1990s (Gharleghi & Popov, 2018; Pomfret, 1995, 2023). This posed a set of development challenges they never experienced before. Not only they had to find new markets and trade routes, but also find new economic policy tools, such as issuing national currencies as they exited the economic union.

Besides implications for the economy, the spatial transition from one entity under the USSR into six independent countries also had implications for bilateral issues among them, particularly arising from competition for resources between countries. For example, the two largest river basins in the region—the Syr Darya and the Amur Darya, shared by Kyrgyzstan, Kazakhstan, Uzbekistan, Turkmenistan and Tajikistan—have become a source of diplomatic disputes (Mosello, 2008). The region has already witnessed several border conflicts, such as between Azerbaijan and Armenia, and between Kyrgyzstan and Tajikistan.

The systemic nature of the transition involved changes in political and economic systems: from authoritarian to "democracy", and from centrally planned to "market" economy. On the political side, they had no history of democratic politics and were emerging from a long period of centralistic and authoritarian Soviet rule. As Richrad Pomfret (2021) noted, in contrast to the situation in eastern Europe and the Baltics, the political or democratic transition in Central Asia was not triggered by a popular revolt. In fact, until November 1991, Central Asian leaders participated in negotiations on a "renewed" Soviet Union agreement with the Soviet president Mikhail Gorbachev (Batsaikhan & Dabrowski, 2017). With the sudden dissolution of the Soviet Union, the incumbent First Secretary of the republican Communist Party retained power as national president, except in Tajikistan.

While the timing of Central Asian countries political independence and transition coincided with a global wave of democratisation, which Samuel Huntington (1991) called "the third wave", they transformed into varieties of authoritarianism in newly independent states. Although they maintained the formality of democratic processes, such as periodic elections, they largely served as a camouflage for authoritarian regimes (Lewis, 2022). Although regular elections took place, they were mostly neither free nor fair. Former leaders of the Communist Party who grasped the opportunity to become new nationalist leaders were fearful of losing privileges (Batsaikhan & Dabrowski, 2017; Pomfret, 2021). In all six countries, political regimes are characterised by the concentration of power around the executives and personalised on the respective presidents (Pomfret, 2021).

In such a political structure, liberalising economic reforms became a means of massive transfer of public wealth and assets to the elite who captured the state, resulting in the rise of oligarchs. Privatisation of state assets and state capture by the elite class in the 1990s reinforced resistance to democracy. Wealth accumulation was mostly associated with privatisation of valuable state assets and with control over natural resource rents, banking and media (Pomfret, 2021). Mariya Omelicheva (2015) confirms the democracy resistant nature of Central Asian states and argues that the governments and citizens of Central Asia have developed their own views on democracy supported by the Russian and Chinese models rather than by Western examples.

The concentration of political power and wealth in the hands of a few created its own political economy dynamics between "losers" and "winners" and a source of violent conflict, especially when these countries are ethnically diverse. Thus, Central Asian countries and Azerbaijan suffered from ethnic and sectarian conflicts and political instability, such as the Tajik civil war in the 1990s, ethnic riots in Osh (Kyrgyzstan) in 1990 and 2010, the popular uprising in Andizhan (Uzbekistan) in 2005, so-called "Tulip revolution" in Kyrgyzstan (in 2005 and 2010). In January 2012 market traders at one of the largest shopping malls in Baku (Azerbaijan) clashed with riot police over increased rent for their stalls. There was also city-wide unrest in Ismayilli (Azerbaijan) in 2012 following a minister son's large sports car colliding with a local taxi.

On the economic side, after the collapse of the central control, these countries had to transit to some form of market-based economy, "with little conception of what they were transitioning to" (Pomfret, 2021, p. 539). Most of them followed a course of liberalisation, economic reforms and deregulation, as promoted by donors and international organisations, such as the International Monetary Fund (IMF), the World Bank and the Organisation for Economic Development and Co-operation

(OECD); but the outcomes were disappointing. Kazakhstan, Kyrgyzstan, Tajikistan, Turkmenistan and Azerbaijan suffered considerable economic collapse and social regress, such as deindustrialisation, high inflation, rise in poverty and declines in life expectancy.

Uzbekistan was an exception. It abandoned the liberalisation prescriptions of the IMF and the World Bank after a brief experimentation, and followed state-guided unorthodox economic policies, characterised by public investment, direct credits and subsidies and social protection. Despite warnings from the IMF and the World Bank of dire consequences and withholding of programme financing, Uzbekistan recovered ahead of all others. Not only its output fell less than in any other former Soviet republics, but also growth turned positive in 1996–1997 (Zettelmeyer, 1998).

In 1993 the World Bank warned of "unnecessary hardship on the population in the medium term represented by a decline in consumption per capita of no less than 30 per cent by 1997" World Bank (1993, p. xx). However, a World Bank research paper comparing Uzbekistan with Kazakhstan acknowledged: "while Kazakhstan's policy performance is definitely superior, economic performance is not so" (Alam & Banerji, 2000, p. 23). In 1998, an IMF research paper described Uzbekistan's performance as "puzzling" given its "hesitant and idiosyncratic reforms" (Zettelmeyer, 1998, p. 1). Still refusing to accept the success of Uzbekistan's so-called "idiosyncratic approach to reforms", the IMF researcher contented, without any convincing counter-factual evidence, "Uzbekistan could have done better by embarking on more decisive structural reforms from the beginning" (Zettelmeyer, 1998, p. 11).

The market reforms in the transition economies were categorised by Yordan Georgiev et al. (2017) into three sequences. First generation (market-enabling) reforms consisted of small-scale privatisation and liberalisation of prices, interest rates and international trade. Second generation (market- deepening) reforms covered large-scale privatisation and establishing the main underpinnings of a commercial banking sector and capital markets. Lastly, the third generation (market-sustaining) reforms to build economic institutions underpinning corporate governance and enterprise restructuring, competition policy, property rights and contract enforcement as well as the framework for regulated sectors and public–private partnerships in infrastructure. The last ones were implemented later with greater variation across countries, and they remain largely incomplete in many countries.

In Central Asia, the reforms stalled around the time of 1998 Russian rubble crisis and with the beginning of resource boom in 1999 (Batsaikhan & Dabrowski, 2017; Pomfret, 2021). According to the European Bank for Reconstruction and Development (EBRD) transition indicators for Central Asian countries, virtually all improvements occurred before 1999 and the indicators changed little in the following decade. These transition indicators track annual progress in the areas of large-scale privatisation, corporate governance and enterprise restructuring, small-scale privatisation, price liberalisation, trade liberalisation and competition policy.

Early reformers, Kyrgyzstan and Kazakhstan started liberalisation reforms in 1994–1995. Tajikistan started market-oriented reform a few years later, after the end of its civil war (1997). Turkmenistan and Uzbekistan resisted market transformation for much longer and retained many of the instruments of a command economy. Tajikistan represents an intermediary case (Batsaikhan & Dabrowski, 2017). However, in retrospect, it seems that, rapid economic liberalisation did not pay off: gradual reformers, Turkmenistan and Uzbekistan, (labelled procrastinators at the time) performed better than the champions of big-bang liberalisation. The quickest recovery was in Uzbekistan, it took about a decade to reach the pre-crisis level of GDP and, since then, the country's long-term growth trajectory has been the most consistent and robust.

The transition crisis is best described by the contractions of the economy. In Central Asia, it took more than a decade for the GDP to recover to the pre-crisis level (Fig. 6.1). Johannes Linn (2004) claimed that the disintegration of the previously unified economic space was a major factor explaining the economic collapse of the transition countries. After the dissolution of the Soviet Union, many industrial enterprises in Central Asia lost their previous markets and were unable to compete under the new market conditions, leading to deindustrialisation in the post-Soviet era (Batsaikhan & Dabrowski, 2017).

As highlighted earlier, Uzbekistan is the first former Soviet Union (FSU) country to restore its GDP to the pre-independence level (Bendini, 2013), and to reach its pre-independence industrial production level in the late 1990s, whereas none of the other FSU economies managed to do so (Islamov, 1998). Vladimir Popov and Anis Chowdhury (2016) claim that Uzbekistan is an economic success story in the post-Soviet space. Its initial transition-stage recession was very mild as compared to other countries of the former Soviet Union: its GDP more than doubled

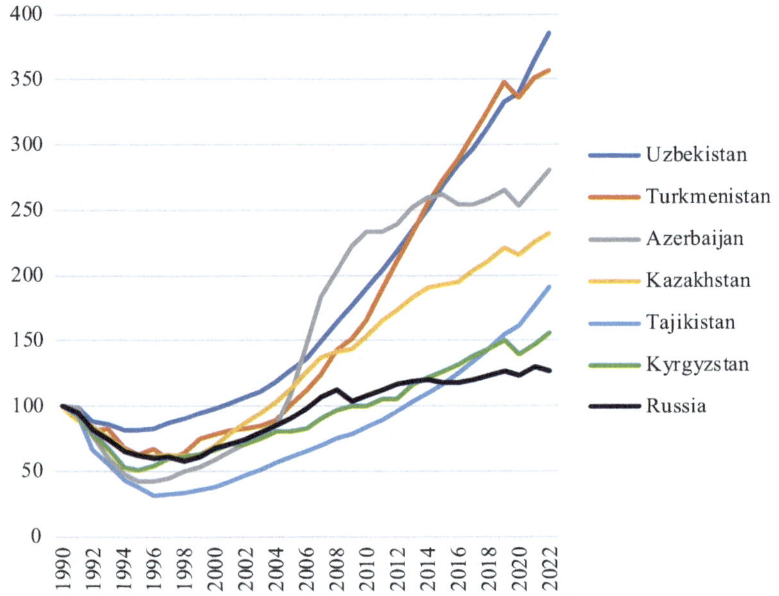

Fig. 6.1 Real GDP change in economies of the Central Asian LLDCs (1990 = 100). *Source*: World Bank online database

in 1989–2012, a better result than even in Central European countries; its life expectancy did not fall as it did in other former Soviet republics in the 1990s. In 2009 during the economic recession, only Kazakhstan and Azerbaijan registered higher economic growth rates than that of Uzbekistan, whereas most post-communist countries experienced economic contractions.

Among the six transition countries, Tajikistan and Kyrgyzstan were the worst performers. They were the poorest among the former Soviet Republics, and experienced the deepest transition crises with the slowest recovery. More than three decades after the transition, their per capita GDP (according to PPP measure) barely increased, while other Central Asian economies have progressed (Fig. 6.2). Tajikistan was a special case as the country descended into civil war following the transition. The war killed tens of thousands people and displaced a million inhabitants in the first year after independence. In 1996, Tajikistan's GDP was less than one-third of the 1990 level. The country returned to the 1990 GDP level only in 2013, more than two decades after its independence and transition journey.

Kyrgyzstan had progressed farthest with economic reforms, was the first Central Asian republic to adopt an independent currency and the first among them to join the World Trade Organization (WTO). However, its recovery lagged behind all other Central Asian transition economies, except Tajikistan until very recently. The relatively better economic performances of the other four transition countries are largely attributed to resource endowment: oil and gas in Azerbaijan, Kazakhstan and Turkmenistan, and oil, gas and cotton in Uzbekistan. As noted earlier, the best performer among the Central Asian transition countries has been Uzbekistan attributed to its gradual approach to reforms. It is not the best endowed country with natural resources, yet has managed to re-industrialise, with the State playing a critical role often discredited by the neo-liberal donor community and international financial institutions as idiosyncratic.

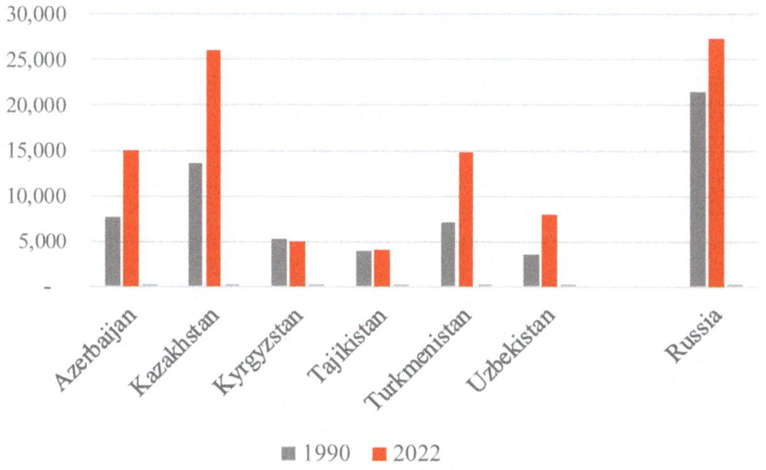

Fig. 6.2 GDP per capita 1990 and 2022, PPP (constant 2017 international $). *Source*: World Bank online database

Growth and Structural Changes

For more than three decades after independence, the Central Asian transition countries have had varied growth experiences—crises in the first half of the 1990s, followed by varied recovery according to each county paths. The long-term real GDP growth as presented in Table 6.1 confirms the best growth trajectory of Uzbekistan, the most populous country in Central Asia. The magnitude of economic contraction during the transition crisis was the mildest; the country recorded the quickest recovery returning to the pre-crisis GDP level; and has managed to grow the economy at consistently higher rates in the long-term.

As revealed in Fig. 6.1 and Table 6.1, the next best performing country in terms of the long-term GDP trajectory is Turkmenistan, the least populous country in the region. The country has been regarded as a slow reformer; and the most reluctant country to market liberalisation in Central Asia. At independence, the country's economy was dominated by two products: cotton and natural gas. By selling their cotton on the world markets, like Uzbekistan, the country benefitted from the buoyant world cotton prices until 1996. With natural gas endowment, the country benefitted from the resource boom during 2000–2014. Apart from cotton and gas exports, Turkmenistan remained the most closed and the least reformed country in the region (Pomfret, 2019).

Table 6.2 presents trends in GDP shares of the primary (agriculture, forestry and fishing), secondary (manufacturing), and services sectors since 1990. The general decline in the role of the primary sector in the economy since 1990 is observable. In most countries, the decline is very dramatic, for example in Azerbaijan (from 27 to 5%), Kazakhstan (from 23 to 5%), and Turkmenistan (from 33 to 12%). All three are resource-rich and resource dependent countries. In fact, they are the richest in Central Asia. Kazakhstan, the richest country in the region, is the largest oil producer in Central Asia and a major gas producer. Azerbaijan is also rich in oil and one of the birthplaces of the oil industry in the nineteenth century (Yergin, 1991), while Turkmenistan is endowed with natural gas. The sector did help in easing the pressure during the transition in the 1990s. However, the contribution of the resource sector in the three countries has been very volatile (Fig. 6.3). The resource boom during 2000–2014, covering the second decade after the transition, had somehow provided less incentives for the diversification of their economies away from the resource sector.

Table 6.1 Real GDP growth, per capita GDP and population

	Real GDP growth (%)								*GDP per capita (current US$)*	*Population*
	1991–95	*1996–2000*	*2001–05*	*2006–10*	*2011–15*	*2016–20*	*2021*	*2022*	*2022*	*2022*
Azerbaijan	− 15.6	7.1	13.4	16.9	2.4	− 0.6	5.6	4.6	7762	10,141,756
Kazakhstan	− 9.3	2.6	10.4	6.3	4.7	2.3	4.3	3.2	11,492	19,621,972
Kyrgyzstan	− 12.6	5.6	3.8	4.5	4.9	2.1	5.5	6.3	1655	6,974,900
Tajikistan	− 17.2	0.5	9.7	6.6	7.0	6.7	9.4	8.0	1054	9,952,787
Turkmenistan	− 8.5	4.9	5.2	10.4	10.6	4.4	4.5	1.7	8793	6,430,770
Uzbekistan	− 4.0	3.9	5.4	8.3	7.2	4.8	7.4	5.7	2255	35,648,100
Russia	− 9.0	1.7	6.1	3.7	1.8	0.9	5.6	− 2.1	15,271	144,236,933

Source: World Bank online database

Table 6.2 Sectoral composition of GDP (%), 1990, 2000, 2010, 2022

	1990	*2000*	*2010*	*2022*
Agriculture				
Azerbaijan	26.5	16.1	5.5	4.8
Kazakhstan	23.3 (1992)	8.1	4.5	5.2
Kyrgyzstan	32.7	34.2	17.4	10.9
Tajikistan	33.3	25.1	19.6	22.4 (2021)
Turkmenistan	33.3	22.5	11.3	11.7 (2021)
Uzbekistan	33.1	30.1	26.9	23.5
Russia	15.5	5.8	3.3	3.9
Manufacturing				
Azerbaijan	17.6	5.3	4.7	5.0
Kazakhstan	14.6 (1995)	16.5	11.3	13.4
Kyrgyzstan	26.4	18.1	16.9	11.3
Tajikistan	24.8	19.6 (1999)	9.7 (2011)	15.0 (2021)
Turkmenistan	38.2 (1995)	9.8		
Uzbekistan			10.2	19.1
Russia			12.8	12.8
Services				
Azerbaijan	34.8	35.8	27.9	32.2
Kazakhstan	25.1 (1992)	48.4	51.7	52.6
Kyrgyzstan	30.6	30.0	49.3	52.4
Tajikistan	29.1	31.5	45.1	33.4(2021)
Turkmenistan	36.7	28.9	28.1	51.1 (2021)
Uzbekistan	34.6	37.2	39.9	35.5 (2021)
Russia	32.6	49.7	53.1	54.0

Source: World Bank online database

In general, the declining role of primary commodity (agriculture) has not been followed by the expansion of the more modern, productive and dynamic manufacturing sector; but was compensated by the general increase in the service sector's contribution. In most cases, manufacturing's contributions to GDP have declined, Uzbekistan being an exception. This indicates a process of rather pre-mature deindustrialisation that is common in the developing world; thus, making the countries more dependent of natural resources (re-primarisation). Resource dependent countries need to diversify their economies for the sustainability of development and to deal with the volatility of resource rents. These countries need to re-industrialise and develop high value service sector. At the same time, the declining shares in agriculture value added were not followed by commensurate magnitudes of the decline in agriculture employment shares indicating low productivity in the sector (Table 6.3). In this case, structural transformation will also require revitalisation of the agriculture sector (Fig. 6.3).

Azerbaijan, which experienced a secular decline in the share of manufacturing from 22% in 1992 to 5% in 2007 and staying around that level up until now, offers an interesting case study of how the big-bang market reforms could possibly go wrong in Central Asian transition countries. Azerbaijan's industrial output index dropped sharply from 100 in 1989 to 26.3 in 1996. Since the industrial output index (in real terms) includes at least part of the hydrocarbon sector itself, the real decline in the non-oil manufacturing sector was even greater than what the index shows. As noted earlier, Azerbaijan was the most industrialised among the Central Asian republics during the Soviet era, with industry accounting for 51% of the Net Material Product (NMP) (as of 1992). More than 70% of the

Table 6.3 Sectoral employment 1991, 2000, 2010, 2022

	1991	*2000*	*2010*	*2022*
Agriculture				
Azerbaijan	43.9	41.0	38.2	35.6
Kazakhstan	36.7	36.1	28.3	12.9
Kyrgyz Republic	35.5	53.1	34.4	24.6
Tajikistan	54.9	60.1	52.4	43.5
Turkmenistan	35.9	35.2	30.3	22.7
Uzbekistan	41.4	37.7	26.8	25.9
Industry				
Azerbaijan	23.0	10.9	13.7	14.9
Kazakhstan	18.2	16.3	18.7	21.5
Kyrgyz Republic	26.5	10.5	21.8	24.6
Tajikistan	21.6	15.6	15.9	20.8
Turkmenistan	30.6	28.1	29.5	33.7
Uzbekistan	21.0	19.9	22.7	24.2
Services				
Azerbaijan	33.2	48.1	48.1	49.5
Kazakhstan	45.1	47.6	53.0	65.6
Kyrgyz Republic	38.0	36.5	43.9	50.9
Tajikistan	23.5	24.3	31.7	35.7
Turkmenistan	33.4	36.6	40.2	43.6
Uzbekistan	37.6	42.4	50.5	49.9

Source: World Bank online database

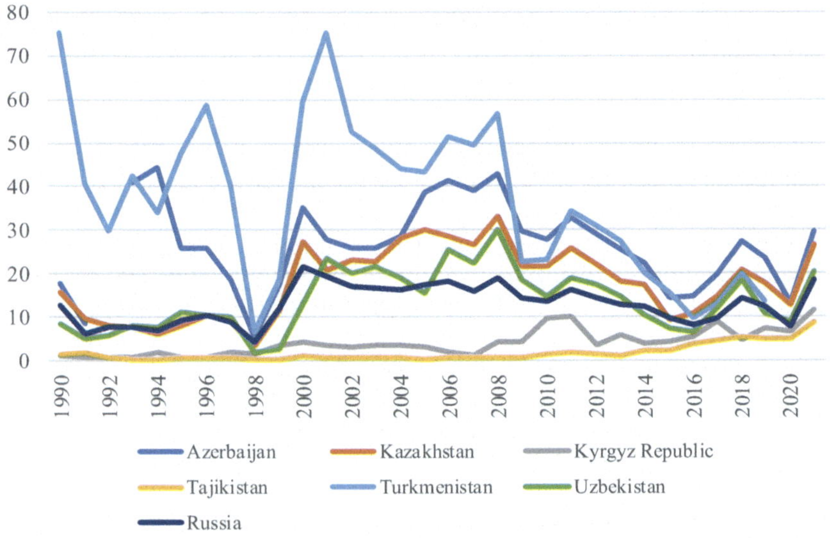

Fig. 6.3 Natural resource rents (% GDP), 1990–2021. *Source*: World Bank online database

equipment used in oil and gas industry, 100% of air conditioners, 100% of electronics (radio and transistor), and 4.5% of all canned food were produced in Azerbaijan during the Soviet era (Chowdhury, 2018).

As noted earlier, with the breakup of the USSR, these industries not only lost captive markets, but also subsidies from Moscow. Thus, faced with competition after the opening up, they collapsed. The mass voucher scheme of privatisation launched in 1997 for finding extra revenue to fill the gap left by earlier tax shortfalls in the government budget also did not help. The new private owners chose to strip off the factories instead of investing in improving their productivity and efficiency.

The declining shares of manufacturing in GDP and of non-oil industries in the industrial output imply that Azerbaijan continued to deindustrialise, despite government's attempt to diversify the economy. The most common explanation for the failure to diversify has been the real appreciation of the currency due to the influx of foreign currencies associated with the oil and gas sector, referred to as the Dutch disease syndrome. The real appreciation makes the tradable sector such as agriculture and manufacturing uncompetitive. Studies have also found that current government spending tends to rise when oil prices rise, and this considerable pro-cyclicality adversely affected the industrial structure or industrial diversification, by pushing up wages and demand in non-tradable sector, such as construction (Chowdhury, 2018).

Contrary to Azerbaijan, Uzbekistan, which recorded the fastest recovery from the transition crisis in Central Asia, offers the case study of the success of a gradualist approach to reforms and the critical role of the State. Not only the country suffered mildest recession and recovered faster than others, it also managed to re-industrialise. Uzbekistan has the highest manufacturing share in GDP in the region and displays an increasing trend in recent years (Table 6.2). The country also has the highest share of medium and high-tech manufacturing value added (MVA) in total MVA (Fig. 6.4). It also was able to upgrade its structure of industrial output; the share of machinery, equipment and chemicals increased at the expense of light industry (Popov & Chowdhury, 2016).

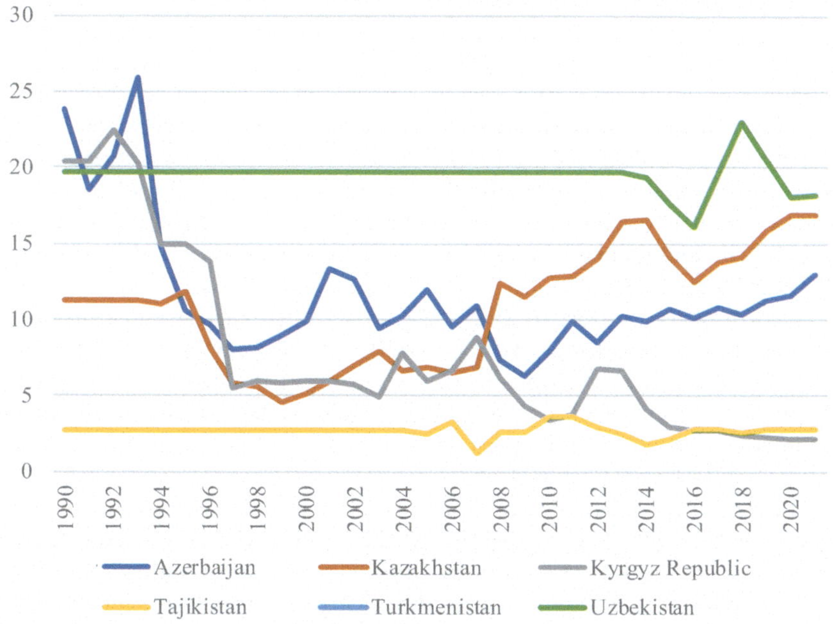

Fig. 6.4 Medium and high-tech manufacturing value added, MVA (% MVA), 1990–2021. *Source*: World Bank online database

Other post-Soviet economies not only experienced the decline of light industry, but also it happened together with the decline of machine building that created space for the expansion of fuel, energy, steel and non-ferrous metals. During the Soviet era, in a centrally planned economy, resource rent was reallocated from resource industries and to secondary manufacturing through the pricing mechanism; prices for commodities and low processed goods were set at levels below the world market, whereas prices for finished goods were established at an artificially high level. Once prices were allowed to be determined by the market after the deregulation in 1992, they got closer to the world levels and terms of trade for resource industries improved, while deteriorated for the secondary manufacturing. However, that did not happen in Uzbekistan due to its gradualist approach and continued state support for manufacturing.

After independence, an automobile industry was created in Uzbekistan from the ground up. Car production was supported by the government and the Korean auto company Daewoo. After Daewoo declared bankruptcy, US General Motors became the government's partner. The government also bought a stake in Turkey's Koc in SamKochAvto, a producer of small buses and lorries. Afterwards, it signed an agreement with Isuzu Motors of Japan to produce Isuzu buses and lorries. In 2014, Uzbekistan produced 250,000 cars and nearly a quarter were exported. In 2013, Uzbekistan sold over 60,000 cars to Russia and 33,000 to Kazakhstan. In 2011, a joint venture of State Auto Company and General Motors, the engine plant in Tashkent, became operational with a capacity of 360,000 engines a year.

According to a report in 2023, Uzbekistan plans to produce up to 1 million units of vehicles per year by 2030. The country planned to invest US$1 billion in the development of the automotive industry, hoping that car production in Uzbekistan would grow from 300,000 to 500,000 over the next two years. With the participation of 13 companies, an automobile cluster would be created in Asaka.[1]

However, Uzbekistan's car industry plan is met with some scepticism. For example, Franco Galdini (2023) argues that Uzbekistan's car industry is a "backward" form of import substitution industrialisation (ISI) in countries integrated into the global economy as exporters of

[1] https://www.uzdaily.com/en/post/81533 (accessed 15/05/2024).

primary commodities. He contends that all manufacturing capitals in the country could stay profitable only via rent subsidisation, the main reason for leading multinational corporations (MNCs) to invest in it.

In recent years, the second round of Uzbekistan's industrial policy focused on heavy chemicals: Shurtan Gas Chemical Complex and the planned production of synthetic liquid fuels based on purified methane together with South African "Sasol" and Malaysian "Petronas"; liquefied natural gas production at Mubarek gas processing plant; Dehkonobod Potash Fertilizer Plant; and Ustyurt gas chemical complex at Surgil deposit. The deepening of the manufacturing sector in Uzbekistan is well reflected by the share of medium and high-tech manufacturing value added (MVA) in the overall MVA, which is the highest in the region (Fig. 6.4).

Due to the climate factors, Central Asia historically has been very favourable for cotton production. Most of the cotton grown in the Soviet Union came from Central Asia, with half of it being produced in the Uzbek Soviet Socialist Republic alone. After the collapse of the Soviet Union in 1991, an independent Uzbekistan diverted cotton production to international markets to accrue hard currency. The country was benefited from the buoyant cotton price in the mid-1990s helping the country during the transition crisis. Cotton production remained the country's main factor endowment for its participation in the international division of labour (Galdini, 2023). Later, Uzbekistan started down-streaming cotton production into the cotton industry. The Government has dedicated significant resources into increasing cotton processing and textile manufacturing, with the aim of capturing more value added though technological upgrading.

The previously state-controlled and regulated cotton supply chain started to undergo significant liberalisation and privatisation reforms in 2017. The cotton cluster system was introduced, where the government allocates a defined geographical area to a private investor who in return commits to growing cotton and to establishing processing facilities in that area. In 2018, the government established 13 cotton clusters, and the number reached 134 by 2022. The clusters are aimed at reducing the role of the government in cotton production, creating jobs and positioning the country as an exporter of textiles and garments rather than raw cotton (Babadjanova & Petric, 2023). According to Government statistics, since 2017, cotton processing has increased from 40% of cotton crop in 2017, to 100% in 2022. In September 2022, the President announced that the quota system for famers had been abolished, and cotton was no longer exported, and was instead processed domestically.[2]

Uzbekistan has clearly pursued an active industrial policy. Since independence, the country encouraged and carried out three important structural shifts in its economy. First, it had previously relied heavily on the monoculture of cotton; but in the 1990s it tried to reduce this heavy reliance on the production and export of cotton. In the meantime, it tried to achieve self-sufficiency in food by increasing grain production. Second, it pursued self-sufficiency in energy and went further, to become a net fuel exporter. Third, it tried to increase the share of industry in GDP and that of machinery and equipment in both total industrial outputs and exports (Popov & Chowdhury, 2016). The government has taken several industrial policy measures, including tax and financial incentives, state orders, policy selectively welcoming foreign direct investment, import protection and export promotion and exchange rate management (Eun & Mah, 2019).

Challenges of Structural Transformation

As structural transformation is synonymous to the process of development itself, the region has been facing a set of challenges emanating from the basic features of the economies. *First* is related to the systemic transition from centrally controlled and planned economy to market economy in independent entities. As has been explained earlier, all Central Asian countries experienced transition crises in varying degrees. The process of the transition was more or less completed in the first decade after their independences with different trajectories of market liberalisation from the most rapidly liberalising Kyrgyzstan to the least reforming Turkmenistan (Pomfret, 2012). Uzbekistan has been labelled as a gradual reformer and regarded as the best performer. Energy exporters (Kazakhstan, Turkmenistan and Azerbaijan) benefited from the shift towards world prices, but at the beginning, the gains were limited by the dependence on Russian pipelines.

Second is the spatial transition from one entity under USSR into six independent economies. This poses the challenge of maintaining

[2] https://kun.uz/en/news/2022/09/22/uzbekistan-is-no-longer-exporting-gas-and-cotton-shavkat-mirziyoyev (accessed 15/05/2024).

economic integration and avoiding conflict between countries. The dissolution of the Soviet Union removed the regional production arrangements, regional economic allocation and inter-regional complementarity previously imposed by the super structure. Although the previous arrangement was not perfect, the currently six independent economies were coordinated as one entity making the economic integration worked. The integration had two meanings: integration among themselves and integration with the rest of the Soviet Union. The dissolution of the union meant that those integrations were dramatically ruptured. Each country would have to navigate their own economies in relations to their neighbouring countries and international markets. The ideal scenario for them would have been to maintain their Soviet era integration among themselves, and the links with other former Soviets republics, while cultivating new economic links with other neighbouring countries, especially China and South Asian countries.

The spatial transition from one entity into six independence countries removed the regional economic integration and complementarity between the countries—among themselves and with the other former Soviet Republics. Before independence, these countries were export-oriented economies within the sphere of the Soviet Union with a free flow of goods and services as well as capital and labour. Such flows of inter-regional trades, finance and labour were significantly reduced due to the increasingly strict border-crossing procedures complicated with petty corruptions by relevant customs officials, increasing the costs for international trade and finance.

While intra-regional trade between Central Asian countries grew five-fold during 2000–2008, the share of intra-regional trade in Central Asia relative to the region's overall trade dropped dramatically after independence whereas it increased in other parts of Asia (Linn, 2012). No doubt that more economic integration would have economic benefits; however, this is subject to cooperation at the political realm among those countries. All the leaders of the newly independent Central Asia countries highly value their sovereignty, while some countries compete with each other for control of resources, especially water and energy as in Tajikistan and Uzbekistan, and for supremacy in regional leadership as in Kazakhstan and Uzbekistan, or prefer to operate in strict neutrality to the point of isolation, as in Turkmenistan (Olcott, 2011).

Over one decade and a half after independence region experienced economic disintegration (Pomfret, 2019), while reports by UNDP

(2005) and ADB (2006) highlighted the cost of regional economic disintegration and potential benefit from regional economic cooperation. Despite many attempts to promote regional economic cooperation, so far, there has been no single regional cooperation framework effectively in place in Central Asia and based in the region as in the case of the Association of Southeast Asian Nations (ASEAN). Several Central Asian countries have been involved in regional cooperations initiated and based outside the region, such as the China-led Shanghai Cooperation Organisation (SCO) and The Eurasian Economic Union (EEU), in which Russia has played a leading role.

The spatial disintegration has also resulted in economic and resource conflicts among those countries. For example, since independence, water has been at the centre of competition and controversy among the downstream countries (Kazakhstan, Uzbekistan and Turkmenistan) and the upstream countries (Kyrgyzstan and Tajikistan). While the downstream countries require more water for their agriculture and domestic needs, the impoverished upstream countries are attempting resource nationalism to accrue benefits using the precious waters (Pradhan, 2022). The spatial disintegration is compounded by the landlockedness nature of their geography. In the past this was not an issue; but after independence, this has become another delicate problem. Such spatial disintegration and landlockedness would require institutionalised regional cooperation that will be critical for managing regional conflicts.

The three-decade long Tajikistan-Kyrgyzstan border conflict will require the presence of regional cooperation entity. Moreover, without a strong regional cooperation among Central Asian countries themselves, they cannot deal with two most important regional powers next to them: Russia and China. They have become increasingly entangled by Russia's coercive diplomacy and China's growing economic presence in the region. Yet despite Russia's coercion, Central Asian countries are still benefiting from economic growth fuelled by increased Russian trade, migration and remittances, demonstrating the region's delicate relationships with global powers (Arduino, 2024). Following Russia's invasion of Ukraine, the Republics have benefitted economically from redirected trade and have striven to reduce dependence on Russia, focusing on East–West links with China, Turkey and the European Union (Pomfret, 2023).

The systemic and spatial transitions have also political economy implications. Based on their survey of literature on research covering the early phase of the transition, David Henderson et al. (2008) concluded income inequality increased in Central Asian countries coinciding with the process of political and economic liberalisation. The trend of increasing inequality was caused by the following factors: (i) the starting point of low inequality in socialist countries was due to socialist egalitarian values, (ii) higher wage differential due to skill and education's premium in a market economy, (iii) the emergence of the private sector and (iv) the growing share of an unofficial or underground economy. Despite the paucity of data, now more than three decades since their independence, available data on Gini index indicate that inequalities did not rise as in the case of most developed as well as developing countries around the world (Popov, 2023). While the reliability of state-controlled data can be questionable, the falling inequality could be attributed to the legacy of the extensive system of social welfare inherited from the Soviet era which was not totally dismantled.

Nevertheless, the transition to market economy has seen privatisation of major state assets to be controlled by political power surrounding the presidents and in turn creating a kleptocratic class (Pomfret, 2021). The way the kleptocratic ruling class in Central Asia reaping the benefits of globalisation while denying civil liberties to their own populations is well documented by Alexander Cooley and John Heathershaw (2017). Three decades after independence, the entrenched kleptocracies will have to deal with younger generations aspiring for better governance and the opening of democratic spaces. The notion of democracy in Central Asia, however, is different from the commonly understood Western style ones. Rather than demanding free elections, political parties and independent parliament, social activism in Central Asia is more motivated by aspiring for transparent and accountable government, even if it is not fully democratic (Stronski & Zanca, 2019).

Martha Brill Olcott (2000) claimed, "the Central Asian region has been a disappointing one from the point of view of democracy-building."[3] A decade later, Jos Boonstra (2012) assessed that Central Asia showed the least inclination towards democratisation compared with the two other former Soviet regions of Eastern Europe and the South

[3] https://carnegieendowment.org/posts/2000/04/democracy-in-the-central-asian-republics?lang=en (accessed 15/05/2024).

Caucasus. The situation has not changed; in 2024 Freedom House classified all five Central Asian countries and Azerbaijan as "not free" pointing to the authoritarian nature of their governance.[4]

While the political transitions in the former Soviet republics were very much within the continuum of the Huntington's (1993) third wave of democratisation, democratic deficit has been an important feature of Central Asia as highlighted in Chapter 3. Prior to their independence, they had virtually no experience of any sort of democratic experiment as they were for centuries under the rule of the Tsarist Russian Empire and for seven decades under the Soviet Union. Assessing the situation, a decade after independence, John Glenn (2003, p. 124) concluded, "although each of the states within the Central Asia region have held elections so that we can speak of some sort of formal democracy having been established, substantive democracy within these states is either absent or falls short of the mark".

The emergence of these newly independent countries in Central Asia has also created a new geopolitical configuration, termed as the New Great Game due to the region's energy resource potential making them serve as a new battleground of sphere of influence among the present-day great powers of China, Russia and the US (Cooley, 2012; Rashid, 2002). A *New York Times* opinion article in 1996 wrote, "Central Asia has again emerged as a murky battleground among big powers engaged in an old and rough geopolitical game. Western experts believe that the largely untapped oil and natural gas riches of the Caspian Sea countries could make that region the Persian Gulf of the next century."[5]The initial Great Game refers the rivalry and strategic conflict between the nineteenth-century British and Tsarist Russian empires over influence in Central Asia that placed Afghanistan as a buffer zone.

Initially after independent, by default, Central Asian countries were within the sphere of influence of Russia given the legacy of the Soviet Union's physical and economic infrastructure. The US invasion of Afghanistan after the September 2001 terrorist attacks on the World Trade Centre in New York should also be seen within the lens of the New Great Game. The US needed Central Asia as a military base and

[4] See https://freedomhouse.org/explore-the-map?type=fiw&year=2024 (accessed 15/05/2024).

[5] https://www.nytimes.com/1996/01/02/opinion/the-new-great-game-in-asia.html (accessed 15/05/2024).

to provide supply supports for the war in Afghanistan. The US-led war against terrorism gave momentum to the USA and Europe (France, Germany and Britain) to actively enhance their ties with Central Asia with an eye on the energy resources. In the new millennium, China has emerged as a new global power challenging the dominance of the US since the end of the Cold War.

With the withdrawal of the US from Afghanistan and declining influence of Russia, this has left China as the most dominant global player in Central Asia, especially since the launch of Belt and Road Initiative (BRI) as China's ambition for global influence (Pradhan, 2018). Key to China's interest is energy. The existing oil and gas pipelines to Russia have been complemented by the development of multiple new pipelines connecting Central Asian countries and China. These developments have been welcomed by Central Asian countries as the new pipelines have offered them alternatives for accessing global energy markets. Central Asian countries have also initiated gas pipeline connections with their southern neighbours: Iran, Afghanistan, Pakistan and India (Tang & Joldybayeva, 2023).

While trade and energy connections with the outside world are important, economic integration and complementarity among Central Asian countries as they used to be during the Soviet era remain the most important challenge. Within the context of currently independent and sovereign countries, economic integration will collectively strengthen their immediate needs for trade facilitation and economic complementarity among one another as immediate neighbours. The most recent initiative on this is the launch of B5 + 1 process to create a unified Central Asian market. Facilitated by the US, the inaugural B5 + 1 forum on 14 March 2024 in Almaty, Kazakhstan, brought together Central Asian government officials, regional business leaders and entrepreneurs.[6] The forum calls for the five countries—Kazakhstan, Kyrgyzstan, Tajikistan, Turkmenistan and Uzbekistan—to take the lead in fostering regional free trade and the diversification of export routes.[7] Such initiative can also be seen as the latest US diplomatic move to balance the much more entrenched influence of China and Russia in the region.

[6] https://eurasianet.org/united-states-launches-initiative-to-foster-central-asian-connectivity (accessed 15/05/2024).

[7] https://eurasianet.org/central-asian-states-easing-trade-barriers (accessed 15/05/2024).

Kazakhstan has been an important regional player with its unique poisoning. Glenn Diesen (2020) suggests, "Kazakhstan has taken a very different trajectory to most other former Soviet Republics. Rather than aligning with Western countries and closing opportunities for trade and cooperation with Russia, it has taken an open approach to cooperation with Russia, China, Middle-Eastern countries and the US/EU. This 'multi-vector' approach has afforded Kazakhstan strong economic growth while maintaining harmonious relations between the ethnic Kazakhs and Russians".

The Way Forward

The six transition economies covered in this chapter have a unique position with regard to the issue of structural transformation presented in this book. They are landlocked, emanating from the collapse of the Soviet Union, and undergoing systemic transition from a centrally planned economy to a market economy. They are resource-rich and have experienced deep economic crises that followed the transition. The enduring lesson that we learn from the transition experiences of these countries is that there is no "one-size-fits-all" approach to reforms. Sequencing and pace are vitally important. Success also depends on compensating the affected people as well as regions. The way forward for Central Asian transition economies is about regional economic re-integration, regional cooperation and democratic institutions building.

While these countries were an integrated economy under the Soviet Union and had an industrial base, after independence, they are now separate entities and deindustrialised to become resource dependent (re-primarisation). As highlighted earlier, the economic disintegration was a major factor for the economic collapse of the transition economies. While political disintegration is inevitable as they are now separate and sovereign political entities, they need to develop meaningful institution of *regional economic re-integration*. This becomes a key factor to re-create economic complementarities among them. Thus, structural transformation of these Central Asian economies is about moving from resource dependence to manufacturing and high value services. To do so, they need to re-industrialise through some forms of industrial policy within the realm of regional economic re-integration for complementarity and economics of scale.

Regional cooperation is also critical for managing conflicts, fostering regional economic integration, and developing complementarity among them. Regional cooperation is needed for navigating geopolitical rivalry and consolidating the region's position vis-à-vis two most important regional powers and their immediate neighbours: China and Russia. As mentioned earlier, Kazakhstan has provided a good example of "multi-vector" approach in maintaining a balance position among strategic global players of Russia, China, the EU and the US. Several new initiatives for regional cooperation have been tried, but none of them have reached sufficiently meaningful outcomes.

As Richard Pomfret (2023) noted, "The longer-term prospect is for Central Asia to return to its historic role as a Eurasian crossroads after 150 years of north–south orientation under Russian hegemony. While the north–south links remain, China, Turkiye and the EU actively collaborated to promote east–west links in 2023. Subject to political developments, the door is open to revitalise southern links to Afghanistan, Iran and Pakistan".

Frederick Starr (2013) in his *Lost Enlightenment: Central Asia's Golden Age from the Arab Conquest to Tamerlane*, reminded us that over a period of about 500 years, from 750 A.D. to 1250 A.D., Central Asia produced some of the world's finest minds and its workshops produced exquisite goods that were recognised and traded across Europe and Asia. As we have argued in previous chapters innovations require experimentations without fear and prejudice. It is highly unlikely that Central Asia can regain its former glory without political reform or genuine democratisation that does not penalise dissent.

Therefore, the region will need to develop *democratic institutions* for managing conflicts and fostering innovation to facilitate a transition to high value added manufacturing and service sectors. Otherwise, they are likely to get stuck at the "factor driven" phase of economic growth as has largely characterised their post-transition economic trajectories rather than upgraded into "innovation-driven" growth as postulated by Michael Porter (1990). Failure to democratise may lead to a "middle-income trap" as seen in some Southeast Asian countries.

References

ADB. (2006). *Central Asia: Increasing gains from trade through regional cooperation in trade policy, transport, and customs transit*. Asian Development Bank.

Alam, A., & Arup, B. (2000), Uzbekistan and Kazakhstan: A Tale of Two Transition Paths? *World Bank Policy Research Working Paper*, 2472

Arduino, A. (2024). Central Asia caught in a geopolitical tug of war. *East Asia Forum*, 26 February.

Babadjanova, J., & Martin, P. (2023). Uzbekistan's cotton clusters in the context of the industrial policy debate. *Eurasian Geography and Economics*. https://doi.org/10.1080/15387216.2023.2267093

Batsaikhan, U., & Marek, D. (2017). Central Asia—Twenty-five years after the breakup of the USSR. *Russian Journal of Economics, 3*, 296–320.

Bendini, R. (2013). Uzbekistan: Selected trade and economic issues. *Policy Briefing*, Brussels: European Union.

Boonstra, J. (2012). Democracy in Central Asia: Sowing in unfertile fields? *EUCAM Policy Brief* No. 23.

Chowdhury, A. (2018). *Azerbaijan: Policy options for sustainable development goals (SDGs)*. Report for UNDP Azerbaijan.

Cooley, A. A. (2012). *Great games, local rules: The new great power contest in Central Asia*. Oxford University Press.

Cooley, A. A., & John, H. (2017). *Dictators without borders: Power and money in Central Asia*. Yale University Press.

Diesen, G. (2020). Kazakhstan: Imagining Globalisation 2.0. *The Astana Times*, 8 May, https://astanatimes.com/2020/05/kazakhstan-imagining-globalisation-2-0/ (accessed 17/05/2024).

Eun Young, B., & Jai, S. M. (2019). The role of industrial policy in the economic development of Uzbekistan. *Post-Communist Economies, 31*(2), 240–257.

Galdini, F. (2023). Backward' industrialisation in resource-rich countries: The car industry in Uzbekistan. *Competition & Change, 27*(3), 429–660.

Georgiev, Y., Piroska N. -M. & Alexander, P. (2017). Structural reform and productivity growth in Emerging Europe and Central Asia. *ADB Economics Working Paper* no 523. Manila: Asian Development Bank.

Gharleghi, B., & Vladimir P. (2018). *Changes in the Geographical Structure of Trade in Central Asia: Real Flows in the 1989–2016 Period Versus Gravity Model Predictions*. MPRA Paper 89041. https://mpra.ub.uni-muenchen.de/89041/ (Accessed 27/04/2024).

Glenn, J. (2003). The economic transition in Central Asia: Implications for democracy. *Democratization, 10*(3), 124–147.

Henderson, D., Robert, M., & Tamas, R. (2008). Did inequality increase in transition? An analysis of the transition countries of Eastern Europe and Central Asia. *Eastern European Economics, 46*(2), 28–49.

Huntington, S. P. (1991). *The Third Wave: Democratization in the Late Twentieth Century*. University of Oklahoma Press.

IMF, World Bank, OECD and EBRD. (1991). *A study of Soviet Economy*. OECD.

Islamov, B. (1998). Systematic transformation reforms in Uzbekistan and Economic. *The Mongolian Journal of International Affairs, 5*, 59–72.

Kalinovsky, A. M. (2022). Development in post-war Central Asia. In R. Isaacs & E. Marat (Eds.), *Routledge Handbook of Contemporary Central Asia*. Routledge.

Lewis, D. (2022). Varieties of authoritarianism in Central Asia. In R. Isaacs & E. Marat (Eds.), *Routledge Handbook of Contemporary Central Asia*. Routledge.

Linn, J. (2004). Economic (dis)integration matters: The Soviet collapse revisited. In *Paper for the conference Transition in the CIS: Achievements and Challenges, at the Academy for National Economy*, 13–14 September, Moscow. https://www.brookings.edu/wp-content/uploads/2016/06/200410linn.pdf (accessed 25/05/2024).

Linn, J. (2012). Central Asian regional integration and cooperation: Reality or mirage? In *Eurasian Integration Yearbook 2012* (pp. 96–117). Eurasian Development Bank: Almaty.

Luong, P. J. (Ed.). (2004). *The transformation of Central Asia: States and Societies from Soviet Rule to Independence*. Cornell University Press.

Mosello, B. (2008). Water in Central Asia: A prospect of conflict or co-operation? *Journal of Public and International Affairs, 19*(March), 151–174.

Olcott, M. B. (2011). Rivalry and competition in Central Asia. In W. Hermann & J. Linn (Eds.), *Central Asia and the Caucasus: At the Crossroads of Eurasia in the 21st Century*. Sage.

Omelicheva, M. (2015). *Democracy in Central Asia. Competing perspectives and alternative strategies*. University Press of Kentucky.

Orlowski, L. T. (1995). Direct transfers between the former Soviet Union central budget and the republics: Past evidence and current implications. *Economics of Planning, 28*, 59–73.

Pianciola, N., & Marianne, K. (2022). Collectivisation, Sedentarism and Famine in Central Asia. In R. Isaacs & E. Marat (Eds.), *Routledge Handbook of Contemporary Central Asia*. Routledge.

Pomfret, R. (2012). Central Asia after Two Decades of Independence. In Gerald Roland, *Economies in Transition: Long-run View*. Helsinki: UNU-WIDER and Palgrave

Pomfret, R. (2023). *Central Asia's gradual economic repositioning*. East Asia Forum, 27 December, https://eastasiaforum.org/2023/12/27/central-asias-gradual-economic-repositioning/ (accessed 25/05/2024)

Pomfret, R. (1995). *The Economies of Central Asia*. Princeton University Press.

Pomfret, R. (2019). *The Central Asian Economies in the Twenty-first Century*. Princeton University Press.

Pomfret, R. (2021). Central Asian economies: Thirty years after dissolution of the Soviet Union. *Comparative Economic Studies, 63*, 537–556.

Popov, V. (2007). Life cycle of the centrally planned economy: Why Soviet Growth Rates Peaked in the 1950s. In S. Estrin, G. W. Kolodko, & M. Uvalic (Eds.), *Transition and beyond studies in economic transition*. Palgrave Macmillan.

Popov, V. (2009). *Lessons from the transition economies putting the success stories of the postcommunist world into a broader perspective*. UNU-WIDER Research Paper No. 2009/15.

Popov, V., & Anis, C. (2016). What can Uzbekistan tell us about industrial policy that we did not already know? *DESA Working Paper* No. 147.

Popov, V. (2023). Recent experiences of successful economic policies: The case of Uzbekistan. In E. S. Reinert & I. Kvangraven (Eds.), *A modern guide to uneven economic development*. Edward Elgar.

Porter, M. (1990). *The competitive advantage of nations*. Free Press.

Pradhan, R. (2018). The rise of China in Central Asia: The new silk road diplomacy. *Fudan Journal of the Humanities and Social Sciences, 11*, 9–29.

Pradhan, R. (2022). Natural resources and violent conflicts: Water and energy in Kyrgyzstan. *Journal of Asian and African Studies, 57*(4), 650–666.

Rashid, A. (2002). *Taliban: Islam, oil and the new great game in Central Asia*. I. B. Tauris.

Starr, F. (2013). *Lost Enlightenment: Central Asia's Golden Age from the Arab Conquest to Tamerlane*. Princeton University Press.

Stronski, P., & Russel, Z. (2019). *Societal change afoot in Central Asia*. Carnegie Endowment for International Peace.

Tang, W., & Elmira, J. (2023). Pipelines and power lines: China, infrastructure and the geopolitical (re)construction of Central Asia. *Geopolitics, 28*(4), 1506–1534.

UNDP. (2005). *Central Asia Human Development Report. Bringing Down Barriers: Regional Cooperation for Human Development and Human Security*. New York: UNDP.

World Bank. (1993). *Uzbekistan: An Agenda for Economic Reform*. The World Bank.

Yergin, D. (1991). *The prize: The epic quest for oil, money & power*. Simon & Schuster.

Zettelmeyer, J. (1998), The Uzbek growth puzzle, *IMF Working Paper*, WP/98/133, September.

CHAPTER 7

Asia–Pacific SIDS: The Tyranny of Geography

> "Indeed, Pacific small island developing States, due to their small nevertheless diverse populations, limited landmass and small economies, as well as geographic locations and remoteness from international markets, are among the most vulnerable countries in the world. They are exposed to a variety of external shocks and internal predicaments that can be classified as economic, environmental, social and political." (Andrzej Bolesta, 2020, p. 27)

The Small Island Developing States (SIDS) are a group of countries facing common social, economic and environmental challenges (UNCTAD, 2014). Small land areas and population size are the most obvious challenges. As the domestic market based is small, these countries are also vulnerability to external market volatilities, such as commodity price fluctuations and hence their economic growth rates are relatively low (Stewart, 2006). In other words, economics of scale and external shocks hamper SIDS' economic structural transformation and poverty reduction.

The SIDS are also challenged by climate change and extreme weather conditions. Climate-related disasters such as severe storms (or cyclones), floods and drought have almost doubled since the turn of the twenty-first century, and they affect SIDS like no other countries (UN-DESA, 2023). SIDS are often described as being on the "frontlines of climate change", as "hot spots of climate change", or as being "canaries in the coalmine"

A. Chowdhury et al., *Structural Transformations as Developing Africa, Asia, and the Pacific*, https://doi.org/10.1007/978-981-97-9092-0_7

(Thomas et al., 2020). Adelle Thomas April Baptiste, Rosanne Martyr-Koller, Patrick Pringle and Kevon Rhiney (2020) reviewed a large body of literature on the patterns of climate change-related hazards, vulnerability and exposure in SIDS and detailed their impacts.

Naturally, the SIDS are highly dependent on aid—for both their developmental aspirations and withstanding extreme climate change vulnerabilities as well as external shocks. Yet, ironically SIDS receive very little Official Development Assistance (ODA) as a share of total ODA. While Pacific SIDS are more aid-dependent, aid received by them amounted to about 10.8% of their Gross National Income (GNI) during 2013–2018 (UN-OHRLLS, 2024). Tonga, Samoa, Vanuatu and Solomon Islands are most aid-dependent with aid/GNI ratio ranging from around 19% (Tonga) to approximately 13.5% (Solomon Islands) during 2017–2019 (Wilkins, 2023).

ESCAP data show that aid flows to Pacific SIDS have been declining in recent years. In 2014, the total amount of aid received by Pacific SIDS was US$2.6 billion. By 2023, this amount has fallen to US$1.9 billion (Basu, 2024). The data also show that the decline in aid flows has been most pronounced for the smallest and most remote Pacific SIDS. Moreover, the ODA flows are not stable or predictable—often responding to crises—while the variability of ODA flows across the countries have increased over the decades. Such aid volatility or unpredictability does not allow these highly aid-dependent countries to undertake long-term development projects. Depending on per capita income levels, the Asia–Pacific SIDS require substantial external assistance to adapt to climate change as well as for loss and damage. However, with the highest need for climate finance, particularly for adaptation and resilience, these smaller countries also have the lowest implementation capacity (Robinson, 2019).

The United Nations Conference on Trade and Development (UNCTAD) classifies 14 SIDS in Asia–Pacific. They are Fiji, Kiribati, Maldives, Marshall Islands, Micronesia (Federated States of), Nauru, Palau, Papua New Guinea (PNG), Samoa, Solomon Islands, Timor-Leste, Tonga, Tuvalu and Vanuatu. While they share many common characteristics of SIDS in other regions, the predicament of Asia–Pacific SIDS is compounded by their remoteness and low connectivity (UN-ESCAP, 2010).

As UN-ESCAP (1989) observed, the structure of the Asia–Pacific Island economies is greatly influenced by the "nature of the colonial and postcolonial relationships between Pacific Island countries and metropolitan powers" (p. 163). The evils of colonialism and the military conflicts devasted the Pacific islands, as the history of sugar cane plantations in Fiji would testify (UN-ESCAP, 2014, p. 96). Fiji's sugar cane plantations were owned by British colonizers and operated with South Asian indentured labour (Ali & Narayan, 1989). The use of Pacific islands for testing nuclear explosions was another horror (Sherril, 2023), as was the totally unregulated exploitation of the peoples and resources of the islands until recent times (UN-ESCAP, 2014).

Peter Fitzpatrick (1980) debunked the conventional narrative of so-called "humanitarian virtue" of Australia's colonial rule of PNG that the Australian administrators did not consider themselves colonists at all, being entrusted with the "sacred trust" of civilising the "lazy" natives, who had to be forced to work. A closer look at the reality shows Australia to be a colonist much like any other even though it ostensibly held some humane attitudes as "a late and little imperialist" (Fitzpatrick, 1980, p. 77). Australian colonial administration's indenture system of labour in PNG was no different from the indenture system that was imposed on Fiji by the British colonial administration. The system, "really rather like slavery" was used to tie PNG societies into the colonial economy by ensuring and maintaining supply of cheap labour. Below subsistence wage caused inadequate dietary standards and contributed to extremely high death rates among labourers, especially on the goldfields.

Australia and the West silently supported Indonesia's invasion of East Timor in 1975, following the leftist Fretilin Party's proclamation of the Democratic Republic of Timor-Leste, Australia recognising the annexation in 1978. By the time Indonesia totally controlled Indonesia in 1979, savage fighting, massacres, large-scale population "re-settlement" and famine had taken a horrific civilian toll. Leongue Tjungue (1985) estimates that possibly one-third of the population of 700,000 in 1975 died during the Indonesian occupation until 1999.

Catharina Brameswari, Tatang Iskarna, Monica Angela Nadine Titaley (2022) studied the effects of colonization of East Timor by Portugal, Japan and Indonesia that changed social structure and relations among the Timorese and brought about physical, social and cultural conflicts. Portuguese colonialism impacted on the socio-political friction among Timorese and destructive vanishing of their culture. Japanese colonialism left trauma amongst them as physical oppression was often used to have domination over the people. Indonesian invasion resulted in horizontal conflicts amongst the Timorese. Violence and corrupt culture became new perspective in solving the problems.

The Asia–Pacific SIDS have become a centre for geopolitical rivalries between China and the US-led alliance of Australia, Japan, India and the UK in recent years, with increased Chinese investment in their infrastructure, climate change adaptations and mitigations as well as in defence and security. France, a former colonial power, and the European Union (EU) are also pivoting to the Asia–Pacific SIDS. Aid is being weaponised to pressurise these smaller highly vulnerable and aid-dependent countries to take a side (Maston & Ramesh, 2021; Keen & Tidwell, 2024a). Legitimately and understandably, there is a risk of militarisation of the region (Keen & Tidwell, 2024a), heightened by the NATO's expression of interest to expand to the region.[1] Japan, in its biggest manoeuvre since World War II, plans to bring 14 strategic South Pacific Island countries into a collective security arrangement, and invited their defence ministers to Tokyo for a multilateral meeting with its Defence Minister Minory Kihara on March 19 and 20, 2024.[2] The militarisation of the region will greatly impact Asia–Pacific SIDS' development trajectory.

However, while this geopolitical competition can breed division, between and within countries and regions, it can also give rise to increased multipolarity, partner country agency and positive competition towards development outcomes (Nath & Klingebiel, 2023). This positive outcome can happen provided the Asia–Pacific SIDS remain neutral and act with solidarity. Furthermore, as Meg Keen and Alan Tidwell (2024b) warn, "Geopolitical competition in the Pacific is intensifying, and left unmanaged it can compromise development and governance".

As argued in Chapter 1, due to the unique nature of these countries, their structural economic transformation has to deviate from the traditional path from agriculture to industry and to services. For the overwhelming majority of Asia–Pacific SIDS, manufacturing is not a viable option due to their remote location and small population size, which

[1] "Nato planning to open Japan office to deepen Asia–Pacific ties—report", *The Guardian*, 3 May, 2023, https://www.theguardian.com/world/2023/may/03/nato-planning-to-open-japan-office-to-deepen-asia-pacific-ties-report (accessed 12/03/2024).

[2] "1st Time Since World War-2, Japan Set To Bring 14 South Pacific Island Nations Under Its Security Ambit", *The EurAsian Times*, 15 March, 2024, https://www.eurasiantimes.com/1st-time-since-world-war-2-japan-set-to-bring-14-south/ (accessed 15/03/2024).

make them unattractive for foreign direct investment (FDI) and thus regional and global value chains. Given the lack of economies of scale as a result of their small sizes, the Asia–Pacific SIDS need to establish "niche markets", targeting high-end products or services. Andrzej Bolesta (2020) argued that the specific type of structural transformation must be underpinned by effective economic policies focusing on building resilience due to their extreme vulnerabilities to climate change and external shocks. This chapter examines the nature of structure transformation in the Asia–Pacific SIDS and the challenges they face in transforming their economy. It begins a brief summary of Asia–Pacific SIDS salient features.

Asia–Pacific SIDS: Salient Features—Unity and Diversity

Contrary to common perceptions, the Asia–Pacific SIDS are a very diverse group of countries. Divided into four geographic sub-regions—Melanesia, Micronesia, Polynesia and South Asia (Maldives), they differ in terms of their national economies, landmass and populations. Their international status and development level also differ. For example, Maldives and Vanuatu graduated from their LDC status, while Kiribati has met the formal, minimal criteria for graduation, and Solomon Islands is scheduled to graduate in December 2027. The Asia–Pacific SIDS can be grouped into either commodity-exporters or tourism-dependent economies. The former includes PNG, Solomon Islands and Timor-Leste, while the latter includes Fiji, Maldives, Vanuatu, Samoa and, to a lesser extent, Tonga. Major commodity exports from the region are oil, gas, gold, timber and copper, while tourism services are worth between 20 and 40% of GDP for tourism-dependent economies (Wilkins, 2023).

Although all Asia–Pacific SIDS face the issues of land and population size, the scale is very different (Chowdhury & Vidyattama, 2008). For example, the Melanesian countries such as Vanuatu, Solomon Islands, Fiji and PNG, are, relatively, larger and mountainous with fertile soils and mineral resources (Barnett, 2011). This means there are better opportunities for these countries to have a reasonable agricultural basis as well as build some industrial or manufacturing capacity. For example, Fiji's sugar cane farming capability should enable its capacity in building sugar industry. Similarly, Solomon Islands may have the capacity to build copra, cocoa and palm oil industry (UN-ESCAP, 1990).

Figure 7.1 illustrates varying land-population conditions of the Asia–Pacific SIDS. PNG is the largest with around 8 million total population in 2016 and a land area of more than 450 thousand km^2. This is followed by Fiji, with an estimated population of a tenth of PNG and total land area of only 18,300 km^2, followed by the Solomon Islands, with an estimated population of around half of Fiji and total land of 28,400 km^2 while the population of Vanuatu is half of Solomon Islands or a quarter of Fiji. This means the scale of production capacity among these countries will be different. The land and population size has already become a constraint for coconut and cocoa production in Solomon Islands according to The March 2009 Roundtable Discussions in Honiara (World Bank, 2009). The scarcity of land and population is event more obvious in the Polynesian SIDS (Tonga, Samoa and Tuvalu) and Micronesian Islands (Marshall Islands, Micronesia, Palau, Kiribati and Nauru). Jon Barnett (2011) characterised these countries with small volcanic islands to low-lying coral atolls.

As can be seen in Fig. 7.1, these islands are spread in the South Pacific Ocean. This increases the transportation cost within the country and directly affect the ability of these countries to build industry. In addition, the rising sea level due to climate change not only threatens the land size, but also their infrastructure especially since the capital cities, major urban centres and most critical infrastructure are in coastal areas. As Clem Tisdell (2000) pointed out, infrastructure is quite inadequate in Pacific SIDS as well as their ability to improve infrastructure. Samoa is the most compact Pacific SID as it mainly consists of two relatively large islands.

This vulnerable situation has led to more people moving out from these countries. Although, the pattern of migration is not always the same, it brings remittances from migrants living overseas (largely in Australia, New Zealand and the US), which have become an important source of foreign currency revenues. Jon Barnett (2011) noted that remittances contributed up to 12% of GDP in Kiribati, 14% in Samoa and 39% in Tonga in 2010. The number was similar in 2019 with 11%, 18% and 37% of GDP in Kiribati, Samoa and Tonga, respectively. The contribution of remittances dropped to 8% in 2020 in Kiribati, likely affected by COVID, but still increased to 25% and 38% in Samoa and Tonga.

Maldives is another Asia–Pacific SIDS. Situated in the Indian Ocean, South of the India Sub-Continent, Maldives is far away from other Asia–Pacific SIDS. However, it still faces similar challenges, especially regarding

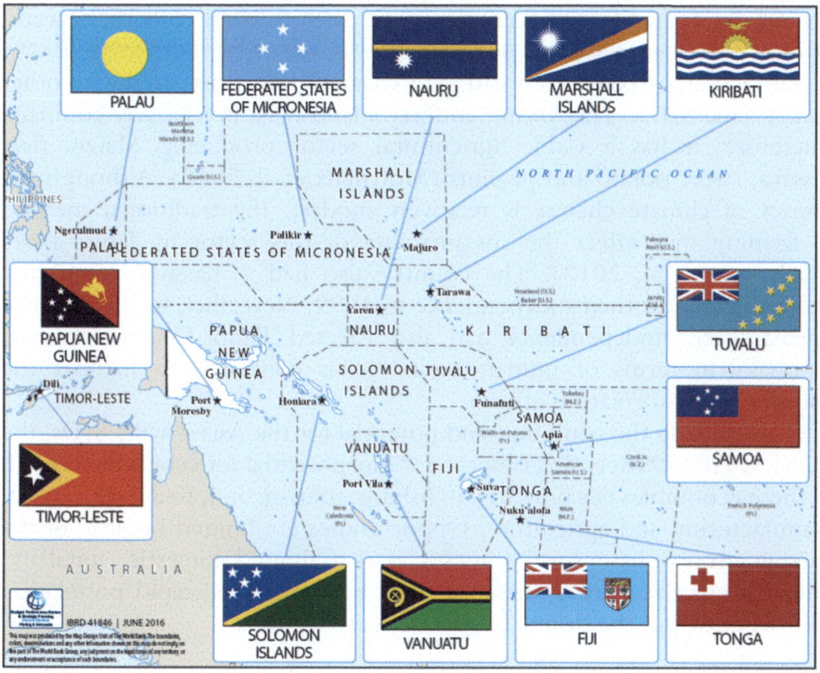

Fig. 7.1 The map of Pacific SIDS (*Source*: Khor, Kronenberg and Tumbarello (2016))

climate change and the rising sea level (Anthoff et al., 2010). To draw attention of the international community to the existential threat of global warning and the urgency to act, the Maldives Government held an underwater cabinet meeting in October 2009, covered by international video media.

As the land mass of Maldives is scattered in the Indian Ocean, the prospect for a viable manufacturing sector is bleak, although it has built a ready-made garments industry sector. Its tourism sector has more viability, but needs secure and good infrastructure. Maldives growing tourism industry has changed the migration behaviour in Maldives and hence, reduced the flow of remittance to this country (Cooray, 2012). In expanding the tourism sector, Maldives faces the problem of pollution and the risk to its fragile ocean environment, such as coral reefs (Scheyvens, 2011).

Timor-Leste has relatively different characteristics compared with other Asia–Pacific SIDS. This young country's land mass is relatively compact. Therefore, it has a viable agricultural sector producing Maize, rice, cassava, sweet potato and peanuts (Molyneux et al, 2012). Although the impact of climate change is relatively modest, the traditional method of farming may affect the sustainability of this sector in Timor-Leste (Molyneux et al, 2012). The country also had a massive reconstruction project after their independence in 1999. Nevertheless, the violence preceding the independence had also affected Timor-Leste's economy especially in terms of human capital. This continues to hamper the country's transformation efforts.

Summarising the condition and potential for the Asia–Pacific SIDs, the UN-ESCAP (1998, p. 35) observed, "The potential for economic growth of these economies lies primarily in fishing, tourism and, to a lesser extent, manufacturing and agriculture. Opportunities are limited because of the narrow resource base, small domestic market, limited domestic capital and skilled human resources, distance from main markets, rapid population growth rates and the dominant public sector".

Volatile and Poor Growth Performance of Asia–Pacific SIDS

Asia–Pacific SIDS experienced fluctuating economic growth rates (Fig. 7.2) for reasons that have been highlighted in the preceding discussion. In general, economic growth has been low, with an average annual growth rate of about 1.6% in the last decade. The COVID-19 pandemic had a significant impact on all Asia–Pacific SIDS, and in 2020 growth rates fell by around −2.5% (Basu, 2024). The most affected among them was Maldives where GDP fell by approximately − 34% in 2020. Fiji was the worst affected economy among the South Pacific SIDS; its GDP contracted by around − 15% in 2020, followed by Palau, experiencing a drop of GDP by close to − 10%. Nauru's GDP growth has been most volatile, followed by resource dependent PNG which also experienced volatility; economic growth rate declined in both since 2013–2014 as commodity prices fell in the international markets.

Even prior to the pandemic, economic growth in the Asia–Pacific SIDS lagged SIDS in other regions, especially those in the Caribbean as well

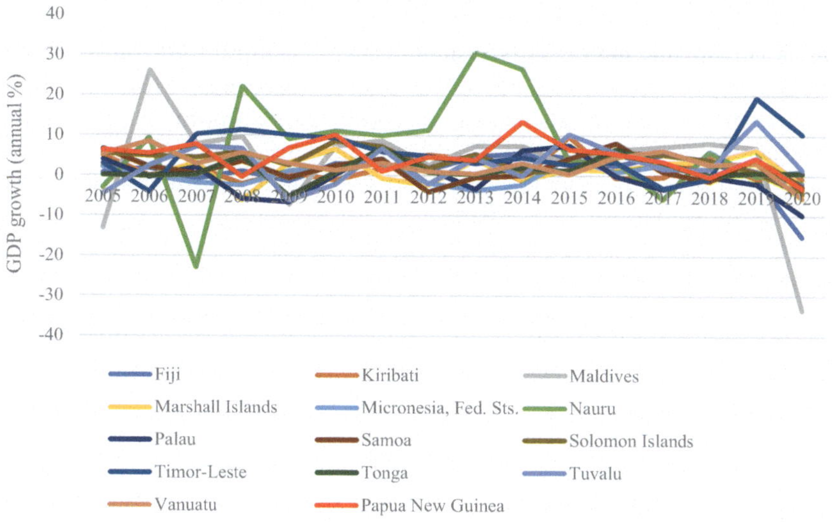

Fig. 7.2 GDP Growth of Asia–Pacific SIDS. (*Source*: World Bank online database)

as other low-income Asian economies, according to Roger Kronenberg and Hoe Ee Khor (2016). Real average income per capita in the Pacific SIDS increased by less than 10% since 1990, compared with 40% in the Caribbean SIDS and 25% in the group of all SIDS, and Pacific SIDS' economic growth in the 2000s was the lowest in four decades (Kronenberg & Khor, 2016). The Pacific SIDS also lagged Asia's low-income countries in recovering from the global financial crisis (GFC). Thus, Asia–Pacific SIDS are facing an increasing level of challenges to create employment opportunities, while the informal sector has seen a significant growth.

However, the general picture masks the differences among them. Rob Stewart (2006) observed that the Polynesian countries (Tonga, Samoa and Tuvalu) generally performed better than Melanesia or Micronesia in terms of per capita GDP growth. As expected, the resource-rich Asia–Pacific SIDS, such as PNG, Solomon Islands, Timor-Leste, outperformed others, especially since 2003, after experiencing sharp declines in the 1990s. Their growth has been also volatile with the fluctuations in global commodity prices. Nauru experienced the most volatility.

Even though the Asia–Pacific SIDS experienced strong post-pandemic recovery—mainly led by Fiji (facilitated by a resumption of tourism) and PNG (benefiting from higher LNG prices)—economic growth slowed significantly. Solomon Islands, the second-largest economy in the group, contracted by − 4.1% in 2022 and managed to grow only by 1.9% in 2023 by hosting the Pacific Games and substantial investments in energy and transport (World Bank, 2024).

Besides commodity price fluctuations, the Asia–Pacific SIDS' growth is also affected by aid uncertainty and volatility as well as low and fluctuating FDI flows. Ron Duncan (2016) suggests that poor or weak institutions and policy failures also contribute to Asia–Pacific SIDS' low and fluctuating economic growth. Dani Rodrik (2004) attributed low economic growth of the Asia–Pacific SIDS to a variety of structural reasons—including macroeconomic instability, weak property right and socio-political instability—exacerbated by global economic conditions.

The low average GDP growth rate and vulnerability have significantly impacted public debt of the Asia–Pacific SIDS, leading to pressures on social protection systems and increased informality of labour markets. This situation has seriously limited their ability to reduce poverty and complicated the momentum of productivity growth, notwithstanding technological advancements globally.

Limited Structural Transformation in Asia–Pacific SIDS

The discussion above shows various challenges for the Asia–Pacific SIDS. These challenges have made it difficult for the Asia–Pacific SIDS to transform their economies. The lingering questions facing these countries are whether they can build a viable manufacturing industrial sector; and if not, what should be their transformation strategies; to what extent could the recent advancements in technology give them a breakthrough in advancing a thriving services sector; what advantage do they have in harnessing the blue economy of the ocean while they face existential threats from climate change and ocean pollutions; what would be the impact of geopolitical tensions, and how can they benefit from the geopolitical rivalries?

Sectoral Share of GDP in Asia–Pacific SIDS

Being unfit for large-scale manufacturing owing to their small economies, almost all Asia–Pacific SIDS are dominated by the services sector, accounting for between 50 and 70% of their GDP (Fig. 7.3). However, this does not mean that the economic structure of SIDS is similar to advance countries (Stewart, 2006). As can be seen from Fig. 6.3, the agriculture sector still has considerable GDP shares in Micronesia Federation of States, Solomon Island and Vanuatu where agriculture sector contributes about 30% to GDP, followed by Kiribati and Tuvalu with around 25% and 20% of GDP, respectively.

The service sector's GDP share is not only high, but also displays an increasing trend in Kiribati, Fiji, Maldives, Palau, Samoa and to some extent in Tonga. This is mainly due to the domination of government services that underline the importance of the State's role in these small economies. This can be seen from the shares of public administration and the defence sector; in many Asia–Pacific SIDS, the sectoral GDP shares of public administration and defence are similar to that of the agriculture sector. This is despite the fact that public administration and defence are only a fraction of government activities; among others, governments also have to deliver education as well as health and social services at the very least.

International tourism is also a contributory factor to high GDP shares of the services sector accounting for up to 30% of GDP in Fiji Samoa and Vanuatu while in Palau it could reach 58% (Kronenberg & Khor, 2016). International tourists spending in Maldives, Marshall Islands, Micronesia, Palau, Solomon Islands, Tonga, Tuvalu and Vanuatu contributes more than 10% of the total export of those countries.

The disappointing aspect of Asia–Pacific SIDS' transformation experiences is not that their industrial or manufacturing sector's low GDP shares, but it is the continuous decline or sluggishness of industry sector's contributions to their GDP. The share of industry sector in GDP was only around 10% for the majority of the Asia–Pacific SIDS in the mid-2010s. Solomon Islands and Tonga are the two countries displaying some progress while Timor-Leste had some boost due to the reconstruction effort following the riot and violence prior to its independence. However, the share of manufacturing component of industry did not show an upward trend.

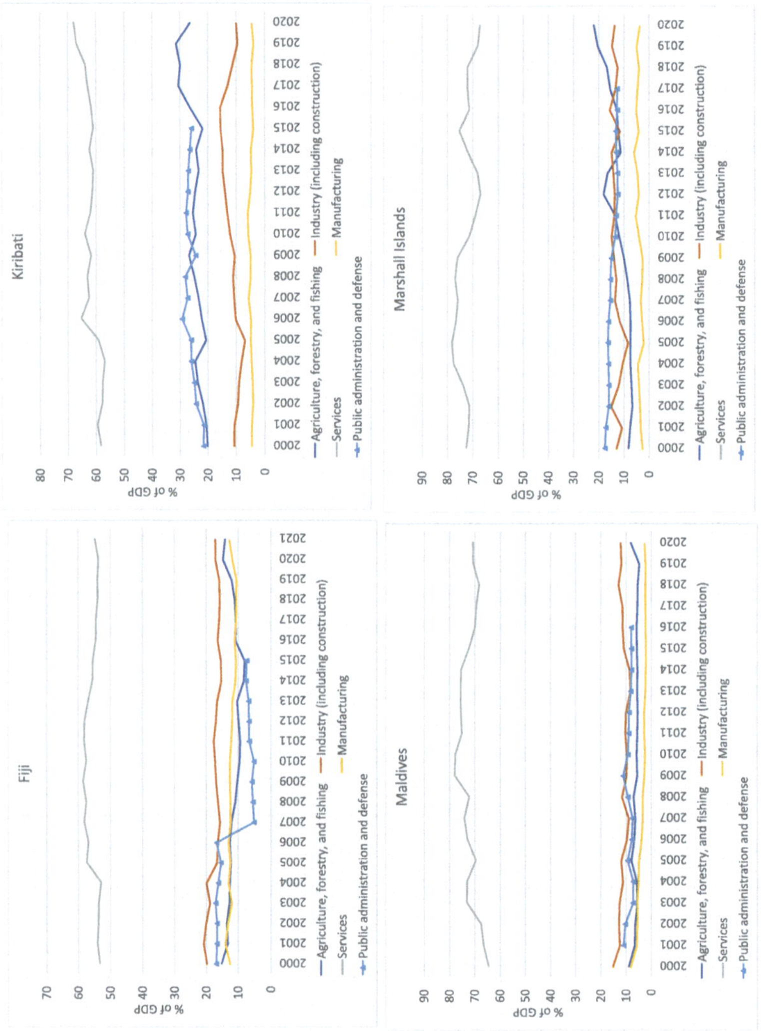

Fig. 7.3 Sectoral GDP share in various Asia–Pacific SIDS. *Source*: World Bank online database

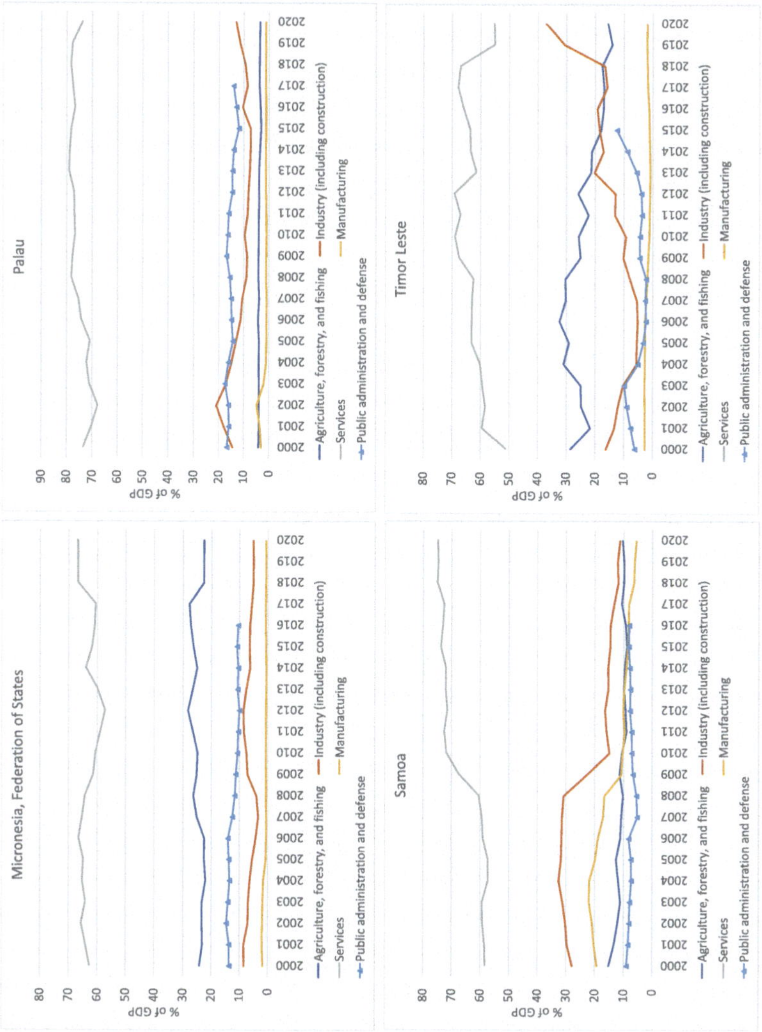

Fig. 7.3 (continued)

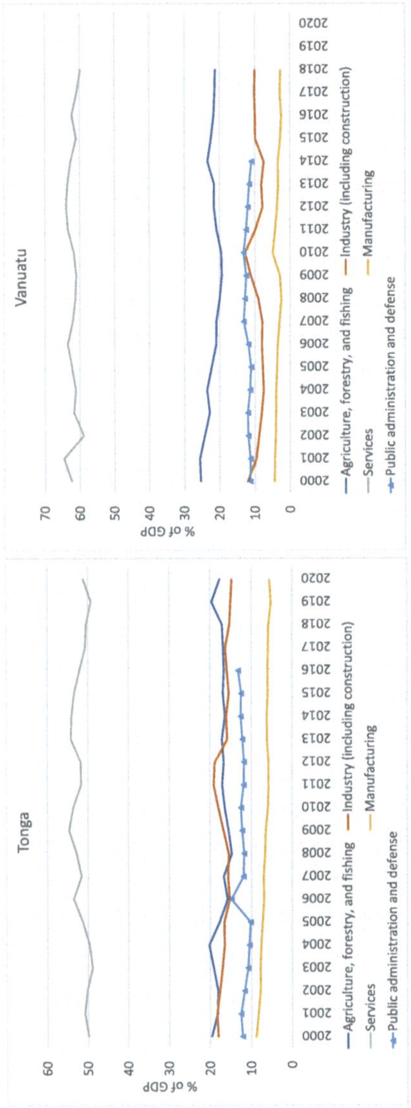

Fig. 7.3 (continued)

Sectoral Employment Shares in the Asia–Pacific SIDS

While the changes in the sectoral GDP share are one of the indicators, the extent of structural transformation can also be gleaned from the movement of labour from the less productive to the more productive sectors. As can be seen from Fig. 7.4, there is not much indication of labour movement from the agriculture to the industrial sector in the Asia–Pacific SIDS although there have been movements of labour from agriculture to the services sector in some countries, for example, Fiji, Timor-Leste and Tonga, and to some limited extent, Samoa, Solomon Islands, Timor-Leste and Vanuatu, indicating variations in their experiences.

The preceding discussion shows that there has been very limited structural change in the Asia–Pacific SIDS, measured by the conventional indicators—the sectoral shares of GDP and employment. Due to limitations of domestic economy and other structural weaknesses, such as remoteness, the traditional path of structural transformation from agriculture to industry and then to services is not viable for the majority of SIDS. Remoteness means the costs of reaching international markets are too high. This impedes the availability of FDI and thus affects capital formation and technology diffusion. Thus, Asia–Pacific SIDS' structural transformation is often characterised by a move from agriculture to services, instead of manufacturing, as was seen historically in larger economies, and also in Asia's newly industrialised economies, e.g., South Korea, Taiwan, Malaysia, Thailand and Indonesia. More worrying is the movement from unproductive agriculture to unproductive services, such as domestic help, delivery services, cleaning, etc. That is, the new jobs of those leaving the rural areas and agricultural activities are as unproductive as those they left behind (UN-ESCAP, 2019). Consequently, despite the move to urban areas and change in type of employment, they remain poor.

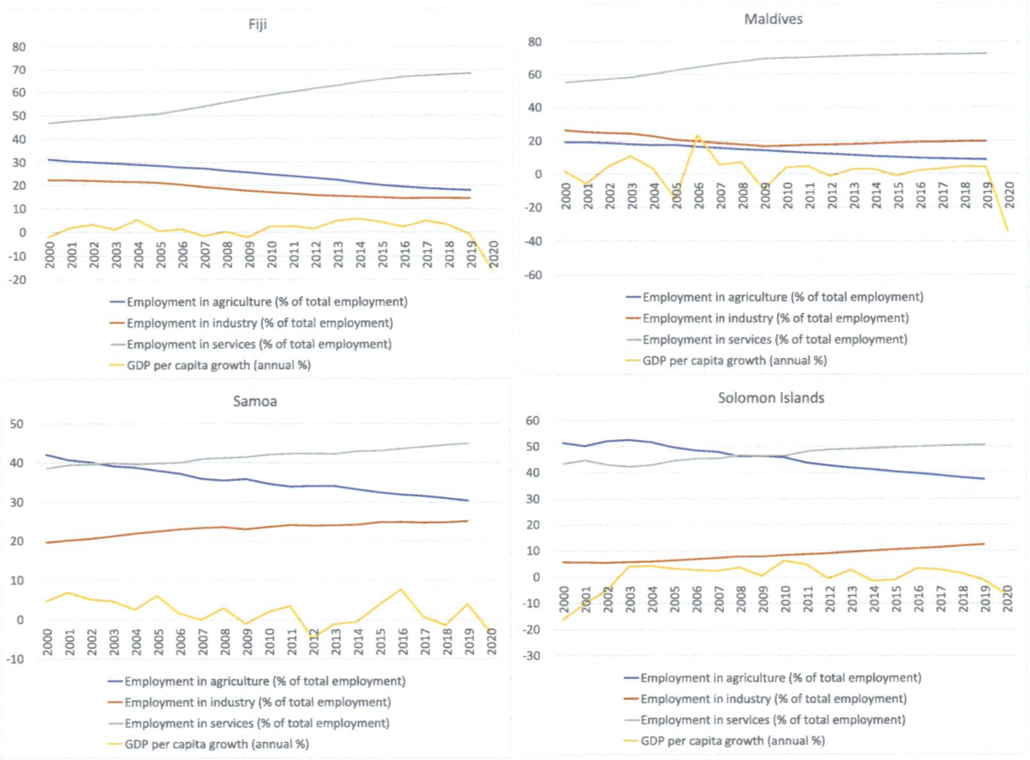

Fig. 7.4 Sectoral Employment Shares in Asia–Pacific SIDS. *Source*: World Bank Online Database

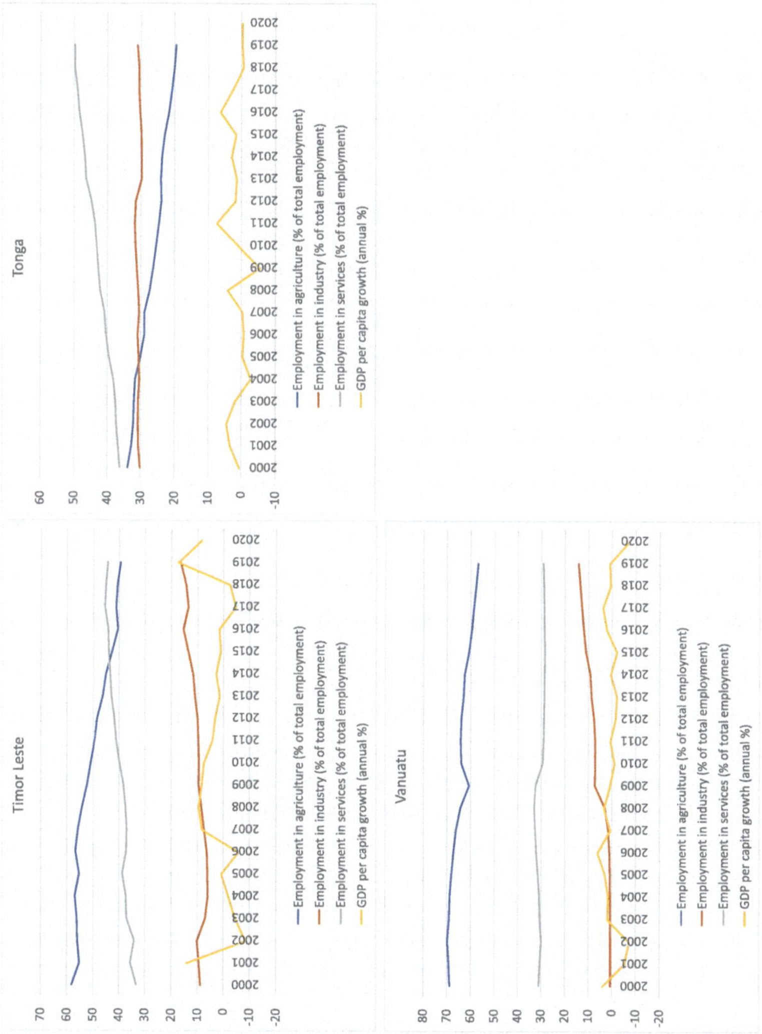

Fig. 7.4 (continued)

Barriers to Asia–Pacific SIDS' Structural Transformation

Resources and Capacity Constraints

Population Dilemma

The population size is often regarded as the weak point for the Asia–Pacific SIDS. Ron Duncan (2014) argues that the Pacific Island countries do not have large supplies of labour that allow them to be attractive for large investments, especially FDI. Therefore, it cannot walk the path of East Asian economies to attract FDI in standard technology, labour-intensive low-wage activities that could provide employment for the large numbers of farm workers being released from the agricultural sector as suggested by 2-sector models *à la* Arthur Lewis.

This is not good news for these smaller Island economies where population growth is projected to escalate, for example in the Pacific SIDS from about 11.9 million to 19.7 million by 2050 (Wilson, 2020). According to Catherine Wilson (2020), "the consequential surge in the youth population—where the current median age is 22 across the region, and half the population is aged under 23—will place an overwhelming fiscal and capacity burden on resource-constrained Pacific Island governments".

Their inability to industrialise and absorb a growing population in productive employment means persistent high open and disguised unemployment as well as low productivity. This has serious socio-political implications, such as increased poverty, persistently low literacy levels and intense competition for educational opportunities and healthcare facilities. This may also accelerate rural–urban migration causing increased pressure on already under-resourced urban areas, thus worsening slums conditions, chronic health problems, crimes and law and order situation.

These conditions are also likely to cause disillusionment with governments, and thus carry higher risks of political grievance and unrests. For example, the study by Aidan Craney (2016) reveals that financial security, failure to complete education and poverty are among the current issues troubling Pacific Islands' youth. Such socio-political instability can create a vicious circle of low growth-high unemployment-social and political instability feeding into low growth. "All of these add to a potent mix in a region that already struggles to achieve even modest improvements in people's quality of life", warns Catherine Wilson (2020).

The lack of opportunity in the Pacific SIDS has led to the culture of migration (Connell, 2010). The SAMOA pathway has recognised the importance of migrants and diaspora in enhancing communities in their home countries not only due to their employment overseas but also through their input to policies and managements (United Nations, 2014). However, increased migration flows to neighbouring countries, especially Australia and New Zealand, and even to some relatively larger economies among the Pacific SIDS, e.g., Fiji and PNG, can have adverse spill-over impacts, such as political and diplomatic tensions. Such developments can affect migration and remittance flows, a significant source of their revenues.

Remittances, Human Capital and Investment Conundrum

Remittance transfers from nationals working overseas) range from 15 to 40% of GDP for Pacific SIDS, compared with around 3% for other small and low-income states (Wilkins, 2023). Thus, remittance has become an important foreign exchange earnings and income source for families in the Asia–Pacific SIDS. Maldives is the only exception where the flow has started to reverse. In addition, remittance has become a major source of foreign exchange. Besides being used for consumption, the remittance is often used to invest in increasing the human capital in the communities, such as for education and healthcare (Tisdell, 2016). In studies involving a large number of low-income developing countries (e.g., Azizi, 2018), it is found that remittances raise per capita health expenditures, and reduce undernourishment prevalence, depth of food deficit, prevalence of stunting, and child mortality rate. Remittances also raise school enrolment and school completion rates, especially for girls, thus, contribute to improving gender parity.

Unfortunately, however, the remittance is unlikely to contribute to investment, especially in infrastructure; the reason being the high likelihood of negative returns. However, Ron Duncan (2016) argues that remittance sometimes can contribute to the infrastructure investment *albeit* indirectly. He cites Tonga in the early 2000s as an example, where with increased remittance flows, the demand for automobiles increased, thus prompting the Tonga government to construct roads. Several Samoan construction projects in the first half of the 2000s were funded from remittances. Nevertheless, Ron Duncan (2016) admits that remittance has not been a long-term source of growth in the Pacific SIDS.

The low returns on investment may not be the only reason for poor investment outcomes in the Asia–Pacific SIDS. Previously it has been mentioned that the lack of appropriate labour force makes it hard to attract investment. The topology of the SIDS is another factor that reduces the productivity of investment. Clem Tisdell (2016) maintains that productive investments are likely to be less in Island nations consisting of atolls (for example, Kiribati and Tuvalu) than in those with Islands that are mainly of volcanic origin (Fiji) or which are primarily of a continental type (New Caledonia). Less favourable business environment, such as highly cumbersome and restrictive administrative regulations is another factor for the lack of contributions of remittance to investment in Pacific SIDS (Browne, 2006; Duncan, 2016). Roger Kronenberg and Hoe Ee Khor (2016) have listed several constraining factors for investment in the Pacific SIDS. They are: absence of positive macroeconomic conditions, capacity constraints, lack of financial depth, inflexible laws and customs towards product and factor markets, high levels of public debt, dependence on foreign aid and remittances, and political instability or lack of security.

Natural Disasters and Climate Challenges

A serious threat for the Asia–Pacific SIDS is the natural disasters. These include major cyclones (mainly affecting Fiji, Samoa, Tonga, Vanuatu), tsunamis (mainly affecting Samoa, Solomon Islands), severe drought (mainly affecting Marshall Islands, Tuvalu), flooding (mainly affecting Solomon Islands), and volcanic eruption (mainly affecting PNG) (Kronenberg & Khor 2016). Cyclone Ami caused over US$35 million in lost crops in Fiji in 2003 (Barnett, 2011; McKenzie et al., 2005) (UN-ESCAP, 2023). Drought and flooding affected food production in Fiji in April 2004 causing damages to between 50 and 70% of crops (Fiji Government, 2004). The threat of natural disasters contributes to the threats of the market (Julca & Paddison, 2010). This is because the destruction of the product will not only affect export but also increase the need to import food. In addition, the destruction also likely to increase import due to reconstruction efforts. Figure 7.5 shows disproportionate economic loss in the Pacific SIDS due to natural disasters.

The impacts of the climate change vary and are less immediate. One of the impacts of climate change is the sea-level rise. Jon Barnett (2001) considered sea-level rise is a mid to long-term problem. However, the

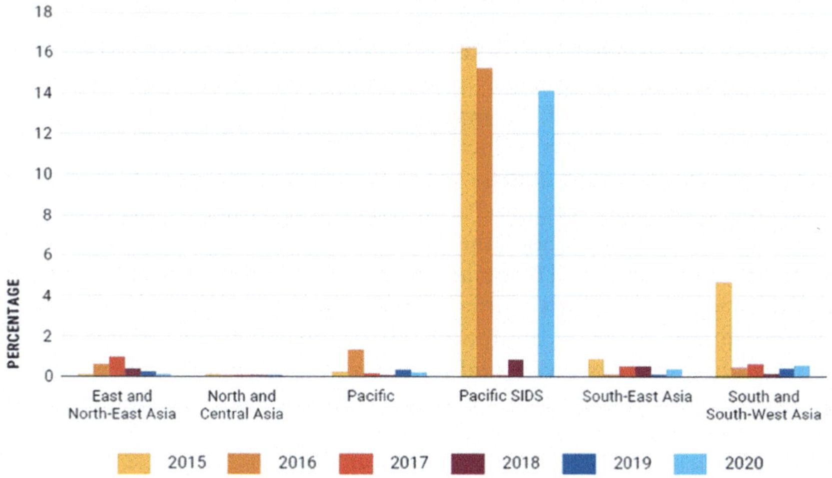

Fig. 7.5 Average economic loss as a percentage of GDP in the Asia–Pacific region due to natural disasters. *Source*: UN-ESCAP (2023)

risk pose is still significant and remains the greatest existential threat for the Asia–Pacific SIDS (United Nations, 2014). The sea-level rise directly threats the survival of these countries.

However, the discussion of sea-level rise often veils other climate change impacts in the Asia–Pacific SIDS (Barnett, 2001). One major impact of climate change is on the food systems involving both agriculture and fisheries, and hence food security which is already precarious in these smaller economies (ADB, 2011). Badjeck, Marie-Caroline, Edward Allison, Ashley Halls and Nicholas Dulvy (2010) discuss several ways climate change affect fisheries including changes in water temperature, precipitation and oceanographic variables, such as wind velocity, wave action and sea-level rise. These factors will directly affect fish population and hence, peoples who depend on the ecosystems. The impact on agriculture and fishing is not only in the subsistence sense as the changes may also disrupt fishing operations and land-based infrastructure. Similarly, climate change affects agricultural production for both direct food supply and commercial purposes. This means the need to buy and import food for daily life if their own production is not sufficient will be great.

It is important to note that natural disasters and climate change also affect the tourism sector of Asia–Pacific SIDS, a vital source of economic activity. For example, global temperature rise is having serious impacts on corals, one of the main tourism attractions. The damages to infrastructures and threats to life can seriously dampen tourism.

Natural disasters and climate change are a great cause of market or economic uncertainty for Asia–Pacific SIDS. Jon Barnett (2001) provides an in-depth discussion about the impact of uncertainty in these remote and smaller economies. The major issue is the inability to plan as all the available options entail with different risk factors depending on what kind of event might occur in the future. He argued that the anticipation of impacts often restricts policy and therefore, the SIDS need to propose a complementary strategy that show the resilience towards the impact of various event and focus on broad policy goals.

External Shocks

The small size of population as well as the size of land means that the Asia–Pacific SIDS need to sell their product outside their country and buy essential products including food from the outside world. This exposes them to the fluctuations of world market. William Easterly and Aart Kraay (2000) argue that a greater degree of openness is likely to be a more relevant source of greater volatility of terms of trade shocks. The global financial crisis (GFC) around 2009 has highlighted the vulnerability of Asia–Pacific SIDS economies, as the high-income economies, their main trading partner, were affected by the GFC. UN-ESCAP (2010) identified the following transmission mechanisms through both trade and financial flows:

- lower commodity prices and reduced demand for commodities,
- decline in tourism numbers and per capita spending,
- fall in remittance flows,
- decline in value of offshore national trust funds,
- decline in FDIs,
- decline in aid,
- decline in terms of trade.

The large distance and isolation of the Asia–Pacific SIDS from the global market also means that price adjustments to get back to the pre-crisis normal in the international market is slow to reach these economies. Additionally, Asia–Pacific SIDS governments' capacity to deal with external shocks is very low, especially due to the high debt burden (Kronenberg & Khor, 2016; Basu, 2024). The public debt burden has particularly worsened due to the COVID-19 pandemic, reaching around 40% of GDP (Basu, 2024). Underdeveloped financial markets and the lack of depth of their financial sector, also limit the effectiveness of monetary and exchange policies to respond to inflation which is mostly caused by supply shocks (Yang et al., 2016).

Neo-liberal Policy Limits

The neo-liberal counter revolution in favour of market-led development that began with the Latin American debt crisis in the 1980s, aided by the Bretton Woods Institutions (IMF and World), regional development banks (e.g., ADB) and donor community also reached the shores of Asia–Pacific SIDS. Thus, these remotely located, smaller aid-dependent economies introduced series of liberalisation and deregulation reforms, including dismantling of public sector.

As noted, Claire Slatter (2006a, p. 27), "The Pacific Islands Forum, formerly the South Pacific Forum, has played a key role in regional economic restructuring, functioning as a channel for the diffusion of neo-liberal economic ideas and thinking among Pacific Island leaders, and as the principal implementing agency in the externally driven programme of 'reforms'". Claire Slatter (2006b) documented the history of donor-imposed neo-liberal reforms in Pacific SIDS, especially the role of Australia and New Zealand, backed by the academics at the Australian National University (ANU) and Pacific SID academics trained in Australia and New Zealand.

Claire Slatter (2006b) critiqued Helen Hughes, a very influential ANU academic who became a senior World Bank economist, for arguing that Australia's Norfolk Island is a model for emulation, ignoring the fact that Norfolk is an Australian territory. Helen Hughes (2004, p. 1) argued that "the best way to support the Pacific is through continuing trade liberalisation to reward the steps necessary to increase exports from the Pacific and thus create incomes and growth". She also argued for the absolute necessity of abandoning communal land ownership in favour of individual property rights (Hughes, 2003).

As can be seen from Fig. 7.6, contrary to the promised growth bonanza, Pacific SIDS' growth plummeted since 1995 and never fully recovered, experiencing wild fluctuations. Roger Kronenberg and Hoe Ee Khor (2016) report that Pacific SIDS' growth rates have also been below other small States and Asian low-income countries (LICs). The proponents of neo-liberal policy package and reforms failed to recognise the uniqueness of Pacific SIDS—they are remote, far away from all major economies, rendering them unattractive for FDI.

The UN-ESCAP annual survey reports—Economic and Social Survey of Asia and the Pacific—consistently highlighted the limits of neo-liberal policies pointing out declining economic growth or stagnations in the Asia–Pacific SIDS (UN-ESCAP, 2014). These annual reports highlighted the need for taking into account these smaller remote economies special circumstances and argued for nationally designed development strategies.

While the neo-liberal policies are imposed through aid conditionally on these highly aid-dependent countries, the actual aid they receive is paltry—far less than what they need for their sustainable development aspirations, especially in the face of climate challenge they face (UN-OHRLLS, 2024). Yet, they had a significant impact on the policy space

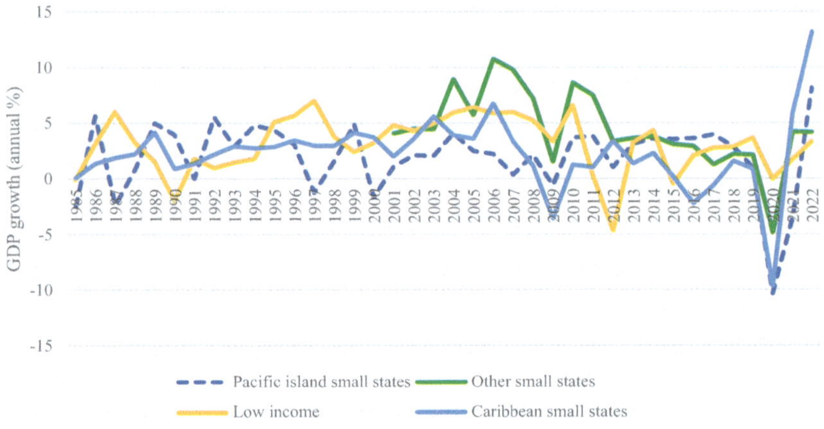

Fig. 7.6 Growth performance: Pacific Island countries and selected comparators (%). *Source*: World Bank online database

as Warwick Murray and John Overton's (2011) study revealed how donors constrained sovereignty of policymaking. They called this, "inverse sovereignty effect", whereby recipient states actually lose control over their development strategies, policies and programmes with aid flows. Furthermore, reporting and planning requirements put administrative strains on small island developing states in the region. Thus, aid served the interest of colonial powers—now donors—instead of the recipients.

The success of sustainable development assistance needs a nuanced understanding of the region's unique cultural, social and environmental landscape—best achieved through genuine, inclusive development partnerships. However, more often than not, donors set aid priorities, ignoring local knowledge and expertise (Keen & Tidwell, 2024b). Teaurere, Rerekura, Siulua Tokilupe Latu, Roxane de Waegh, Mark Orams and Michael Lück (2023) argue that aid has increased the level of dependence of Pacific SIDS on donor countries not only in terms of fund allocation decision, but also in terms of foreign consultants to implement the aid-based projects. Yet, recipient countries are blamed for aid-led development failure or aid ineffectiveness by the proponents of neo-liberal policies, e.g., Helen Hughes (2003) who ridiculed the Pacific SIDS and argued for continuing trade liberalisation instead of aid.

Claire Slatter (2006b) provided a critique of neo-liberal policies in the Pacific SIDS. She highlighted the neo-liberal bias against states as political entities with regulatory and other powers that can be used against the interests of free enterprise. The neo-liberal policy or reform paradigm downplays the sovereignty of States and conceptualises these Island States as economic entities, presumably run by free market technocrats. This suggests island populations not of citizens with rights, but simply of producers and consumers, or buyers and sellers. That is, within the neo-liberal paradigm, societies are defined and governed by the market, where local culture, traditions or concepts of societal well-being become subservient to global culture, defined and governed by transnational corporations. Thus, Pacific Islanders were dispossessed of the communally held land that is the basis of their semi-subsistence livelihoods by a rush of land sales to wealthy foreigners and corporations, resulting in acute inequality, food insecurity and persistent poverty. Claire Slatter (2006b, p. 176) concluded, "The time is long overdue for critical investigation and public debate on the long-term implications of following a course set by outside navigators whose final destination is not of our choosing".

Geopolitical Playground

For centuries, the US and European colonial powers, and their outposts—Australia and New Zealand—have been key players in different parts of the Pacific. Western engagements, rooted in historical colonial ties and a liberal internationalist perspective, have shaped the region's development landscape (UN-ESCAP, 2014; Keen and Tidwell, 2024a, 2024b). While for some Western powers, these small remote islands were nuclear testing sites, for others these resource-rich islands were places for extractive activities and sources of vital minerals for their industries (UN-ESCAP, 2014). Thus, sustainable development of these vulnerable smaller remote Island States suffered with endless fallout from nuclear testing (Sherril, 2023). In many respects, their fate is very similar to that of Africa's structurally underdeveloped countries, determined by their past colonial exploitations (Jacobson, 1960; Schneewind, 2020)) and is continued to be constrained by neo-colonial arrangements, such as neo-liberal economic system (Slatter, 2006b).

Besides resources and neo-colonial exploitations, the geography of island nations across the Indian and Pacific Oceans also made them attractive for great powers' strategic interests (Keen & Tidwell, 2024a). Thus, these small Island nations are at the strategic crossroads of great power competition. Traditional powers—Australia, France, Japan, New Zealand and the US—and are now competing with China for geopolitical influence in the Pacific Islands. With the NATO's explicit desire to expand to the region, there is an increased risk of militarisation or "strategic manipulation" (Keen & Tidwell, 2024a).

Maldives, too, is caught up in the geopolitical rivalry, especially between China and India. Michael Kugelman (2021) termed Maldives as "Island battleground" for India-China competition. In February 2020, the US Secretary of State Michael Pompeo visited Maldives to announce plans to open a resident US embassy in the country. That same year, the US also entered into a "Framework for Defence Cooperation" with Maldives. While bilateral relations between the two countries date back to 1966, this will mark the first time Washington will have resident diplomatic representation in Maldives, symbolising the US' strategic interest in the Island State. Amit Ranjan (2023) discusses the geopolitical rivalry between India, China and the US in the Maldives, particularly in the economic and military spheres, and its impacts on Maldives domestic politics and economy.

Increasingly aid is being weaponised by both traditional Western donors and China for their respective strategic political and economic interests (Regilme & Hodzi, 2021). For example, in 2018, India offered US$1.4 billion in aid to Maldives in exchange for the Maldives distancing itself from China (Marston & Ramesh, 2021). The US budget for 2024 included more than US$7.1 billion in funding for the Marshall Islands, Micronesia and Palau to counter China.[3] At the 2021 QUAD Summit in Washington, leaders from Australia, the US, India and Japan agreed to ramp up infrastructure investment across more than 30 countries in the Indo-Pacific to compete with China's Belt and Road Initiative (BRI).[4]

Mihai Sora (2022) believes actions by powerful nations from their geopolitical interest perspective can cause social and political destabilisation. He used the example of Honiara riots in November 2021 to illustrate his point. As recent elections in some Asia–Pacific SIDS, such as Fiji and Maldives, demonstrated, the relative roles of geopolitical players in the country can also cause political polarisation. George Carter (2022) believes that great power geopolitics is undermining island unity. According to George Carter, the great power rivalry is also marginalising the issues that are critical to these smaller Island States, such as climate change, plastic pollution, illegal, unreported and unregulated fishing practices, piracy and the threat of oil spills.

Options for Structural Transformation

The analysis in this chapter has emphasised the uniqueness of the problems faced by Asia–Pacific SIDS, especially those in the remote South Pacific, still largely under the influence of colonial metropolitan powers. As highlighted in various UN-ESCAP reports and summarised in UN-ESCAP (2014), their developmental problems are paradigmatically quite different from those of other economies in Africa, South Asia, Southeast Asia and Central Asia, as discussed in previous chapters. The scope for Asia–Pacific Island economies' structural transformation following the

[3] "Biden budget includes billions for Pacific islands to counter China", Public Broadcasting Service (PBS), 9 March, 2024, https://www.pbs.org/newshour/world/biden-budget-includes-billions-for-pacific-islands-to-counter-china (accessed 15/03/2024).

[4] "Quad steps up response to China's Belt and Road", Australian Financial Review, 27 Sept., 2021, https://www.afr.com/policy/foreign-affairs/quad-steps-up-response-to-china-s-belt-and-road-20210926-p58uu1 (accessed 15/03/2024).

traditional route—from agriculture to industry and to services sector is thus considerably limited. However, for larger Pacific economies, such as Fiji, Solomon Islands and PNG, policy options "for economic restructuring are broadly similar to those available for Asian least developed and other developing countries" (UN-ESCAP, 2014, p. 102).

A major distinctive feature of Asia–Pacific Island economies, in contrast with most commodity-producing and-processing economies of the region is their heavy dependence on "what are in essence external rental incomes—budgetary support, emigrants' remittances, interest on investments, resource rents(for example, fishing and site-leasing fees), and tourism (which can be regarded partly as rents of location)...Related to this is the question of how these rental incomes are to be disbursed among the population, bearing in mind incentive effects on local production as well as the realization of external rents, and the desire to preserve the traditional mode of production and the cultural values that it embodies" (UN-ESCAP, 2014, p. 102).

The transformation problems of the Asia–Pacific SIDS are connected with the much broader issues of sustainable, inclusive and resilient development in light of the fact Natural capital in many of these island countries has steadily eroded over the past few decades due to poor waste management; overexploitation of natural resources; abundance of invasive species; and increasing damage from natural disasters and climate change. Resource-extractive activities, including commercial fishing, logging and mining, have resulted in extensive environmental degradation and loss of biodiversity.

Within these constraints the Asia–Pacific SIDS can develop high value niche products, such as ecotourism and sustainable ocean-based activities, now being referred to as "blue economy". As Sudip Basu (2024) notes, the Asia–Pacific SIDS already relies heavily on ocean ecosystems and resources for economic development and people's livelihoods. Oceans are a source of income generation across (i) sustainable fisheries, (ii) coastal and ocean tourism, (iii) marine transport and (iv) marine ecosystem conservation. For the blue economy to continue to be an effective source of economic growth and employment generation in the future, sustainable management of the blue economy is key to delivering SDGs for these smaller Island States.

Tourism

As mentioned at several places in this chapter, tourism is a major activity in most of the Asia–Pacific SIDS. Tourism has become an essential part of the Asia–Pacific SIDS economy and is a key sector in their national development plans (Roberts & Ali, 2016). This is despite the remoteness and isolation of these Islands, making transport and development very costly (Connell, 2010). In Fiji, Palau, Samoa and Vanuatu, tourism receipts on average account for about 30% of GDP while in the other Pacific countries, tourism is still in relatively early stages of development, but the potential is large. UNCTAD (2014, p. 14) have a similar calculation of the contribution of tourism to SIDS, between 20 and 50% of GDP and over 30% of employment.

The tourism sector could also bring investment into the SIDS. UNCTAD (2014) argues that one area that has been less explored by the Pacific SIDS compared to those in Caribbean and Indian Ocean is the linkages to the information and communications technologies (ICTs) sector and offshore financial services. While the investment in terms of hotel and resort is important, the ICTs investment could increase travel routes and connectivity with major tourism origin countries. In addition, public–private partnerships with key airlines or tourism operators could reduce travel costs and improve the overall competitiveness of the sector.

However, there are concerns about the sustainability of this sector especially in the face of climate challenge, ecological and environmental degradation. Therefore, the Asia–Pacific SIDS governments need to develop policies that promote responsible, resilient and sustainable tourism. The concentration of tourism in certain areas of the countries and disconnection between the tourism sector with the communities is also a concern. Therefore, policies on tourism need to consider how to include the participation of all peoples in SIDS (United Nations, 2014). One of the options is to diversify the tourism sector especially from concentrating on beach resorts. Activities such as traditional fishing experience would have invited more participation from the communities. Another option is through utilising products and services that come from communities, instead of large transnational supply chains.

Another policy option to connect tourism and communities could be integrating sustainable tourism development projects with human settlements so that the efforts to build infrastructure that protect the tourism areas can also benefit the settlement. As a matter of fact, the SAMOA pathway mentions as a strategy to bring together tourism, environment, health, disaster risk reduction, culture, land and housing, transport, security and immigration, planning and development responsibilities and expertise (United Nations, 2014). This will also help enable a meaningful partnership approach between the public and private sector and local communities.

Ocean and "Blue Economy"

While small land masses and remoteness are barriers to economic growth of Asia–Pacific SIDS, the vast area of ocean may provide important resources for the countries. Therefore, the governments and regional agencies especially in Pacific SIDS have started to focusing on sustainable oceans management, programmes and policies (Keen et al., 2018). The adoption of the 2050 Strategy for the Blue Pacific Continent has provided a significant opportunity to advance sustainable development. The blue economy is a source of income, food and a way of life for Pacific people.

However, the concept of "Blue Economy" needs to be further developed especially in terms of the implementation steps. It still puts the attention mainly on the fisheries sector such as small-scale fisheries, urban fish markets and onshore tuna processing while Keen, Meg R., Anne-Maree Schwarz and Lysa Wini-Simeon (2018) points out that it should include mining and tourism activities.

There are also concerns that the huge resources often invite many stakeholders. For example, Mads Barbesgaard (2018) worries that the external stakeholders are coming not only to seek access to the resources, but also to have some control on the resources. This is because there are opposing interests and contradictory dynamics between the search for growth, economic profit and conservation from three different sides of conversations—coastal communities, investors and the environment. Mads Barbesgaard (2018) argues that at least two major components have to be put forward, sustainable fisheries and food sovereignty. This is because the current policy may hurt "ocean health" with major impacts on small-scale users, while large-scale, capital-intensive uses gain the most.

The concern is not without a basis. Jon Barnett (2011) notes that only a small proportion of the fish caught in the Exclusive Economic Zones of Pacific Island countries landed on the Pacific Islands. The Pacific Island governments ask access fees for around US$60–70 million a year (Gillett et al., 2001; Petersen, 2001; Tarte, 1999). The most valued target species of these deep-water fishing operations is tuna. The value of the tuna is approximately US$0.9 billion with the final market value that can reach US$4.5 billion. Another value that can reach the Pacific Island countries is through the remittances from the people who worked in the large-scale fishing boat.

Therefore, the "Blue Economy" strategies should be able to provide clear policy solutions to promote national control, inclusive economic growth, reduce poverty and improve people's lives and well-being. Individual countries are unlikely to have power and ability to deal with large transnational companies. The small size of Asia–Pacific Island economies is a major hindrance to their ability to plan on their own or to have an effective bargaining position with foreign investors. Therefore, they need to act together as a joint force.

In this regard, during the preparatory meeting for the 4th International Conference on SIDS for the Pacific Region, held in Tonga from 16 to 18 August 2023, the Nuku 'alofa Outcome Document highlighted the importance of cooperation to rejuvenate socio-economic aspirations and climate action in the Pacific SIDS. The gathering cited the 2050 Strategy for the Blue Pacific Continent as the blueprint to advance Pacific regionalism for the next three decades—articulating the region's long-term vision, values and thematic priorities.

FiamèNaomi Mata'afa, Prime Minister and Minister of Foreign Affairs of Samoa, has highlighted that "Pacific countries need to stand together as a region to protect from the current geopolitics and power play".[5] Regional cooperation is vital to deal with the emerging geopolitical threats from global and regional powers.

The Way Forward

The financing need for Asia–Pacific SIDS infrastructure and addressing climate challenge is huge, running into billions of dollars (UN-OHRLLS, 2024). Given their limited capacity to meet this need from domestic sources, Asia–Pacific SIDS' sustainable structural transformation will

[5] "No one asked us"—PM Fiamē on Geopolitics and the Pacific Region, Talamua Online News, 31 May, 2022, https://talamua.com/2022/05/31/no-one-asked-us-pm-fiame-on-geopolitics-and-the-pacific-region/ (accessed 15/03/2024).

remain highly aid-dependent. This combined with their geographic position at the geopolitical strategic crossroads, the Asia–Pacific SIDS cannot avoid great power rivalries.

While great power competitions can significantly undermine Asia–Pacific SIDS structural transformation prospects, as mentioned earlier, geopolitical rivalries can also be leveraged for positive development outcomes. As Hunter Marston and Akhil Ramesh (2021) observed, emerging great power competition provides small states with the opportunity to balance their economic and strategic ties with countries vying for influence such as China, the US, India and Japan.

So, most Asia–Pacific Island states welcome the increased attention towards them. They see it as an opportunity to pit wealthy countries in competition with each other to extract favour for them. For example, Solomon Islands and Vanuatu have been able to extract highly favourable communications infrastructure deals from Australia after first agreeing to a deal for Huawei to serve as a provider.

The leaders of the Pacific Islands Forum announced in 2018 the Boe Declaration, which draws attention to non-traditional security issues such as climate change and transnational crime, as an explicit alternative to the Cold War-style framing of the US and its allies. The Asia–Pacific Island governments have also refused to buy into the polarising logic of recent increased geopolitical attention. The more outspoken leaders have stated that they welcome China's interest and will continue to build ties with Beijing, while still maintaining close relations with others. The Asia–Pacific SIDS leaders repeatedly insist of being "friend to all, enemy to none"; but the rhetoric requires careful navigation to maintain sovereignty and avoid falling into a dependency trap or becoming pawns in a larger geopolitical game.

Hunter Marston and Akhil Ramesh (2021) warn, "small states must wield agency to find viable economic strategies that simultaneously protect states' sovereignty by avoiding overexposure to any one powerful country" (Marston & Ramesh, 2021). They can easily fall into self-defeating race to the bottom among themselves competing to offer advantages to the rival global and regional powers, compromising their own sovereignty or agency, in the hope of getting more economic or financial help.

George Carter (2022) points out that the SIDS depend on multilateral institutions to survive as sovereign states, but their capacity to engage and achieve national goals through international organisations is limited.

Moreover, the risk is that Asia–Pacific SIDS become embroiled in conflicts not of their own making, and that geopolitics leads to fragmentation, reducing the strength of Asia–Pacific SIDS' collective voice.

Therefore, maintaining unity and common agenda is vital for the Asia–Pacific SIDS' if they do not want to be reduced to mere bystanders and demonstrate agency and strategic thinking. Only then can they leverage their position to extract maximum benefits from both sides. As George Crater (2022) notes, SIDS as a group of countries through the Alliance of Small Island States (AOSIS) have quite effectively used various international fora and mechanisms to draw attention to their unique condition, especially climate change vulnerability. For example, AOSIS successfully secured a dedicated window of funding—equivalent to US$3 million per SIDS from 2022 to 2026—through the Global Environment Facility (GEF)for 30 SIDS that are not LDCs. Similarly, regional alliances such as the Caribbean Community (CARICOM) and Pacific Islands Forum (PIF) have been active in asserting a collective voice and agenda on regional issues.

Despite this, George Crater (2022) acknowledges that successes have been largely confined to environmental issues. While core sustainable development challenges are widely recognised by the international aid and trade system, special and differential treatment (SDT) at the World Trade Organisation (WTO) has been more difficult to secure. As larger developing states fear that SDT for SIDS will set a dangerous precedent, and affect their own competitiveness, the WTO has struggled to adequately address trade and development issues faced by SIDS.

The Asia–Pacific SIDS need to balance the scales of financing, ensuring their development agendas are not overshadowed by the interests of the more powerful nations, often harnessing financial flows in favour of ruling elites. China may offer an attractive alternative with its touted no-strings-attached aid, especially for politically prized development projects to the traditional aid models of the West with conditionality normally related to reforms, accountability and governance.

However, China is accused of "debt-trap diplomacy" by the West. For example, a study by the Washington-based Center for Global Development (Gelpern et al., 2022) claims that Chinese contracts include "unusual confidentiality clauses", but do not promise collective debt restructuring. Also, their debt cancellation-related clauses would allegedly allow China to "influence debtors" domestic and foreign policies'. On the other hand, Meg Keen and Alan Tidwell (2024b) note, *Partners in the*

Blue Pacific—an informal coordination initiative among the US, Australia, Japan, New Zealand, the UK, Germany, Canada and the Republic of Korea– has been criticised for undermining existing regional institutions as regional and global powers compete for strategic advantages.

While the discourse is clouded with geopolitical lens, the Asia–Pacific SIDS need to strengthen their solidarity. The intra-SIDS cooperation and partnership arrangements provide critical opportunity to reflect, rethink and revise the SIDS' partnership strategies and avoid harmful race to the bottom. They must maintain neutrality and work towards global and regional multilateralism. Forging partnerships should be the cornerstone during the current era of geopolitical rivalries.

Finally, as UN-ESCAP (2014, p. 102) argued, the interests of the great powers as well as the people of these smaller ecologically fragile Island States will be best served under a global/regional public-good umbrella. That is, "the habitat of the island peoples should be treated as a global public good and the peoples should be empowered to become custodians of that ecological space, a space that can give those peoples a dignified standard of living without breaching their freedom. While these small island States are threatened by climate change, the livelihoods of their people must be protected and their human development must be advanced, making sure that they are not forced to abandon their habitats and cultures and are not left at the mercy of profit-hungry transnational corporations or volatile financial flows".

References

ADB. (2011). *Food security and climate change in the Pacific: Rethinking the options*. Asian Development Bank.

Ali, R., & Jai, N. (1989). The Fiji sugar industry: A brief history and overview of its structure and operations. *Pacific Economic Bulletin, 4*(2), 13–21.

Anthoff, D., Robert, J. N., & Richard, S. J. T. (2010). The economic impact of substantial sea-level rise. *Mitigation and Adaptation Strategies for Global Change, 15*(4), 321–335.

Azizi, S. (2018). The impacts of workers' remittances on human capital and labor supply in developing countries. *Economic Modelling, 75*(November), 377–396.

Badjeck, M.-C., Edward, H. A., Ashley, S. H., & Nicholas, K. D. (2010). Impacts of climate variability and change on fishery-based livelihoods. *Marine Policy, 34*(3), 375–383.

Barbesgaard, M. (2018). Blue growth: Savior or ocean grabbing? *The Journal of Peasant Studies, 45*(1), 130–149.

Barnett, J. (2001). Adapting to climate change in Pacific Island countries: The problem of uncertainty. *World Development, 29*(6), 977–993.

Barnett, J. (2011). Dangerous climate change in the Pacific Islands: Food production and food security. *Regional Environmental Change, 11*(1), 229–237.

Basu, S. R. (2024). Pacific preview: Current trends and trajectories. *Asia-Pacific Sustainable Development Journal, 31*(1), 1–20.

Bolesta, A. (2020). Pacific islands: Development vulnerabilities, international response and structural transformation. *Journal of International Studies, 13*(3), 25–40.

Brameswari, C., Tatang, I., & Monica, A. N. T. (2022). The effects of colonialism toward the Timorese as depicted in Nesi's *Orang-Orang Oetimu. Journal of Language and Literature, 22*(1), 163–178.

Browne, C. (2006). *Pacific Island Economies*. International Monetary Fund.

Carter, G. (2022). With geopolitics undermining development in Small Island Developing States, stronger alliances are needed more than ever, ODI Global expert comment, 13 July. https://doi.org/en/insights/with-geopolitics-undermining-development-in-small-island-developing-states-stronger-alliances-are-needed-more-than-ever/ (accessed 05/01/2025)

Chowdhury, A., & Yogi, V. (2008). Macroeconomic policies for growth in small Pacific Island economies. *Pacific Economic Bulletin, 23*(2), 124–144.

Connell, J. (2010). Pacific islands in the global economy: Paradoxes of migration and culture. *Singapore Journal of Tropical Geography, 31*(1), 115–129.

Cooray, A. (2012). The impact of migrant remittances on economic growth: Evidence from South Asia. *Review of International Economics, 20*(5), 985–998.

Craney, A. (2016). Avoiding a lost generation: Understanding the social and economic impacts of the Pasifika youth bulge. *ANU College of Asia & the Pacific*, 24 October, http://dpa.bellschool.anu.edu.au/news-events/events/4625/avoiding-lost-generation-understanding-social-and-economic-impacts-pasifika (accessed 13/03/2024).

Duncan, R. (2014). Reflections on constraints to growth in Pacific Island countries. *DEVPOLICYBLOG*, http://www.devpolicy.org/reflections-on-constraints-to-growth-in-pacific-island-countries-20140626/ (accessed 21/10/2018).

Duncan, R. (2016). Sources of growth spurts in Pacific island economies. *Asia and the Pacific Policy Studies, 3*(2), 351–365.

Easterly, W., & Aart, K. (2000). Small states, small problems? Income, growth, and volatility in small states. *World Development, 28*(11), 2013–2027.

Fiji Government. (2004). *Preliminary estimates of flood affected areas*. Press release April 17. Ministry of Information. http://www.fiji.gov.fj/cgi-bin/cms/exec/view.cgi/19/2282/printer.

Fitzpatrick, P. (1980). Really rather like slavery: Law and labor in the colonial economy in Papua New Guinea. *Contemporary Crises, 4*, 77–95.

Gelpern, A., Sebastian, H., Scott, M., Brad, P., Christoph, T. (2022). How China lends: A rare look into 100 debt contracts with foreign governments. *Economic Policy* 15 November, https://doi.org/10.1093/epolic/eiac054 (accessed 10/05/2023).

Gillett, R., Mike, M., Len, R., & Josie, T. (2001). *Tuna: A key economic resource in the Pacific Islands. A report prepared for the Asian Development Bank and the Forum*.

Hughes, H. (2003). *Aid has Failed the Pacific*. St Leonards: The Centre for Independent Studies.

Hughes, H. (2004). *The Pacific is Viable*! St Leonards: The Centre for Independent Studies.

Jacobson, H. (1960). Our 'colonial' problem in the Pacific. *Foreign Affairs, 39*(1), 56–66.

Julca, A., & Oliver, P. (2010). Vulnerabilities and migration in Small Island Developing States in the context of climate change. *Natural Hazards, 55*(3), 717–728.

Keen, M., & Alan, T. (2024a). *Geopolitics in the Pacific Islands: Playing for advantage*. Lowy Institute.

Keen, M., & Alan, T. (2024b). *Navigating the tides of geopolitical rivalries: Challenging times for Pacific Islands*. Australian Outlook, Australian Institute of International Affairs, 05 February. https://www.internationalaffairs.org.au/australianoutlook/navigating-the-tides-of-geopolitical-rivalries-challenging-times-for-pacific-islands/ (accessed 13/03/2024).

Keen, M. R., Anne-Maree, S., & Lysa, W.-S. (2018). Towards defining the blue economy: Practical lessons from Pacific Ocean governance. *Marine Policy, 88*, 333–341.

Khor, H. E., Roger, K., & Patrizia, T. (2016). *Resilience and growth in the small states of the Pacific*. IMF.

Kronenberg, R. P., & Hoe, E. K. (2016). Economic growth in the Pacific Island countries: Challenges, constraints, and policy responses. In H. E. Khor, R. P. Kronenberg, & P. Tumbarello (Eds.), *Resilience and Growth in the Small States of the Pacific* (pp. 3–14). IMF.

Kugelman, M. (2021). The Maldives: An island battleground for India-China competition. *Georgetown Journal of International Affairs*, 16 July, https://gjia.georgetown.edu/2021/07/16/the-maldives-an-island-battleground-for-india-china-competition/ (accessed 15/03/2024).

Marston, H., & Akhil, R. (2021). Great power competition and small state leverage in the Indo-Pacific. *East Asia Forum*, 16 September, https://eastasiaforum.org/2021/09/16/great-power-competition-and-small-state-leverage-in-the-indo-pacific/ (accessed 13/03/2024).

McKenzie, E., Biman, C. P., & Atu, K. (2005). Economic impact of natural disasters on development in the Pacific. In *Volume 1: Research Report*. University of the South Pacific (USP), The South Pacific Applied Geoscience Commission (SOPAC).

Molyneux, N., Da Cruz, G. R., Williams, R. L., Rebecca, A., & Neil, C. T. (2012). Climate change and population growth in Timor-Leste: Implications for food security. *Ambio, 41*(8), 823–840.

Murray, W., & John, O. (2011). The inverse sovereignty effect: Aid, scale and neostructuralism in Oceania. *Asia Pacific Viewpoint, 52*(3), 272–284.

Nath, E., & Stephan, K. (2023). *Geopolitical competition in the Indo-Pacific: Managing development cooperation.* German Institute of Development and Sustainability (IDOS), Policy Brief, 8/2023, https://www.idos-research.de/uploads/media/PB_8.2023.pdf (accessed 10/03/2024).

Petersen, E. (2001). Governance of the South Pacific tuna fishery. *Pacific Economic Bulletin, 16*(2), 63–76.

Ranjan, A. (2023). The Maldives' geo-political dilemma: India-China rivalry, and the USA. *Asian Affairs, 52*(2), 375–395.

Regilme, J., Salvador, S. F., & Obert, H. (2021). Comparing US and Chinese foreign aid in the era of rising powers. *The International Spectator, 56*(2), 114–131.

Roberts, J. P. & Ali, A. (2016). The blue economy and small States. *Commonwealth Blue Economy Series* No. 1. London: Commonwealth Secretariat.

Robinson, S.-A. (2019). Mainstreaming climate change adaptation in small island developing states. *Climate and Development, 11*(1), 47–59.

Rodrik, D. (2004). *Rethinking growth policies in the developing world.* Draft of the Luca d'Agliano Lecture in Development Economics, mimeo, Harvard University, Harvard, MA.

Scheyvens, R. (2011). The challenge of sustainable tourism development in the Maldives: Understanding the social and political dimensions of sustainability. *Asia–Pacific Viewpoint, 52*(2), 148–164.

Schneewind, C. (2020). *Colonialism is at the root of the diabetes epidemic in the Pacific Islands.* State of the Planet, Columbia Climate School, 19 June, https://news.climate.columbia.edu/2020/06/19/colonialism-pacific-diabetes-epidemic/ (accessed 20/03/2024).

Sherril, L. (2023). Endless fallout: The Pacific idyll still facing nuclear blight 77 years on. *The Guardian*, 25 August.

Slatter, C. (2006a). Treading water in rapids?: Non-governmental organisations and resistance to neoliberalism in Pacific Island States. In S. Firth (Ed.), *Globalisation and Governance in the Pacific Islands: State, Society and Governance in Melanesia*. ANU Press.

Slatter, C. (2006b). Neo-liberalism and the disciplining of Pacific Island States: The dual challenges of a global economic creed and a changed geopolitical order. In M. Powles (Ed.), *Pacific Futures*. Canberra: ANU Press.

Sora, M. (2022). Geopolitical competition among the larger powers in the Pacific. *Journal of International Affairs, 74*(2), 111–125.

Stewart, R. (2006). An economic survey of developing countries in the Pacific region. Australian Treasury, https://treasury.gov.au/publication/economic-roundup-spring-2006/an-economic-survey-of-developing-countries-in-the-pacific-region/ (15/04/2024).

Tarte, S. (1999). Negotiating a tuna management regime for the Western and Central Pacific: The MHLC process 1994–1999. *The Journal of Pacific History, 34*(3), 273–280. https://doi.org/10.1080/00223349908572912

Teaurere, R., Latu, S. T., de Waegh, R., Orams, M., & Lück, M. (2023). Foreign aid, human agency, and self-reliance in the Pacific: Lessons from the pandemic. *Development Policy Review, 41*, e12727.

Thomas, A., April, B., Rosanne, M.-K., Patrick, P., & Kevon, R. (2020). Climate change and small island developing states. *Annual Review of Environment and Resources, 45*(October), 1–27.

Tisdell, C. (2000). Poverty in the Pacific Islands. *International Journal of Sociology and Social Policy, 20*(11/12), 74–102.

Tisdell, C. (2016). Models of the international economic dependence of pacific microstates: A critical review with important implications for international policies and relations. *Journal of Self-Governance and Management Economics, 4*(2), 7–27.

Tjungue, L. (1985). The Indonesian occupation: 1975–1999. Western Australian Museum, https://museum.wa.gov.au/debt-of-honour/indonesian-occupation-1975-1999. (15/04/2024).

UNCTAD (United Nations Conference on Trade and Development). (2014). The oceans economy: opportunities and challenges for SIDS. New York and Geneva: United Nations.

UN-DESA. (2023). Islands of the Pacific meet to assess development progress and tackle shared crises spotlight is on assessing development progress and proposing new solutions for Small Island Nations, https://www.un.org/ohrlls/news/islands-pacific-meet-assess-development-progress-and-tackle-shared-crises-spotlight-assessing (accessed 10/03/2024).

UN-ESCAP. (1989). *Economic and Social Survey of Asia and the Pacific*. Bangkok: UNESCAP.

UN-ESCAP. (1990). Patterns of economic growth and structural transformation in the least developed and Pacific Island Countries of the ESCAP region: Implications for development policy and planning for the 1990s. *Economic and Social Survey of Asia and the Pacific*, pp. 103–164.

UN-ESCAP. (1998). *Economic and Social Survey of Asia and the Pacific*. New York: United Nations.

UN-ESCAP. (2010). Sustainable development in the Pacific: Progress and challenges. *Pacific Regional Report for the MSI + 5 Review'*. ESCAP Subregional Office for the Pacific, Suva, Fiji

UN-ESCAP. (2014). *Asia and the Pacific: A Story of Transformation and Resurgence*, Bangkok: UNESCAP.

UN-ESCAP. (2019). *Asia–Pacific Countries with Special Needs Development Report 2019: Structural Transformation and its Roel in reducing Poverty*. Bangkok: UNESCAP.

UN-ESCAP. (2023). *Seizing the Moment: Targeting Transformative Disaster Risk Resilience, Asia Pacific Disaster Report 2023*. Bangkok: UNESCAP.

UN-OHRLLS. (2024). *Financing for development of Small Island Developing States—Advance Unedited Copy*. https://www.un.org/ohrlls/sites/www.un.org.ohrlls/files/financing_for_development_for_sids_report_advance_unedited.pdf (accessed 10/03/2024).

United Nations. (2014). *Draft outcome document of the third International Conference on Small Island Developing States*. 1–4 September, Apia, Samoa.

Wilkins, K. (2023). Economic developments in the South Pacific. *Reserve Bank of Australia Bulletin*. (pp. 72–81).

Wilson, K. (2020). *Demanding the future: Navigating the Pacific's youth bulge*. Lowy Institute, 8 July, https://www.lowyinstitute.org/publications/demanding-future-navigating-pacific-s-youth-bulge (accessed 13/03/2024).

World Bank. (2009). Solomon Islands Sources of Growth, Roundtable Meetings: Background Materials prepared for 5–6 March, Honiara.

World Bank. (2024). *Pacific Economic Update March 2024: Back on Track?—The Imperative of Investing in Education*. World Bank.

Yang, Y., Hong, C., Shiu Raj, S., & Baljeet, S. (2016). The Pacific speed of growth: How fast can it be and what determines it? In H. E. Khor, R. P. Kronenberg, & P. Tumbarello (Eds.), *Resilience and Growth in the Small States of the Pacific*, (pp. 45–70).

CHAPTER 8

Empowering Citizens and Enabling the State

"[To]... accelerate progress towards self-sustaining growth of the economy of the individual nations and their social advancement … in each underdeveloped country … each country [should be] setting its own target [and policies]" (United Nations General Assembly resolution 1710 (XVI))

"…each member shall endeavor to direct its economic and financial policies … with due regard to its circumstances." (Articles of Agreement of the International Monetary Fund; Article IV)

In the concluding chapter, it is generally expected that authors offer policy solutions to the problems discussed in previous chapters. However, we are refraining from the common practice; because as we said at the outset that we reject the "one-size-fits-all" approach. The causes for the persistence of underdevelopment are varied and widespread. The literature lists a plethora of them ranging from unconducive culture, difficult geography, inappropriate institutions, wrong policies, unfair global economic governance structure to colonial and neo-colonial exploitations. While some may be relatively more important in certain countries, none can be an absolute determinant. We believe in the agency of citizens and the State in determining the fate of a nation.

Therefore, we respect the sentiment expressed in the above quotes from the United Nations and International Monetary Fund. The emphasis on "individual nations" and on "each member" [country] as

A. Chowdhury et al., *Structural Transformations as Developing Africa, Asia, and the Pacific*, https://doi.org/10.1007/978-981-97-9092-0_8

well as on the consideration of "its circumstances" for target setting and policy decisions is very significant in our views. Furthermore, we reiterate the right of the State and its citizens to set their own development targets and policies as affirmed in the United Nations Declaration on the Right to Development (henceforth, the declaration).[1]

The declaration implies a new social contract between the State and its citizens. Therefore, we believe that it is vitally important to empower citizens and the State in order that they can together find effective solutions to practical problems of underdevelopment.

This resonates with Amartya Sen's (1999) notion of "development as freedom" and Duncan Green's (2008) notion of active citizens and effective states for development. For this reason, we are devoting this chapter to a broader discussion of democratic consolidation and building State capabilities in order for the Sate to be developmental and democratic.

The Declaration also calls for States to co-operate to remove all barriers to development. Therefore, in this final chapter, we reflect on the role of international community as set out in key agreed action programmes and declarations of the United Nations.

Democratic Consolidation

The inalienable right to development means democracy and development are inseparable. Thus, the logic of democracy is not only about abstract political rights, but inputs into economic decisions that affect the lives of the people. It is meaningless for citizens to have the right to choose leaders (presidents/prime ministers); but they are denied the right to participate in economic policymaking that affects their lives and livelihoods, in short, capabilities.

Electoral democracy does not constitute a magic bullet for economic progress and social transformation. Rather, it is the content of democracy and the way it is constituted that has some implications for development. Therefore, democratic consolidation must go beyond regular elections to include citizens' right to actively participate in policy or decision-making for making "development as freedom" meaningful—freedom to choose without fear or prejudice (democracy's intrinsic value) and freedom from

[1] Adopted on 4 December, 1986.

hunger, illiteracy, malnutrition, etc., that influence their life chances (democracy's instrumental value).

In other words, democracy in its constitutive elements must give practical expression to an organised and predictable life for the people, engender equity and fairness both in power and resource distribution, and facilitate the empowerment of the people. In short, democracy must be the kingpin of the interactive framework between various right-holders and institutions of the social system, including the State. Only then can democracy provide a base or conducive environment for socio-economic development. Therefore, following elements are critical for democratic consolidation:

Constitutionalism and the Rule of Law

The constitution of a country determines the nature of the constitutive and regulative rules for social and political interactions among individuals and groups. It sets the rules for property.

rights, the fundamental rights of the citizens, the nature of political authority, etc. The process of drafting and adopting must not be seen as a purely technical or legalistic affair, but essentially as a political process. Thus, drafting and adopting of a country's constitution must be thorough, highly inclusive, open and subjected to the test of popular will.

However, a good constitution is not enough; it has to be well popularised, with a new culture of the rule of law. This is the only way citizens can make their elected leaders accountable, so that the elected leaders can be bound by set rules and governance can proceed in a stable and predictable way. In short, a new civic culture of constitutionalism and the rule of law are germane to a democratic polity and its consolidation.

Decentralisation and Democratisation of Local Governance

Political decentralisation of power, responsibilities and resources to the local level is critical to prevent democratic slides or tendency for a strong leader to centralise power. Besides widening empowerment, decentralisation provides sustaining force for political competition at the local level, ensures local accountability and enhances the efficiency of local service delivery.

However, decentralisation may not necessarily engender good local governance or enhance the participation of the people in the management of their affairs. It may simply create a local elite or oligarchy, which usurps local power and resources for itself. Therefore, decentralisation at the local level must be accompanied by local democratisation, consisting not only of local elections, but also involving of local interests, groups and civil associations in the process of local governance.

Sharing Democracy's Dividend

Support for democracy can quickly drop as citizens become disillusioned when they do not see any tangible improvements of their lives or living conditions. As the Economist (2023) magazine observed, "When people lose hope that their lives will improve, they become impatient for change and the risk of coups and civil wars increases sharply".

Austerity programmes that involve cuts in social spending, like social protection or public provisioning of basic services to meet aid conditionality can accelerate people's disillusion about democracy. This is extremely important, especially when growth and structural transformation create "winners" and "losers".

However, there are tendencies to pursue populist policies in the name of protecting the losers. At the end, such policies and programmes become unsustainable and can precipitate economic and political crises. Governments can avoid such situations by carefully designing redistributive fiscal systems that tax the beneficiaries for compensating the affected communities in the process of structural transformation. People should see that fairness is upheld and their socio-economic rights are progressively met. This requires State capabilities.

Building State Capabilities

The immediate question that arises is how States are to address the fundamental challenge and, more importantly, what factors will determine their relative success. The answers to these questions vary depending one's view about the State. Those in the tradition of neo-classical political economy who see the State as a leviathan suggest institutional constraints on the State's behaviour, such as an independent central bank or fiscal rules, as vital to free the State from predatory capture by narrow vested interest groups. The new-institutionalists do not differ much in this regard.

Thus, in the late 1990s, the "good governance" agenda emerged in response to acknowledged failure of SAP as a prerequisite for an effective State. It is alleged that SAP's "stabilise, privatise and liberalise" reform agenda did not produce professed results due to "poor" governance or lack of good governance. Among others, the good governance agenda focused on accountability, political stability, regulatory quality, rule of law and control of corruption.

Good Governance Not Good Enough

Research claiming that "good governance" is essential for an effective State suffers from serious methodological or conceptual limitations. Existing definitions are extremely broad, suffer from functionalist tautology, or mainly refer to corruption.

Invoking a functionalist definition (such as "good governance" is "good-for-economic-development"), one cannot define a country's "quality of government" without measuring its effects. As *The Economist* (June 4, 2005) noted, defining "good governance" as "good-for-economic-development" may generate tautological explanations and meaningless policy implications: "What is required for growth? Good governance. And what counts as good governance? Whatever promotes growth. And what is required for growth?".

Attempts to define Quality of Governance (QoG) as multi-faceted also suffer from tautology: "What is required for the quality of life enjoyed by citizens? Quality of governance. What is quality of governance? That which promotes the quality of life....". If good governance or "QoG is everything, then maybe it is nothing". Those who have defined "good governance" as what can be shown to be "good-for-economic-development" illustrate this problem. Many important non-economic attributes of good governance, such as trust and subjective measures of well-being, are left out by such definitions.There is a good discussion on this in Musukhal, Vidyattama, Sutiyono and Graham (2023) in the context of Indonesia.

Thus, "good governance" cannot be defined precisely, and hence, cannot be meaningfully or usefully monitored. Furthermore, many countries that have performed well in terms of growth, structural transformation and equity, have fallen short on the most widely used World Bank's "good governance" indicators. Also, not all good governance reforms are similarly feasible or beneficial, let alone necessary or desirable in all circumstances.

In today's developed countries, governance did not improve significantly until they had become quite affluent (Jomo & Chowdhury, 2012). Contrary to the frequently exaggerated claims about how much "institutions matter", greater transparency, accountability and participation are often a consequence, rather than a direct cause of faster development. Small governments are not synonymous with the absence of corruption while countries with very low levels of corruption have relatively large governments, as in Scandinavia and the Netherlands.

Poor countries suffer a multitude of constraints, and effective interventions for accelerated structural transformation must address the most binding bottlenecks. Thus, as a rule, broad good governance reforms are neither necessary nor sufficient for growth.

Unfortunately, the long and lengthening good governance agenda often means that a multitude of reforms needs to be undertaken urgently, typically with little thought to their sequencing, interdependence, or relative contributions to reforming governments to be more efficient, effective and responsive, let alone to accelerate development and alleviate poverty. There is typically little guidance about what is considered essential and what is not, what is feasible and what is not.

The good governance agenda is particularly demanding on poor countries. In some cases, it may not be possible to make much progress on one dimension without prior or simultaneous progress on others. And if certain institutional and policy reforms matter more for development, these should probably receive priority. Selectively concentrating resources would then be better than spreading limited resources thinly across a whole range of ostensible good governance reforms—as some international development agencies tended to do.

A Pragmatic Evolutionary Way Forward[2]

In many developing countries the capability of the State to implement its policies and programmes is a key constraint to structural transformation. As Peter Evans (1998) notes, a number of lessons can be learned from successful East Asian countries in addressing these key constraints.

[2] Draws on UNCTAD (2014).

1. *Institutional capacity develops over time through learning*. The technical capacities of Governments were not particularly advanced when East Asian developmental States embarked on their development process.[3] They were built up over time, through policies of meritocratic recruitment, continuity of personnel and an incentive-based career structure commensurate with the private sector. Significantly, even in successful developmental States all the bureaucracy was not necessarily super-efficient. Policy learning was an integral aspect of the process of building developmental State capability.
2. *Focus on a small number of key agencies and institutions*. There was a deliberate strategy to build a few strategically important agencies instead of improving government effectiveness across the board and all at once.[4] This is consistent with Dani Rodrik's findings from his cross-country analysis of the relationship between institutions and growth that "large-scale institutional transformation is hardly a prerequisite for getting growth going. ... Countries do not need an extensive set of institutional reforms in order to start growing" (Rodrik, 2007, p. 191).
3. *There is no one-size-fits-all magic bullet*. One major lesson of efforts at institutional reform is that "institutional innovations do not travel well" (Rodrik, 2005, p. 994). Matt Andrews, Lant Pritchett and Michael Woolcock (2015, p. 124) also found, "There are no easy or quick-fix solutions. Building state capability is an idiosyncratic process that looks different in each and every country; the specific institutional structures that come to have local legitimacy and effectiveness are highly dependent on a complex interplay of local context, history, politics and culture".[5]

[3] Evans (1998, p. 71) noted, "Public bureaucracies capable of fostering effective public performance in global markets were not some kind of natural resource, immediately available to East Asia following the Second World War. Modern bureaucracies were constructed through intense prolonged struggles for reform and endless experimentation over the course of the post-Second World War period".

[4] As Evans (1998, p. 73) observed: "a substantial share of the benefits of superior bureaucratic performance may be obtained by focusing reforms on a relatively small set of economic agencies".

[5] Also see Andrews, Pritchett and Woolcock (2017).

Therefore, the Governments in structurally underdeveloped countries should not imagine that they can simply take policies and institutions from successful East Asian developmental States, and transplant them for guaranteed success. In building developmental State capabilities in structurally underdeveloped countries, it is necessary to identify which principles and practices of the successful models provide a "good fit" with the circumstances of each of them. This is different from the wholesale transfer of best practice as in the case of onerous "good governance" agenda. Again, what constitutes a "good fit" to a particular country circumstances will change over time. Therefore, it is important to have a pragmatic and evolutionary approach in which policies and institutions are adapted to the level of development of both productive capacities and governance capabilities. A pragmatic evolutionary approach also implies that institutions should build on what exists within a country rather than identifying what does not exist, compared with some external norms of best practice.

Therefore, a pragmatic evolutionary approach to building developmental State capabilities in structurally underdeveloped countries would involve the adoption of a small number of institutional reforms that fit well within the existing context. Figure 8.1, drawn from Ole Therkildsen (2008), shows the factors that need to fit well for any type of public sector reforms to work. In short, reforms will progress: (a) if their outputs and outcomes are well matched with political demands; (b) if there is a good fit between the political capacity and technical capacity for specific reforms; and (c) if technical competencies fit the requirements of the reform tasks.

Both technical and political capacities matter, in applying this approach to building developmental State capabilities. It is necessary for Governments to have an overall development vision that maps where they are going. However, most significantly, developmental State capabilities should be built up over time through a strategic incrementalistic approach,[6] building on islands of excellence in public administration or executive agencies, promoting policy learning and nurturing growth coalitions (Fig. 8.2).

According to Mushtaq Khan (2008), particular effort should be focused on building the governance requirements to address factors that are slowing down capital accumulation, technological upgrading, sectoral

[6] Strategic incrementalism—between big bang and "muddling through"—is also advocated in World Bank (2005).

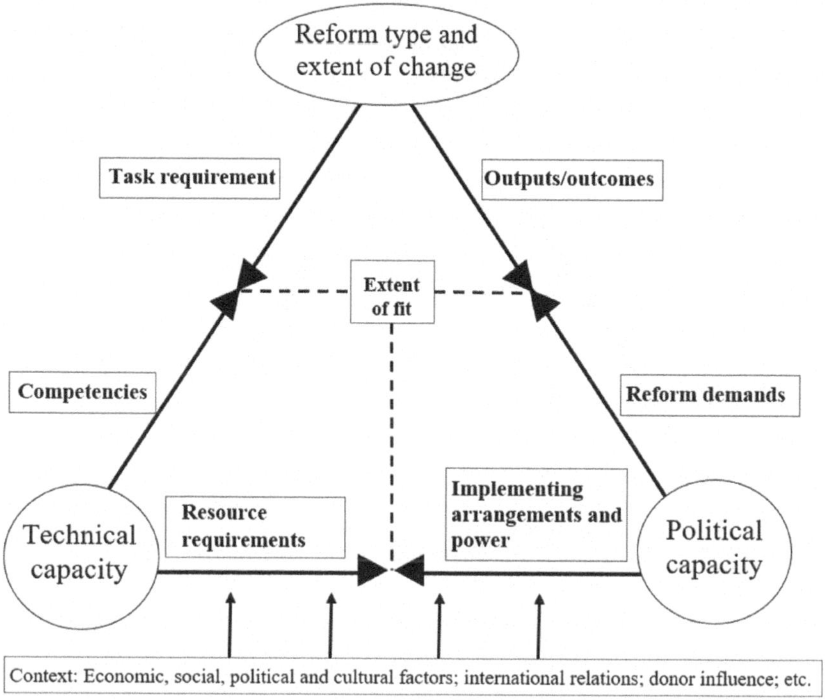

Fig. 8.1 Schematic representation of fit requirements in public sector reform. *Source*: Therkildsen (2008)

diversification and structural change. Khan illustrates this idea using the example of Bangladesh's garments sector. He discusses how through discussion with entrepreneurs, efforts were made to identify market failures in the allocation of key resources—namely investment funds, labour skills and land—and which governance reforms might help resolve these problems. He then discusses how an incremental approach can address these critical market failures.

Complementarities in State Capacity

There is a clear link between tax-GDP ratio and state capabilities. A study at the IMF reveals that countries with higher tax revenue-to-GDP also tend to have stronger protection of property rights, higher quality

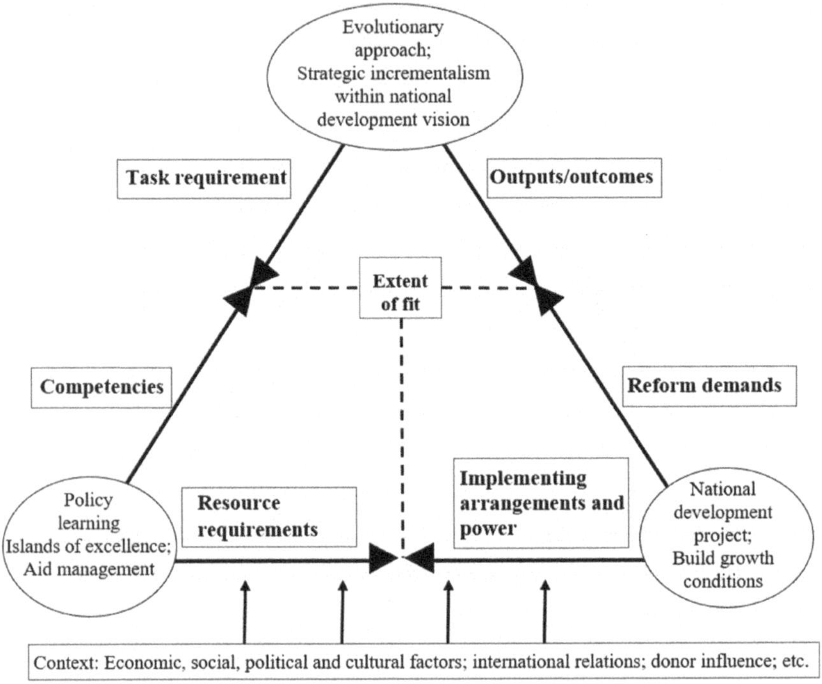

Fig. 8.2 Building developmental State capabilities in structurally underdeveloped countries: Public sector reforms. *Source*: UNCTAD (2009), adapted from Therkildsen (2008)

of government policies and regulation and greater government transparency and accountability (Gaspar, Jaramillo & Wingender, 2016). It presented the tax revenue's role in the link between state capabilities and development in an infographic (Fig. 8.3).

Timothy Besley and Toresten Persson (2011, 2013, 2014a, 2014b) emphasise the broader concept of state capacity to stand for a range of capabilities that are needed for the state to function effectively. State capacity incorporates investment by the government in building three key dimensions: (i) fiscal capacity, by increasing collection of taxes, especially broad-based taxes, through stronger tax enforcement; (ii) legal capacity, which refers to market-supporting regulation, enforcement of

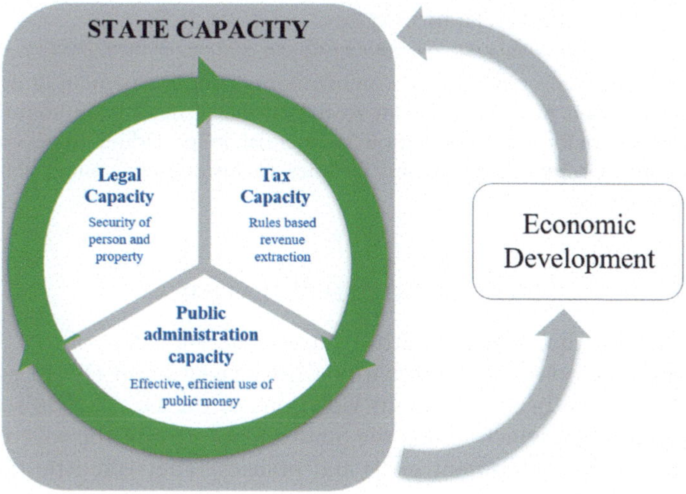

Fig. 8.3 Complementarities in State capacity. *Source*: Gaspar, Jaramillo and Wingender (2016)

contracts and protection of property rights; and (iii) collective capacity by augmenting markets, mostly by supplying public goods.

Robert Barro (1990) discusses how the economy can be made more productive when tax revenues are spent on public goods and investments. Robert Barro and Sala-i-Martin (1992) show that well-designed tax systems can raise the GDP growth rate. Christian Ebeke and Helene Ehrhart (2012) find that the instability of tax revenue leads to the instability in public investment and reduces the level of public investment.

Development Partnership

Article 3.3 of the Declaration states:

> "States have the duty to co-operate with each other in ensuring development and eliminating obstacles to development. States should realize their rights and fulfil their duties in such a manner as to promote a new international economic order based on sovereign equality, interdependence, mutual interest and co-operation among all States, as well as to encourage the observance and realization of human rights."

Article 4.2 of the Declaration states:

> "Sustained action is required to promote more rapid development of developing countries. As a complement to the efforts of developing countries, effective international co-operation is essential in providing these countries with appropriate means and facilities to foster their comprehensive development."

North–South Relations

Unfortunately, the North–South relations or the role of the donor community, including the International Monetary Fund (IMF) and the World Bank, have been in flagrant violations of the Declaration's Article 3.3 and Article 3.1 which grants the State and its citizens the sovereign to determine their development goals and policies. They often tie their aid to projects which are not the priority of the nations. Their policy conditionality of aid often has been too onerous and overwhelming. The donor community also miserably failed in fulfilling their commitments to agree development aid and climate finance.

An important lesson from the failure of past donor supported policy reforms, such as the "good governance" agenda is the critical role of country ownership. Reforms were often seen as imposed externally by donors, even during the Poverty Reduction Strategy Papers (PRSPs) era. To begin with PRSPs were part of IMF/World Bank loan conditionality, and secondly, the stakeholder consultations for PRSPs, too, were donor driven. As Matt Andrews, Lant Pritchett and Michael Woolcock (2015) noted, donors not only define and codify so-called best-practice solutions, but also either implicitly or explicitly compel recipient countries to copy. The recipient countries comply, putting on the appearance of change without changing.

Ole Therkildsen (2008, p. 46) states that "there is no doubt that many reform initiatives have grounded to a halt because donors push too hard on issues that had a limited domestic constituency". This has been a particular feature of past efforts to build general State capacity. It has been observed that the types of capacity development that donors are likely to do well normally do not lead directly to significant improvements in State capacity (Teskey, 2005).

Therefore, development partners must abandon this approach, including aid-tying, and become a genuine partner by providing budgetary support for nationally designed and owned development strategies. Solving development problems and creating development opportunities requires the participation of a wide range of informed and interested stakeholders. Participatory democratic processes, which might take various forms, can provide the basis for a more inclusive societal mobilisation behind a national development project, including structural transformation.

Building State capabilities need human and financial resources which many structurally underdeveloped countries do not have. To gauge the scale of the issue, UNCTAD (2009) estimated domestic resources available for financing (DRAF) governance and investment. In 2006, the DRAF in the LDCs, when measured at current prices and market exchange rates, was on average 41 cents per capita per day. There are quite large variations among the LDCs in the sample with the median value of 18.4 cents per capita per day. In other words, half the LDCs had less than 18.4 cents a day available per capita to spend on private capital formation, public investment in infrastructure, the running of vital public services such as health, education and public administration, as well as the provision of law and order. For the sake of comparison, the average sum of domestic resources available for financing development in lower–middle-income countries in 2006 amounted to $3.2 per capita per day, while in high–income countries it was $38.4 per capita per day. An alternative measure shows that compared with $295 in lower–middle-income countries, LDCs had only $60 (or 16 cents per person per day) to cover all government current expenditures for purchases of goods and services (including compensation of employees).

The situation has become worse since 2008–2009 global finance crisis (GFC) due to declining aid flows, volatile and falling commodity prices and increasing cost associated with climate change vulnerabilities (loss and damage, and recovery). The COVID-19 pandemic dealt further blows to the fiscal space of structurally underdeveloped countries, in particular LDCs and SIDS. This has forced many countries to borrow externally; thus, the debt-to-GDP ratio of LDCs grew from 48.5% in 2019 to 55.4% in 2022 (the highest since 2005) (UNCTAD, 2023). Shrinking fiscal space limits structurally underdeveloped countries', especially LDCs and SIDS, ability to implement development policies and forces tough choices, such as choosing between paying their external debt or investing in health, education, climate action and institutions.

This clearly shows the critical importance of development assistance and meaningful debt-relief. Therefore, urgent, bold action from the international community is critical to ensure LDCs and SIDS have better access to affordable, long-term international financing, especially from public sources. The development partners must deliver on their commitments made at the 3rd International Conference on Financing for Development held in Addis Ababa in 2015. Besides increasing aid, in Addis Ababa, development partners pledged support for improving tax administration and stem illegal transfer of funds, which is crucial for enhancing domestic resource mobilisation. However, unsurprisingly solutions offered through OECD's so-called Inclusive Framework for tackling TNC's tax avoidance and evasion benefits are biassed towards rich countries as highlighted in Chapter 1.

Climate finance for adaptation and recovery from loss and damages is extremely important for LDCs and SIDS which are disproportionately impacted by climate change crisis. Unfortunately, the rich countries also have failed their commitment made at the 15th Conference of Parties (COP15) of the UNFCCC in Copenhagen in 2009 to a collective goal of mobilising USD 100 billion per year by 2020 for climate action in developing countries. Anis Chowdhury and Jomo Kwame Sundaram (2022) show climate finance is not only awfully inadequate, but also in a mess as donors take advantage of the absence of a clear universal definition of what should be counted in climate finance.

South–South Cooperation

South-South cooperation, especially between the successful Asian and lagging Sub-Saharan countries, offers significant opportunities for structural transformation in structurally underdeveloped countries. Asian has been world's fasted growing for the past few decades and a number of countries have accumulated significant amounts of foreign reserves in their sovereign wealth funds. The newly industrialised economies in the region, including China, have joined Japan in offering substantial aid to developing countries. China's Belt and Road Initiative (BRI) is one of them. The BRI is not only financing much needed infrastructure, but also connecting the countries, especially LLDCs. The BRI, which is part of China's strategic trade policy (Krugman, 2017) offers excellent opportunities for some of the structurally underdeveloped countries to become a communication or transportation hubs as well to participate more effectively in the global value chain. Thus, it is likely to help these countries, especially those which lack economies of scale by linking them to larger regional and global markets.

However, in recent years there have been concerns about debt sustainability of a number of recipient countries. Such concerns are amplified by geopolitical rivalry between the US-led traditional donors and China. China is accused of engaging in "debt-trap diplomacy". A Harvard University study (Parker & Chefitz, 2018) claimed that through a process, "debtbook diplomacy", China intends to leverage accumulated debt of poor countries to achieve its strategic objectives. Similarly, Sebastian Horn, Bradley Parks, Carmen Reinhart and Christopher Trebesch (2023) implied nefarious motives for China's refinancing of debt distressed countries. Yet, other independent studies (for example, Vines, Butler & Jie, 2022; Brautigam & Rithmire, 2021; Jones & Hameiri, 2020; Rajah, Dyanat & Pryke, 2019) did not find evidence of hidden strategic motives of China.

While geopolitically motivated accusations do not help and poor countries should stay away from geopolitical rivalries, countries seeking foreign funding for their structural transformation should be cautious. They should, instead, try to maximise their funding options arising from geopolitical rivalries, for example, Japan initiated "Free and Open Indo-Pacific" (FOIP) strategy in the Asia–Pacific regions, the US-led India-Middle East-Europe Economic Corridor (IMEC), the EU-led "Global Gateway" project.

As cautioned by Helen Hughes (1979) and Gershon Feder (1980) decades ago that seeking funds for infrastructure, developing countries should be aware that over-ambitious project selections, poor project management or governance and regulatory framework can lead to project failures and unsustainable accumulation of external debts. This situation is often exacerbated due to the absence of a formal debt-management-restructuring mechanism. Transfer of skills and technology as well as social (especially employment) and environmental impacts should also be considered when seeking foreign investment. These are relevant regardless of sources of funding—China or other Western countries. A cooperative approach, hopefully, can overcome many of the geopolitical and project-related concerns, to yield "win–win" outcomes for all stakeholders.

A New Social Contract: Right to Development and Freedom

The United Nations Declaration on the Right to Development, in fact, demands a new social contract between citizens and the State which is developmental as well as democratic. Article 2.1 of the Declaration states: "The human person is the central subject of development and should be the active participant and beneficiary of the right to development". And Article 1.1 of the Declaration states:

> The right to development is an inalienable human right by virtue of which every human person and all peoples are entitled to participate in, contribute to, and enjoy economic, social, cultural and political development, in which all human rights and fundamental freedoms can be fully realized.

Freedom, in Amartya Sen's "development as freedom", is both the primary end and the principal means of development. Sen argues that the only acceptable evaluation of human progress is primarily and ultimately enhancement of freedom—freedom to participate in social, economic and political activities in order to attain one's full potential as a human being. The achievement of development as freedom, in turn, is dependent on the free agency of people—ordinary citizen's ability to choose the course of actions she or he deems best for her or his advancement. Thus, when development is seen as "freedom" as Amartya Sen (1999) argued, then the citizens become the focal point as articulated in the Declaration on Right to Development.

Article 2.3 states: "States have the right and the duty to formulate appropriate national development policies that aim at the constant improvement of the well-being of the entire population and of all individuals, on the basis of their active, free and meaningful participation in development and in the fair distribution of the benefits resulting therefrom". Article 8.2 states: "States should encourage popular participation in all spheres as an important factor in development and in the full realization of all human rights".

Thus, the Declaration requires empowering citizens and enabling the State. Ultimately the State has to strive to develop human potential in expanding the choice set available to its citizens and in making available human freedoms to them through democracy. This also means a State which is strong and capable.

"Yet", as Amartya Sen (2008, p. x) reminds, "the state is not the only responsible agency that can make a difference, nor is it the only instrument for tackling the general evil that society tends to tolerate and accept… '[A]ctive citizenship' can be a very effective way of seeking and securing solutions to these pervasive problems of powerlessness and unfreedom". Duncan Green (2008) presented case studies of a number of different types of initiative around the world that have enhanced and expanded the powers of the ordinary citizens and enabled the State to successfully reduce the unfreedoms that characterise the poverty of the deprived.

References

Andrews, M., Lant, P., & Michael, W. (2015). The challenge of building real state capability. *Harvard University Center for International Development Working Paper* 306.

Barro, R. (1990). Government spending in a simple model of endogenous growth. *Journal of Political Economy, 98*(5), 103–125.

Barro, R., & Sala-i-Martin, X. (1992). Convergence. *Journal of Political Economy, 100*(2), 223–251.

Besley, T., & Torsten, P. (2013). Taxation and development. In A. J. Auerbach, R. Chetty, M. Feldstein and E. Saez, (Eds.), *Handbook of Public Economics* Vol. 5. North Holland.

Besley, T., & Torsten, P. (2011). *Pillars of Prosperity: The Political economics of development clusters*. Princeton University Press.

Besley, T., & Torsten, P. (2014a). Why do developing countries tax so little? *Journal of Economic Perspectives, 28*(4), 99–120.

Besley, T., & Torsten, P. (2014b). The causes and consequences of development clusters: State capacity, peace and income. *Annual Review of Economics, 6*, 927–949.

Brautigam, D., & Meg, R. (2021). The Chinese 'debt trap' is a myth. *The Atlantic*, 6 February, https://www.theatlantic.com/international/archive/2021/02/china-debt-trap-diplomacy/617953/ (accessed 23/08/2023).

Chowdhury, A., & Jomo Kwame, S. (2022). The climate finance conundrum. *Development, 65*(February), 29–41.

Ebeke, C., & Helene, E. (2012). Tax revenue instability in Sub-Saharan Africa: Consequences and remedies. *Journal of African Economies, 21*(1), 1–27.

Economist. (2005). *Special Report: A regime changes—Paul Wolfowitz at the World Bank*. 4 June.

Economist. (2023). *Why Africans are losing faith in democracy: The alternatives will undoubtedly be worse*. 5 October.

Evans, P. (1998). Transferable lessons? Re-examining the institutional prerequisite of East Asian economic policies. In Y. Akyüz (Ed.), *East Asian development: New perspectives* (pp. 66–86). F. Cass.

Feder, G. (1980). Economic growth, foreign loans and debt servicing capacity of developing countries. *Journal of Development Studies, 16*(3), 352–368.

Gaspar, V., Laura, J., & Philippe, W. (2016). Tax capacity and growth: Is there a Tipping Point? *IMF Working Paper*, WP/16/234, https://www.imf.org/en/Publications/WP/Issues/2016/12/31/Tax-Capacity-and-Growth-Is-there-a-Tipping-Point-44436 (accessed 24/08/203).

Green, D. (2008). *From poverty to power: How active citizens and effective states can change the world*. Oxfam International.

Horn, S., Bradley, P., Carmen, R., Christoph, T. (2023). *China as an international lender of last resort*. Kiel Working Paper No. 2244, March. https://www.ifw-kiel.de/publications/kiel-working-papers/2023/china-as-an-international-lender-of-last-resort-18075/ (accessed 29/03/2023).

Hughes, H. (1979). Debt and development: The role of foreign capital in economic growth. *World Development, 7*(2), 95–112.

Jomo, K. S., & Anis, C. (2012). *Is good governance good for development?* Bloomsbury Academic.

Jones, L., & Shahar, H. (2020). *Debunking the Myth of 'Debt-trap Diplomacy'. How Recipient Countries Shape China's Belt and Road Initiative*. London: Chatham House

Khan, M. (2008). Investment and technology policies. In *National Development Strategies: Policy Notes*. United Nations Department for Economic and Social Affairs, New York.

Krugman, P. (2017). Belts, roads, and strategic trade policy. *The New York Times*, 20 May, https://krugman.blogs.nytimes.com/2017/05/20/belts-roads-and-strategic-trade-policy/ (accessed 24/08/2023).

Musukhal, W., Yogi, V., Wahyu, S., & Peter, G. (2023). Accountability in variation of agency-based governance reforms: The case of Indonesia. *International Journal of Public Administration, 46*(14), 1020–1032.

Parker, S., & Gabrielle, C. (2018). *Debtbook diplomacy*. Paper, Belfer Center for Science and International Affairs, Harvard Kennedy School, 24 May, https://www.belfercenter.org/sites/default/files/files/publication/Debtbook%20Diplomacy%20PDF.pdf (accessed 24/08/2023).

Rajah, R., Alexandre, D., & Jonathan, P. (2019). *Ocean of Debt? Belt and Road and Debt Diplomacy in the Pacific*. Lowy Institute.

Rodrik, D. (2005). Growth strategies. In P. Aghion & S. Durlauf (Eds.), *The Handbook of Economic Growth*. (Vol. 1). Elsevier.

Rodrik, D. (2007). Industrial development: Some stylized facts and policies. In *Industrial Development for the 21st Century: Sustainable Development Perspectives*. United Nations.

Sen, A. (1999). *Development as freedom*. Oxford University Press.

Sen, A. (2008). Foreword. In *Duncan Green, From Poverty to Power: How Active Citizens and Effective States Can Change the World*, (2nd Edition). Oxford: Oxfam International.

Teskey, G. (2005). *Capacity development and state building: Issues, evidence and implications for DFID*. Department for International Development.

Therkildsen, O. (2008). *Public sector reforms and the development of productive capacities in LDCs*. Study prepared for UNCTAD as a background paper for The Least Developed Countries Report 2009, New York and Geneva.

UNCTAD. (2009). *The Least Developed Countries Report 2009: The State and Development Governance*. UNCTAD.

UNCTAD. (2014). *The Least Developed Countries Report 2014: Growth with structural transformation: A post-2015 development agenda*. UNCTAD.

UNCTAD. (2023). *The Least Developed Countries Report 2023: Crisis-resilient development finance*, The United Nations, New York & Geneva.

Vines, A., Creon, B., & Yu, J. (2022). *The response to debt distress in Africa and the role of China*. Chatham House.

World Bank. (2005). *Economic Growth in the 1990s: Learning from a Decade of Reform*. World Bank.

Index

A. Chowdhury et al., *Structural Transformations as Developing Africa, Asia, and the Pacific*, https://doi.org/10.1007/978-981-97-9092-0